Women on Ice

CRITICAL ISSUES IN CRIME AND SOCIETY
Raymond J. Michalowski, Series Editor

Critical Issues in Crime and Society is oriented toward critical analysis of contemporary problems in crime and justice. The series is open to a broad range of topics including specific types of crime, wrongful behavior by economically or politically powerful actors, controversies over justice system practices, and issues related to the intersection of identity, crime, and justice. It is committed to offering thoughtful works that will be accessible to scholars and professional criminologists, general readers, and students.

For a list of titles in the series, see the last page of this book.

Women on Ice

METHAMPHETAMINE USE AMONG SUBURBAN WOMEN

MIRIAM BOERI

RUTGERS UNIVERSITY PRESS
New Brunswick, New Jersey, and London

LIBRARY OF CONGRESS CATALOGING-IN-PUBLICATION DATA

Boeri, Miriam.
Women on ice : methamphetamine use among suburban women / Miriam Boeri.
    p. cm. — (Critical issues in crime and society)
  Includes bibliographical references and index.
  ISBN 978-0-8135-5460-0 (hardcover : alk. paper) — ISBN 978-0-8135-5459-4 (pbk. : alk. paper) — ISBN 978-0-8135-5461-7 (e-book)
  1. Women—Drug use. 2. Methamphetamine abuse. 3. Women drug addicts. 4. Drug addiction—Treatment. I. Title.
  HV5824.W6W64 2013
  362.29'952082091733—dc23

                                                  2012012096

A British Cataloging-in-Publication record for this book is available from the British Library.

Copyright © 2013 by Miriam Boeri

Visit our website: http://rutgerspress.rutgers.edu

For the women

We first crush people to the earth,
and then claim the right to trample on them forever,
because they are prostrate.
Lydia Marie Child (1856)

Contents

Figures and Tables

PREFACE

BASED ON MY CURRENT education, occupation, and residential zip code, I appear to be far removed socially and culturally from the women I interviewed, analyzed, and wrote about in this book. Yet, as I heard their stories, I often thought of my own childhood, my siblings, and my not too distant past living in the suburbs on food stamps. I was not on Skid Row, where I used to look for my father. I was not in prison, where I visited my brother. I was not an abused wife, like my alcoholic sister who died from a head injury, allegedly an accident. I was on a Pell grant and penniless, but I was in college.

Like many idealists who are attracted to the academic discipline of sociology, I wanted to learn how to stop the social injustices I saw around me, starting with those against my brother. Serving a thirty-year sentence due to the "three strikes and you're out" laws, the root of his crime was drug addiction, probably depression that started in youth. It was no surprise that my graduate education led me to study drug users, fortunately with some of the best drug researchers in the United States.

After I got my Ph.D., a university position, and a federal grant, I was back in a suburban landscape similar to where I had lived in a trailer during my college years. Now, though, I was studying women who used methamphetamine—an increasing social problem in these suburban communities. Conducting research in this area, I often felt my past chillingly close. I cried many times after hearing the painfully dismal stories from hopeless women who I knew had few options, but was I weeping for them or for my brother, who as an ex-felon parolee entered society with no prospect of employment? Or were these tears of guilt because I was safe and they were not?

Poor, marginalized, and vulnerable females are not the only women presented in this book, but they are the most desperate and forgotten in the suburbs. Anecdotes of abuse and violence are not the only stories depicted here, but they are the most poignantly told and intensely remembered. These were also the women and the stories that resonated most with my own experiences. Some of these women had lives of pain and suffering that I knew would probably never stop. Their vulnerability was tangible. Their despair and hopelessness would continue long after the interviews were over.

My research on suburban drug use began in 2007, the same year my brother was released from prison and could not find employment. In 2008, he started to attend community college and we finally glimpsed hope. He stopped treating his depression with illegal drugs and reduced his dependence on alcohol so he could learn to study instead of trying to forget. I worked with him to deconstruct the wall of his past and reconstruct a future—a brick at a time. He wanted to be an addiction counselor. We joked that we would start a new program called *one-step*. Audaciously, I envisioned his rise from the ashes as a model for those I studied. He was shot and killed in his room at the boardinghouse where he lived on October 3, 2009, by someone who knew him from prison. It was called a burglary. I continued my research, hoping to make sense of seemingly senseless situations.

Acknowledgments

SOME WHO READ THIS book might change their views on drug users and the decisions they make regarding drug policy. For the women I interviewed, any positive results stemming from this book based on their lives will be too late to have much influence on them. Although the women received a small recompense for their time and the difficult emotional work of recounting painful and challenging periods of their lives, it was merely a token of respect for the knowledge they imparted. More than a few of the women told me, "We are doing this to help others." I hope that my honest portrayal of their candidly told stories provides a more humane justice in the lives of those who come after them. I would like to thank many people for their help with this book, but first among them are the women who shared their lives and stories with me, to whom this book is dedicated.

Next I want to thank Claire E. Sterk and Kirk W. Elifson, who believed in me when I was a nontraditional graduate student and mentored me to a career in drug research. Claire served as an advisor on the two research studies I conducted to collect the data needed for this book. Additionally, I am especially appreciative of Annette Bairan, coinvestigator on one of the studies, who conducted most of the focus groups and read through the first very rough draft of this book, and Elle Ballard, my colleague and friend, who helped collect data on community services when I was too emotionally involved to do this objectively.

I want to express great thanks and appreciation to my research staff, starting with David Gibson, a student with incredible insight on life and politics, who worked in various research roles, including ethnographer, interviewer, transcriber, coder and writer throughout both studies; Ben Tyndall, the best project manager in the world, who organized the mountain of data into controllable files and kept me focused; Denise Woodall, a woman with extraordinary energy and resiliency, who continually reminded me of the broken state of our social services, health services, and legal aid for the poor; and Nick Zeller, Sarah Goehler, and Jason Rodriquez, temporary research assistants of excellence. I also greatly appreciate Jan Morian, my intern and friend, who checked my references and conducted a final reading of the manuscript with great attention to detail. Of course, I thank the anonymous reviewers who offered suggestions on my proposal and favorably reviewed the submitted manuscript, and the Rutgers University Press editors.

One of the findings of this book is the devastating effect methamphetamine use has had on suburban families, so it is with a deeper appreciation of family that I thank my husband, Michael, who showed his love and support by cooking my meals, doing the weekly shopping, and helping me find my way when I was lost in the suburbs before I had a GPS. I also thank my daughter, Jasmine Boeri, who spent a week holed up in a cottage during her vacation time to read an earlier draft of this book with an outsider's fresh perspective.

Finally, I thank the National Institute on Drug Abuse (NIDA) at the National Institutes of Health (NIH) for providing the funds to conduct this research, and NIDA program officer, Elizabeth Lambert, a defender of research on women. Through generous support from NIH, the voices of the most disempowered and vulnerable individuals in our society can be heard, and progress toward a more socially just and healthy society can be possible. This research was funded by award numbers 1R15DA021164 and 2R15DA021164. Views expressed are those of the author and do not necessarily reflect the position of NIDA.

Women on Ice

Chapter 1

Methamphetamine

The Perfect Drug for Suburban Women

Maggie

Maggie looked like the typical housewife next door in a suburban community. No one but an experienced user might guess she had injected methamphetamine almost every day during the last six months. She looked younger than her forty-seven years, and her easy smile revealed strong white teeth, inconsistent with the pictures of toothless "faces of meth" displayed on highway billboards by anti-meth campaigns. She looked as if she had just stepped out of the beauty salon with her stylish haircut, manicured nails, and just enough makeup to accent her best features. Maggie was very personable, and we quickly developed affinity over common concerns for people with drug problems. Some of the suburban women I met were reluctant to open up about their personal lives because of the social stigma of their drug use, and it took time to develop a trusting relationship with them. I did not have this problem with Maggie. Her frank turns of phrase, amiable demeanor, and candid communication style conveyed a sense of camaraderie that engendered trust. Having already established good rapport with Maggie, I did not think she would be offended when I asked if her beautiful teeth were her own. "Yeah, I got all my own," she replied, with a smile that reassured me she understood why I had asked. Tooth decay was a common problem among methamphetamine users.

Maggie lived most of her life in the same suburban area where she lives today. She was close to her family, especially the grandmother she cared for until her death. She had three children and was extremely bonded to her family and loved ones. Her otherwise conventional suburban life included dealing cocaine and methamphetamine, which supplemented her husband's income.

Compared to many drug users, Maggie started her drug career relatively late. Believing the antidrug warnings she had heard in high school, she never used marijuana, which she called pot—the slang term used by her generation. It was not until she graduated from high school that she tried pot at a party, mainly because she did not like to drink alcohol. She discovered that marijuana did not give her the stomach problems she got from drinking, and it made her feel relaxed and more sociable. She also experimented with a trendy drug at the time, Quaaludes (methaqualone), available in pill form, for much the same reason she used marijuana occasionally—they were a depressant but did not give her a hangover.

Illegal drugs were used in her social network and offered to her at different points in her life. Typically, drugs held no appeal when she first tried them. For example, Maggie experimented with a homemade type of methamphetamine, known as crank, a few times as a young adult, but she never liked it. The motivational push that led to her continued use of methamphetamine came years later when she was a young mother. Trying to lose weight after having kids, she sought help from a doctor. Like many women who marry, have children, work at home, and live in suburban communities where errands and shopping are done in a car, Maggie had little time or opportunity for physical exercise, and she gained more weight than she wanted. Her plump figure put a damper on what was otherwise the perfect suburban housewife role she adeptly occupied.

In our society, the symbolic wife is expected to keep a clean house, cook delicious and varied meals, help with the children's schoolwork and extracurricular activities, uphold the family's social reputation, and contribute to the household income by holding a flexible job with little career opportunity. Beyond this, the postmodern wife is expected to be a ready and prepared sex partner with a model figure at any age. A television show popular early in the twenty-first century, *Desperate Housewives*, depicts this type of suburban woman with an edgy twist but lacks the "supermom" role most real suburban mothers have to maintain. Maggie's story was not far removed from the script of this television phenomenon. To help her lose weight, the doctor prescribed diet pills. When she moved and could not find a doctor who would give her a prescription, a friend offered her a drug that was better and cheaper—and that was her first taste of a form of methamphetamine called ice: "At that time a quarter gram was fifty dollars. I was like, wow. And having done crank, I was like, what? Crank was okay, but I didn't like it. That was really what they call bathtub crank, and I mean it could kill you. It was like lye and acid and all this other stuff. Whereas ice was supposed to be something that you could do one line and be up twelve hours."

Maggie used ice occasionally to lose weight and keep trim. She started regular use of the drug because it helped relieve her depression. Although typically an extrovert, who described herself as a "social person," she entered an emotional slump and stopped participating in many social activities after her grandmother's death, which was followed by the death of another close relative. A doctor prescribed Paxil, but Maggie soon discovered that ice made her feel better: "I was the kind of depressed that a hairbrush would be sitting there and it was just like heavy to pick it up. I couldn't even pick it up. It was like I didn't even want to go out. I didn't want to do nothing. And they put me on Paxil, and it just didn't seem to be getting it . . . and I did ice and I started getting up, and I started being social again." It was easy for Maggie to obtain ice in her suburban neighborhood. Methamphetamine was being called an epidemic by the local the newspaper and police in this southeastern region of the United States, where federal funding for anti-meth campaigns and special law enforcement task forces helped to focus attention on this emerging drug problem.

Maggie started using methamphetamine fairly regularly, but in her mind, ice was a functional drug rather than a recreational one. Her husband worked in hard physical labor and he used ice to help him work even harder and longer hours. Together, he and Maggie managed to start two successful businesses: one legitimately and the other covertly.

Their illegitimate business was not part of their original business plan, but it helped them maintain their middle-class status. Maggie learned that her neighbors were selling cocaine from their house. She tried cocaine a few times, but she never used it regularly. When her neighbors discovered she was good with math, they asked her do the accounting for their underground business. She could use the extra money. Eventually, Maggie and her husband started dealing cocaine to supplement the money he made from their legitimate small home business. "It's unbelievable what you can do. Because I mean I could break it down by how many quarters or how many sixteenths. . . . We were dealing so much my husband was like, 'we could quit work.' And I was like, 'no, no.' He called me at lunch and I said I made five hundred dollars already, and he's like, 'what?' And I'd still have dinner cooked and still be at the PTA. I was mother of the year and volunteer of the year at my daughter's school. . . . We banked close to fifty thousand dollars in a few months." Maggie and her husband were low-key. Unlike the stereotypical drug dealer, who is often depicted as indulging in his newfound wealth, splurging on luxuries, and arousing the suspicion of the police, a type that has been documented in some literature as well (see for example the crack dealer in Bourgois 2003), Maggie possessed social and cultural capital that not only enabled her to bridge diverse social networks but also provided the skills and understanding needed to maintain her middle-class status. With her strong background in the values, beliefs, and behaviors learned from her middle-class parents and grandparents, she embraced the norms of modern suburban living that developed over the last century throughout the U.S. social landscape. Whereas many of the other drug dealers I had met spent their money on transient pleasures that drained their assets, while simultaneously attracting the attention of drug enforcement officers, Maggie knew better.

Avoiding the trappings of the suburban nouveau riche, Maggie used the extra money made from drug dealing to save for unexpected family expenses, such as hospital bills, and started saving for her daughter's college fund. Maggie and her husband eventually saved enough to buy a house. Their middle-class dealing activities stayed well under law enforcement radar, and since cocaine was not her drug of choice, she never used up their supply or secretly cut their product to cheat customers and keep more for personal use, which was a common practice according to stories I heard from other suburban drug dealers. Maggie also seemed to be able to control her methamphetamine use behaviors. Even though she used almost daily, she never binged. Her husband did not have an addictive personality: "My husband is the type that can do it once a month, maybe two. I mean if it was just left up to him, he'd never do drugs again."

Maggie's peculiar yet tranquil suburban life was shattered when accumulated family tragedies instigated her deep depression. She tried to commit suicide with prescription pills but woke up in the hospital instead. During her fight for life in the intensive care unit (ICU) of the hospital, she saw her deceased relatives in a vision:

> They brought my family in to basically say good-bye and I came to, because my youngest daughter was sitting there saying, "Mom," and they were taking the tubes out of me at the time, and the nurse was, I remember, the nurse hollering for the doctors . . . and I remember I had blisters from the tubes in my mouth and pneumonia in both my lungs when I came to from the ventilator, you know, the machine doing all my breathing. I remember cause I'd had a conversation earlier that crossed—that experience, it wasn't the light and all—but I remember having a conversation with my grandmother right before I came in, and I don't know if it was a dream. I don't know if it was the actual vision or whatever, but I do remember her telling me to get out of here, "You're not welcome here. Go. Go. Go!" And I know they were trying to get rid of—trying to make me come back is what I feel like. And my grandmother wouldn't look at me. She just kept looking down at the ground, but if she [had] looked at me, I think I wouldn't have come back because I wouldn't have wanted to.

Maggie revealed that after this vision she realized, "God had a purpose in my life." But it did not stop her from continuing her use of methamphetamine, which she felt she had under control with her newfound belief in the twelve-step philosophy. The juxtaposition of being an ambassador for twelve-step, an abstinence-only model of drug treatment, while still using methamphetamine was just one of the contradictions she revealed.

Maggie's attempted suicide changed her life. She went to a residential treatment home after the pill-taking incident that had left her in the emergency room. It was here that she was introduced to the support group recovery model known as the twelve-step program. Maggie had always been a person who bonded easily with strangers and bridged social gaps that often divide those of different social status, and she bonded just as easily with her recovery sponsor while embracing the twelve-step program. She told me about her first twelve-step meeting at the residential recovery program, where she honestly revealed in her matter-of-fact way to all that her entire social network was composed of suburban methamphetamine users:

> The first thing that they told me when I walked in was they gave me a sponsor, and she turned around, and I mean I was scared to death. She said, "Tomorrow night I want you to come in here with your phone-book. Bring your phonebook in here." I was like "okay." I came in here the next night, she hands me a permanent magic marker and she said, "I want you to take this phone book and I want you to mark everybody in that book that uses." And I looked at her, and everybody was looking at me, and I threw it on the floor. And she said, "Now we have rules, this is how," and I said, "Oh no ma'am, I got my sister's number memorized by heart. Everybody else in the book is all users." And she said, "You got to be kidding me." And I said, "No ma'am, everybody else is users." . . . And I called every person I know and said, "No, I'm not a narc [under-cover drug cop], and no, I didn't get busted. But I wish you well, and I want you to wish me well. I'm going to try this out [twelve-step]. Remember me telling you I wanted to find out who I am? I'm fixing to try out." And that's what I did. And I just—I love it. . . . Yeah, "My Name is Bill." Bill's the one that wrote the book, and actually the whole step. It's a spiritual program. It's an awesome program.

Maggie became what could be called a twelve-step zealot. She ceased all her drug use and developed a missionary-like calling to help those less fortunate than herself.

Ironically, although her self-proclaimed spiritual experience roused by the twelve-step program led Maggie to acquire the role of a savior for other addicts, she herself began using methamphetamine again—she relapsed with a peculiar twist. As Maggie described her own recovery path and relapse, and how she "saved" others from self-destruction, her religious fervor caused a change in her previously sincere self-reflective and subdued demeanor. She became visibly energized while she unconscientiously preached the twelve-step philosophy like a convert at a revival meeting. She linked every incident of her own personal story to the story of Bill W, the alcoholic who started the twelve-step program known as Alcoholics Anonymous. For example, when I asked about her relapse, her story was interspersed with twelve-step ideology:

> Because when they say you can't get back around anybody, they really mean, I don't care how strong we are. It's like Bill said, "Oh I can go

into this bar, and I can sit there and say I don't have to drink." Bull! You're there. Maybe the second time, maybe you think, "Well I'll just take a sip of it and eat my sandwich." And the next thing you know you're drunk, and you're sitting there, and you're only fooling yourself . . . and I thought, well, I can't go to the school today to help my daughter unless I have some ice. And I know better, but that's the mind thing of me saying—I'm trying to fool myself is what it is.

I pressed her to describe what was going on in her mind when she relapsed:

> Well, I was on the way over there [the house of a friend who was a user] and I wanted to prove to them that I could be—and my husband said, "'Don't go over there." And I said, "'Oh no, I've been clean for a year and a half, I'm never going to do ice again. I've got sponsors." I was sponsoring people and I just, I can do this—I'm thinking now that's what Bill said when he went into that bar—I can do this and be the only one in the world that can do it.

Maggie said she felt guilty after relapsing. Although she did not see a relationship between her guilt and her new role as a missionary for the twelve-step philosophy, the two appeared connected in her narrative. Every mention of her current use was linked to how she was going to quit using by bringing another person into the twelve-step program. For example, Maggie had introduced me to a young woman who was staying at her house. The girl's tiny body belied her nineteen years, and in contrast to Maggie, she looked eerily like one of the "faces of meth" photos I saw on the highway billboards. Maggie explained her current mission with this young woman:

> I mean, see poor old Julia. She's been through hell, and I gave her an intervention. She actually looks better now. She got raped last week over at a friend's house. And he left, and she was there by herself. And the guy had a grudge against this other guy and came in and raped her in the process of it . . . I feel so sorry for her because she is just—she's alone. Just met her at some friend's house. I went over there and next thing I know I brought her home . . . and I kept trying to tell her, "Julia, you are an addict," and we [twelve-steppers] are not supposed to call each other addicts. And I keep trying to say [to Julia], "I can't call you an addict but I'm telling you, from experience, that you need to go [to a twelve-step program], and I'll take you" . . . I love being clean to be honest with you. I know in my heart I like being clean [drug-free] . . . I tell Julia all the time. "Shit," I said, "forget that I'm using." I tell her all the time, "I'll go in with you . . . when you work the program, when you get to step four, all of a sudden you wake up one day and world is just all out there. It's like God opens miracles for you." . . . I keep telling Julia to go clean with me, "Julia, you know,

when we get to step four [of the twelve-steps], if you are not seeing miracles happening in your life, I'll go buy your dope [local slang term for methamphetamine] and we'll go out and get high again.

Though Maggie's behavior of using methamphetamine while encouraging others to stop using might seem hypocritical, she was truthful about her use. Some might interpret this behavior as dishonesty or a petty excuse to continue using. Yet the sincerity of her confessional belief in the twelve-step program and her candid portrayal of herself as a recovering "sinner" did not give the impression that she was what some women in twelve-step called a *poser*. Instead, Maggie appeared to be a woman trying to bridge two worlds that held meaning for her but were, unfortunately, incompatible.

To complicate her recovery further, Maggie bonded easily with members of divergent social networks. Maggie displayed unusual social characteristics that can be both helpful and harmful. She seamlessly wove her intimate primary relationships in suburban middle-class networks with her drug-using relationships that bridge legal and illegal activities. She understood the motivations and needs of disenfranchised drug users while embracing the strictly conventional norms of middle-class society endorsed by the twelve-step practice. Therefore, while Maggie appeared to be firmly grounded in the suburban social landscape, her association with many young methamphetamine users influenced her to engage in behaviors that conflict with middle-class conventions. For example, when revealing that she is a daily injector, she explained that she cannot inject herself and asks someone else to do it. Her reasons for injecting methamphetamine instead of smoking or another route were also unusual:

Because it [methamphetamine] was like dirty and 'cause everything filters through the kidneys and liver and all that. I know all that. And when you get bad dope you get kidney infections, or you get backaches, and that's your kidney, cause it's filtering through that. I knew that, and I was like, "There's got to be another way." That's when she [a friend] was like, "Well, let me show you." And I was okay, and then it was like, wow, I can do it once in the morning and I'm fine all day. A lot of people, they do it all day long. Now I'll do twenty dollars in the morning and I'll be good all day. I'll go to sleep at night, go home and eat dinner.

Most of Maggie's close friends used methamphetamine, and those she came in contact with who were not close (teachers, PTA parents) could not tell that Maggie was on ice. She looked like every other mother, and her behavior did not give her away.

While Maggie talked, I hardly noticed any behaviors that would indicate methamphetamine use, except for the vast knowledge she recounted of every aspect of a user's life. She sat calmly in her chair during the two-hour interview, except when recounting her twelve-step stories and advocating its philosophy with slogans and quotes she memorized and repeated with an uncharacteristic display of animation. I attributed this to twelve-step enthusiasm more than the influence of methamphetamine. I had met enough twelve-steppers to recognize that her behavior was learned, but it was her otherwise composed state that was more curious.

Daily methamphetamine users were, if not agitated and unable to sit still for long periods of time, often more frenetic in their behavior than Maggie. I had seen this composed nature before among the few women who had been using methamphetamine regularly for years but not in a bingeing pattern of intense use for days. Some women who used in a controlled manner over years even gained weight and said they had little trouble sleeping, which seems contrary to the physical effects common to methamphetamine use. Typically, as tolerance increases, women increased their dose or frequency, but not Maggie. She had learned her lesson. She told me that previously she had been the type of methamphetamine user who did occasionally binge. She lost weight and was always agitated. She recounted the first time she met an old using friend after her recovery: "I went over to a friend's house I had not seen for a year and a half, and I'm like, you know, I want them to see the new me, because my sponsor had showed me a picture of myself at one of the meetings on the very first time I came and I was like 'wow.' I wonder if I would, I wonder if everybody else would see me that different. And I ran into a girlfriend at a flea market and she said, 'Oh my God, I can't believe that's you. It was like your complexion, everything about you is different.'" Although her former use had taken a toll on her body, by current appearances her looks had been restored. Moreover, the infamous "meth mouth" that so many women feared had not affected Maggie. Her teeth were all her own and pearly white. Her clear complexion was smoother than was to be expected of a woman nearly fifty years old.

An explanation was needed to understand how Maggie could continue using methamphetamine and still maintain a relatively healthy body and a social life unaffected by the well-documented medical consequences of methamphetamine use and unharmed by the harsh legal repercussions that hurled many of the actively using women I interviewed into eventual abject poverty. One explanation is that she learned how to use drugs in a controlled manner, which is a harm-reduction approach that will be further explored in this book.

Maggie's drug path is not over, and her goal is obviously complete abstinence, but unlike many women I interviewed, she appeared to be comfortable with the fact that she promoted abstinence while still using. Before Maggie left I asked her how long she thought she would she be using methamphetamine. She answered forthrightly, "Every day I wake up and I'll say—like what I told Julia, I'll go with you and start over—I'll stop because I'll start back at step one. I mean relapse is a part of recovery. I think I'm ready to recover."

I had heard this from many of the women I interviewed. And knowing the current treatment options and recovery rates for methamphetamine users, I understood why she seemed facetious about relapse. Being a woman on ice was not an easy path to follow, but it was even more difficult to leave. While our knowledge of methamphetamine use and treatment is increasing, little is known regarding its use among residents living in a geographic setting that is traditionally regarded as a haven for law-abiding middle-class families—the U.S. suburb. Yet on closer inspection, the social landscape of the suburbs is a potential breeding ground that fosters attraction to use a drug with the effects provided by methamphetamine—energy, weight loss, and happiness.

SUBURBAN WOMEN

For five years I conducted ethnographic research in the suburbs of a large metropolitan area in the southeastern United States to learn more about suburban use of methamphetamine, a drug also known as ice, speed, crystal, shards, and a variety of other street names. During the last two years of the study, I focused on suburban women exclusively in order to better understand their use of this drug from their own perspectives and changes that occurred in their lives over time. The purpose of this book is to portray the everyday reality of methamphetamine use by suburban women from a diversity of social settings, social classes, race/ethnicities, and age groups. I aim to unravel what being a methamphetamine user, or addict, means to these women by examining the trajectories of their drug use within the context of suburban life.

Maggie was one of the women who seemed to navigate the world of drug users and mainstream suburban middle-class more successfully than others. Some of the women decided to leave the drug-using environment either to avoid various consequences such as loss of family or employment, adverse health effects, involvement with the criminal justice system, or as part of what seemed like a process of "maturing out" of drug use (Winick 1962). Others continued in their drug use despite serious consequences that often left them homeless, abandoned by family and friends, and facing repeated or extensive periods of incarceration. Treatment, whether coerced or voluntary, worked for some but not for others. Many women recited the sayings that I had come to recognize as the philosophy of twelve-step: "Once an addict, always an addict" or "You have to hit rock bottom first." Yet empirical evidence shows that not all drug abusers remain addicts or recovering addicts for life, and some stop having a problem with alcohol or other drugs before they hit rock bottom (Akers 1991; Boshears, Boeri, and Harbry 2011). However, many of the women I interviewed who had relapsed multiple times repeated the twelve-step phrase I often heard—that they needed to hit rock bottom first. Maggie was unusual in that she expressed a strong belief in the twelve-step model but did not embrace the rock-bottom mandate that was part of twelve-step lore.

Another faithful twelve-step believer who accepted this tradition was Mia, a fifty-year-old woman who had been a homeowner when she held a semiprofessional work role. After years of problematic drug use, she lost it all. "I haven't hit rock bottom yet," Mia told me, although she was currently homeless and had resorted to prostitution on a busy suburban highway to pay for her daily motel room, the suburban version of what are known as single-room occupancies in the city.

I could see that Mia had been a beauty in her younger years, but she lost her looks as a result of her constant drug use and intermittent poverty. She had no teeth; the last remaining teeth had been pulled at a free clinic that promised her a set of dentures but never delivered, and her sunken cheeks made her appear even older. "I will always be an addict," she told me. When I asked her what "addict" meant, she said if she knew, she would not be one.

Mia said she never thought she would wind up in a shady motel taking strange men into her bed for thirty dollars. She started to cry in my car as she recounted her story—an emotional outpouring I had seen many times. As we sat in silence in the parking lot of a fast-food restaurant, I let Mia's sobs subside on her own time. I knew she had already seen many professional addiction counselors over the years, having been in and out of both private and public treatment facilities. She had heard every addiction explanation available, yet she could not tell me what it meant. I also could understand why the rock-bottom philosophy worked for her—it gave her hope for the future.

Typically it was the older women who cried as they remembered their many losses and acknowledged they had so little time left to turn around their lives. In contrast to the younger women, who were full of hope despite their current desperate situations, the older women had seen too many of their dreams broken by circumstances beyond their control. Younger women were just as clueless about what being an addict meant and what to do about it, but they all believed they would never be "like one of those addicts" they saw on the streets or on the highway billboards.

Dee was one of the younger women whose social and economic situation was similar to Mia's—basically penniless and without a job or home—but she had more hope and more positive social capital thanks to her age. She was new at being homeless and new at being addicted. She thought she was not going to end up like the women she saw gathered outside the only homeless shelter in the suburbs. Although she was now going to the homeless shelter for the hot meal they gave at lunchtime, she was adamant that this was a very temporary situation. The hot meal was the only free resource available to the homeless, since a bed in the shelter required the homeless to have a photo ID and pass an alcohol Breathalyzer and drug test, which eliminated many.

At the time, Dee was sleeping in her car in a parking lot, where an improvised Hooverville of old cars, instead of tents, was parked behind a big-box retail store. "Hooverville" was the term used to describe the shantytowns of makeshift dwellings that sprang up in public parks during the Great Depression. Now, in the Great Recession (Grusky, Western, and Wimer 2011), the Hoovervilles I saw in suburban areas were made up of old cars in deserted parking lots. Dee had no gas money, and she left her car in the parking lot while she walked to the shelter for food. At the shelter she talked with some other young people in a similar situation, who referred her to a trailer park. There she met a group of youths living in one small trailer. All were using methamphetamine supplied by the young man who rented the trailer. It was not clear how the drugs were paid for, although interviews with other women who lived there indicated that some of them got methamphetamine in exchange for sex. At their young age, they did not consider this exchange prostitution but instead consensual casual sex.

Dee was raised in a solidly middle-class suburban family and had lived in a tranquil suburban neighborhood all her life. She said she was ashamed of living in this run-down trailer park inhabited primarily by immigrant families and the suburban poor, and she swore that this was only a temporary situation. But she did not want to return to her mother's house. Apparently, her mother, who lived only half an hour away by car, would not speak with her and told the rest of the family that Dee was a "thieving crazy junkie" who could not be trusted.

Dee's flawless skin and pearly white teeth gave no indication that she had been injecting methamphetamine for the last two years. Having learned her drug skills from an ex-boyfriend, she was relatively clueless about the drug-using world outside her former group of suburban high school kids who used drugs. For example, despite having shared syringes in the past, she had never been tested for HIV or hepatitis C and did not know where to go to get tested. I learned that she had been subjected to severe domestic violence at the hands of a much older boyfriend.

As we sat in my car surrounded by 1960s-era mobile homes squeezed next to each other in a haphazard fashion, she revealed that she hated her current situation. "I'm in a place where I don't really belong, but I am choosing to do this." I asked her why she chose this. "Because I'm a drug addict," she said without a thought, as if she had heard this reason before. She could not explain to me what that meant. "But I will never get to the point of stealing or prostituting myself," she assured me. "My rock bottom is before that."

Contrast Dee with a group of women I interviewed who are part of the suburban poor, the suburban brand of the "urban outcast" found in marginalized urban communities (E. Anderson 1999; Wacquant 2008; Wilson 1987). The suburban poor typically lived in what were essentially hidden areas of the suburbs. Many of these communities were no more than a collection of dilapidated trailers more isolated than the middle-class trailer parks where residents enjoy private pools, laundry services, and a residential custodian. The suburban poor trailer parks were typically without any of these features, and no custodian was present to ensure the residents' safety or address their complaints. Most were not walking distance to any public transportation, which is essential for employment and access to the social services for people without cars. Often located at the end of a dirt road and buried in the woods, they became enclaves of danger as well as poverty. Having conducted fieldwork in urban, rural, and suburban environments, I noted the similarities and differences between these poor neighborhoods.

In contrast to the poor in rural and suburban enclaves of poverty, the poor in urban areas often have access to a vast array of social services accessible via public transportation. In fact, recent studies on the migration of the urban poor to suburban areas find a dire lack of access to needed health and social services for the suburban poor (Allard and Roth 2010). As I became familiar with the exurbs, the area outside the initial suburban ring surrounding the city, I learned what it means to live in communities that are intentionally or inadvertently overlooked by the publicly funded social safety net. Being invisible to public services, the residents in suburban and exurban enclaves of poverty were left to rely mainly on aid provided by religious organizations. This private support was not enough, and as more and more suburban homeless began to appear at their doors, many of the local churches decided to provide for the poor by giving their donations to the one local homeless shelter that controlled all distribution in the area. The shelter divided the deserving poor from what it identified as the undeserving poor, and anyone who screened positive to a drug and alcohol test were part of the latter.

The lives of women from the suburban enclaves of poverty were typically a consequence of intergenerational rural poverty unaddressed by social services. Their current proximity to the suburbs, which had spread to incorporate their communities, seemed to have provided little additional social support. These women had been exposed to domestic violence as children, often were exploited sexually before they became adults, and had experienced violence at the hands of men throughout their lives. Those over forty years old had few teeth left and suffered from chronic disease or the cumulative effects of previous injuries. Many were raised in communities where drug use was the norm and surrounded by relatives who used and/or produced methamphetamine, which was part of some rural communities for decades.

The theories that explain problematic drug use by the suburban poor are different from those that explain methamphetamine use by middle-class suburban kids like Dee or the suburban middle-class and working-class housewives like Maggie. They face a lifetime struggling with depression and self-medicating with drugs and alcohol like Mia. But unlike Maggie, who still had mainstream social capital that provide networking resources, the marginalized poor suburban women typically have only each other to count on for help—people who were just as poor and without resources.

The women in this book represent a range of methamphetamine users with a range of reasons why they use methamphetamine. Their stories also illustrate the structural forces and structural violence that affect drug users in the United States, which is more detrimental in many ways for women than for men (Bourgois, Prince, and Moss 2004). For example, the stigma attached to a woman who is incarcerated for drug use is greater than it is for a man, especially if the woman is a mother. Later chapters of this book depict the insider's view of the lives of women who use methamphetamine, framed in sociological perspectives. Throughout the presentation and interpretations of their lives, I use scholarly theories to inform my analyses. My goal, however, is to look beyond the explanations of scholars and professionals by using the voices of the women and their interpretation of their lives as revealed in the interviews. In the interplay between analysis and narrative, I depict the everyday reality of suburban women who use ice with a goal toward understanding how to reduce the problems and suffering merely glimpsed here.

While I draw from many theories, my purpose is not to support one side or another of a current theoretical debate but instead to engage theory so that it becomes useful for the people being studied (Bourgois 2002). To this end, I use the typology of drug-use phases I developed, informed by life course, social control, and self-control theories (Boeri 2004). This typology illustrates phases in the drug-use trajectory conceptualized as a drug career (Becker 1953). The in-depth stories recounted by the women illustrate the divergent pathways taken, influenced not merely by choice but also by structural constraints and the social capital resources available to them. A more detailed explanation of this typology is provided in appendix B.

In the rest of this introductory chapter, I give an overview of methamphetamine-use literature to set this qualitative study in historical and contemporary context. I start with a synopsis of the history of methamphetamine and its pharmacological-based effects, followed by epidemiological reports of data collected in the United States. Next I review the literature on drug use and women who use drugs, focusing on the literature pertaining to the use of methamphetamine by women. I end with a discussion of the literature on HIV/AIDS and how the spread of infectious diseases affects women who use illicit drugs. This background material is precursory and meant only to provide a current academic perspective of methamphetamine use and the use of methamphetamine and other drugs by women. The women's stories are the heart and soul of this book.

METHAMPHETAMINE: A BRIEF HISTORICAL AND PHARMACOLOGICAL BACKGROUND

Methamphetamine is similar in chemical structure to amphetamine and can be smoked, snorted, injected, taken orally, or taken anally. The fastest-acting and most potent methyl group of amphetamines, chemically known as methamphetamine hydrochloride, became the popular street drug known as "meth," "crystal meth," "tina," or "speed." Another type of methamphetamine, known as "crank," is typically produced in small labs and usually associated with users living in rural areas or among motorcycle gangs. A smokable and chemically purer form of methamphetamine, called "ice," was reportedly first produced in Asia and smuggled into the United States (Abadinsky 1997). The popularity of ice and its rapid spread across the globe, particularly in the United States, is reportedly due to its smokability, which, as with smoking cigarettes and crack, results in more addictive behaviors.

Methamphetamine epidemics have more than a forty-year history in the United States (Anglin et al. 2000; Weisheit and White 2009). As with other epidemic drugs, the popularity of methamphetamine rises and falls over time, often linked to a particular subculture (Agar 2003; Reinarman and Levine 1997). Ice first received national attention when a near epidemic in Hawaii spread to California in the late 1980s and continued to diffuse across the United States from the West Coast to the East Coast. Concern over methamphetamine use decreased during the 1980s as a growing crack epidemic dominated national attention. Attention returned to methamphetamine during the 1990s when a form of methamphetamine made from anhydrous ammonia, often used in fertilizers, was produced in labs built on farms in the U.S. heartland, devastating communities affected by economic downturns (Reding 2009). As the increased use of the drug continued across the country, methamphetamine abuse became known as an "American disease" (Sloboda, Rosenquist, and Howard 1997).

Often, as the popularity of one drug wanes, a new drug trend appears to attract public attention. Andrew Golub and colleagues warn that while drug epidemics come and go, "journalists and politicians commonly abuse the term 'drug epidemic' to arouse concern and serve political agendas" (2004, 364). While we should use the term *epidemic* with caution, methamphetamine use did continue to increase and spread into all U.S. geographic regions. Public concern over methamphetamine's infiltration across social and economic barriers is now supported by empirical evidence.

Methamphetamine is a stimulant that affects the central nervous system and releases dopamine neurotransmitters to the brain while simultaneously inhibiting their uptake. This produces a pleasurable experience along with increased activity and decreased appetite. In low doses, its effects are perceived to improve functioning (Lende et al. 2007), but in high doses it becomes extremely dysfunctional (Weisheit and White 2009). Effects of methamphetamine may include insomnia and loss of appetite—pursued for functional reasons. Adverse physical effects include increased blood pressure and hyperthermia. High doses can increase body temperature to dangerous levels and cause convulsions. Long-term psychological effects of methamphetamine may include violent behavior, anxiety, confusion, insomnia, paranoia, auditory hallucinations, mood disturbances, and delusions (National Institutes of Health [NIH] 2005). While there is little evidence of methamphetamine withdrawal symptoms similar to those based on the classical definition of withdrawal from heroin (Lindesmith 1938), methamphetamine withdrawal reportedly may produce "fatigue, anxiety, irritability, depression, inability to concentrate and even suicidality" (Barr et al. 2006, 303). The severe dental problems attributed to extensive use of methamphetamine, popularly known as "meth mouth" (Shaner et al. 2006), have been shown to be associated with poor dental hygiene combined with the dry mouth and teeth grinding associated with using this drug (Donaldson and Goodchild 2006).

Methamphetamine users expose themselves to risk of HIV infection through injection and unsafe sexual practices (Compton et al. 2005; Urbina and Jones 2004; Semple et al. 2005). Treatment studies find that methamphetamine users typically show more severe mental and health problems than other drug users entering treatment, and more effective strategies for treating methamphetamine users are needed (Brecht, Greenwell, and Anglin 2005; O'Brien 2003; Rawson et al. 2004).

Methamphetamine production is of particular public health concern because of the frequent explosions, fires, and toxic fumes resulting from clandestine production labs (Connell-Carrick 2007; Hannan 2005). Unlike cocaine and heroin, methamphetamine is not derived from a plant but is instead synthetically produced in a laboratory. A methamphetamine lab inventory might include pseudoephedrine, which is found in over-the-counter decongestants, and chemicals such as hydrogen peroxide, lye, and red phosphorus. Because it is relatively cheap and easy to manufacture, methamphetamine has been produced in clandestine labs in rural areas for years; however, makeshift labs are increasingly found in suburban and urban areas, notably in motel rooms, trailers, and vans (Ward et al. 2006). The literature on methamphetamine highlights the health hazards to the users, their family, and the community posed by clandestine methamphetamine labs (Lineberry and Bostwick 2006; Potera 2005).

The government responded to the meth lab problem through the Combat Methamphetamine Epidemic Act (CMEA) of 2005. While the majority of states had already passed laws curtailing the sale of some precursors, these restrictions varied by state (Goetz 2007). The CMEA was incorporated into the Patriot Act and was enacted at the federal level on March 9, 2006. Under this legislation, over-the-counter products containing ephedrine, pseudoephedrine, and phenylpropanolamine are subject to strict purchasing regulations. These anti-meth provisions introduced safeguards to make certain ingredients used in methamphetamine manufacturing more difficult to obtain in bulk and easier for law enforcement to track (Bren 2006).

The unintended consequence of recent policy aimed to reduce availability of methamphetamine appears to be increased small-batch production. Studies conducted after the law was passed show that more users are self-producing small batches of poorer-quality methamphetamine, which may result in problematic health effects (Sexton et al. 2006). As a result of increased regulation, methamphetamine producers are attempting novel ways to concoct precursors. One method, called the "cold cook method," is cheaper but uses ingredients that may be more toxic than those found in the purer forms of the drug produced in large labs (Boeri, Gibson, and Harbry 2009). This method involves mixing toxic ingredients in a container (usually a fish tank) and burying it in the ground for thirty days. Crystals forming along strings hanging from the lid of the tank have methamphetamine qualities, according to field reports. Since the cold cook method produces less noxious gas and fewer explosions, production is less detectable by law enforcement officers. The new methods of producing methamphetamine also make it harder to know the estimated number of current users, since epidemiological indicators rely on reports from police and public health records.

Drug Use, Social Context, Health, and Women

The women in this book who initiated and continued use of methamphetamine were influenced by the increased use of methamphetamine in the southeastern region of the United States. The use of illegal drugs by women should also be set in historical perspective, however. Only recently have women been the focus of research on drug use. What these studies show is that the effects of drug use and the social context of drug use are different for women than for men.

Illicit drug use among women began receiving greater attention in the 1970s, which is late compared to their male counterparts. A key aspect for female drug users is their stigmatization as bad women because they violate gender-role expectations (Campbell 2000; Ettore 1992; Zerai and Banks 2002). This stigmatization is encountered not only in society at large but also within the drug scene (Boyd 1999; Sterk 1999). Several studies show women's drug use to result in further victimization (Chesney-Lind and

Sheldon 1992; McElrath, Chitwood, and Comerford 1997; Stewart, Elifson, and Sterk 2004).

Just as the emancipation of women that started in the 1970s resulted in an increased involvement of women with deviant activities, including drug use (F. Adler 1975), it also resulted in the cultural reproduction of female roles. Lisa Maher found that the "cultural understandings that continue to shape the legitimate world of glass ceilings" are reproduced in street-level drug and sex markets (1997, 206). More recent literature emphasizes the women's agency and empowerment (T. Anderson 2005). While it is important to recognize the extent to which social conditions impact female drug users' access to power and agency, we cannot ignore how structural violence is also reproduced in the drug scene (Bourgois, Prince, and Moss 2004).

Much of our early knowledge about drug users derived from studies of prison, treatment, or street-based populations that were primarily male samples (Preble and Casey 1969; Waldorf 1973). During the latter part of the twentieth century, a number of empirically based books provided additional insights on female drug users. For example, Marsha Rosenbaum (1981) interviewed one hundred female heroin users and found narrowing role options for women in both mainstream and drug societies as their drug use continued. She also found that prostitution was the fastest way for female heroin users to make money, since few legal work options were available to them. Subsequent literature supported these findings but revealed increasing diversification of female drug roles.

Maher's (1997) inner-city sample included forty-five female crack users in New York City involved in sex work. Maher identified three types of hustles that contributed to the women's income: "drug business hustles, non-drug hustles, and sex work" (83). Like Rosenbaum, she found that only sex work provided a reliable and consistent means of income generation for the drug-using females. Preferring the known routines involved in sex work, females engaged in subordinate work compared to males, who more often became high-level dealers in the drug-using culture. Maher contends that the hierarchy found in the drug-using culture strengthened the reproduction of existing gendered relations.

Studies on female drug users usually are made up of samples recruited from low-income neighborhoods. A Miami sample of street-based female sex workers (Surratt and Inciardi, 2004) focused on the social context of homelessness. Compared to women who were not homeless, the homeless women had more reports of childhood abuse and higher levels of victimization in the past three months. Female prostitutes who use heroin were found to be primarily polydrug users who often migrated to using crack cocaine (Inciardi, Lockwood, and Pottieger 1993).

Avril Taylor (1993) conducted an in-depth study of twenty-six crack-using females recruited from inner-city streets. Taylor found that females typically were initiated into drug use by male partners, and they usually learned to provide illegal sources of income from male partners, although some learned from female friends in the drug world as well. In Taylor's sample, only six women used prostitution as a means of acquiring drug money. The women in her study generally viewed prostitution as a shameful occupation engaged in only when their drug use increased.

Claire Sterk (1999) developed a typology of female drug roles in her study on 149 inner-city women who were active users of crack cocaine. Sterk found that the women in her sample fell into four main income-production categories: (1) women who cooked crack for drug dealers; (2) women mainly engaged in prostitution; (3) women involved in illegal activities other than prostitution; and (4) women who started crack at a late age and had few income-generating skills. The women in the last category usually bartered sex for crack.

As the average age of drug users increased, largely because of an aging baby boomer cohort, research focused on the influence of age on female drug users (T. Anderson and Levy 2003; Boeri, Sterk, and Elifson 2008). While younger female drug users may find increased agency and empowerment through their involvement in the underground economy, since their youth supplies bargaining power, older women generally face a reduction in resources in the drug-using world. Moreover, female drug users of all ages are at greater risk than males for being victims of violence and for contracting HIV, hepatitis C, and other infectious diseases through heterosexual contact—a risk that increases with age (Lorvick et al. 2006).

Since epidemiological data report statistics collected from known populations of drug users, such as those in the criminal justice system, treatment, or hospitals, we know less regarding illicit drug use among hidden populations (Page and Singer 2010). Suburban areas have less direct oversight by the criminal justice system or public health care services, and methamphetamine users in these areas remain less visible. Moreover, many middle- and upper-class users are able to avoid detection and are therefore not included in drug treatment and criminal justice records, and female drug users often are veiled from public view in suburban and rural communities. Recent studies call for a greater understanding of methamphetamine use in diverse social contexts, specifically use by women (Dluzen and Liu 2008; Sheridan et al. 2006).

Women and Methamphetamine

According to epidemiological data, female participation in the methamphetamine-using social culture increased at rates similar to those of males (Substance Abuse and Mental Health Services Administration

[SAMHSA] 2007). However, as a result of their double stigmatization in both the mainstream and drug world, females have fewer resources to help them cease drug use and are more vulnerable to the numerous health risks associated with methamphetamine use (Substance Abuse and Mental Health Services Administration [SAMHSA] 2010). Moreover, little is known regarding patterns of cessation of methamphetamine use that are specific to women.

A study by Patricia Morgan and Karen Ann Joe (1996) comparing male and female methamphetamine users provides increased insight into gendered use patterns among this hidden population. Their study sample of 450 methamphetamine users included 141 women who worked in the drug economy in three cities: San Francisco, San Diego, and Honolulu. The women in this sample played a larger role in the illicit drug economy than found in previous studies. More than 30 percent of males and 22 percent of females received their primary source of income from illegal drug activities. Furthermore, the women reported that their involvement in drug dealing increased their self-esteem and help them to control their drug use. Many of the women participated in mainstream society as citizens with traditional female roles while concurrently participating in the drug economy as sellers of illicit drugs. The authors concluded that research on drug use should move beyond the traditional disenfranchised minority groups, since many drug users, both male and female, do not live on the "extreme marginal edge of society" (139).

Findings from studies conducted on gender differences among methamphetamine users show that females generally start earlier, are affected differently, appear more dependent on methamphetamine, suffer more adverse effects, and respond more favorably to treatment than do males (Brecht, Greenwell, and Anglin 2005; Westermeyer and Boedicker 2000). Female methamphetamine users also show more indicators of depression than male users and are more likely to report that they use methamphetamine for self-medication and to lose weight (Hser, Evans, and Huang 2005; Lorvick et al. 2006). Remarkably, although some women who use methamphetamine endure greater stress in family relationships due to gendered social roles, recovering female methamphetamine users show significantly better improvements in family relationships than do males (Dluzen and Liu 2008). They are also more vulnerable to the adverse health effects of drug use, however.

HIV/AIDS, Infectious Diseases, and Women

Drug use presents a primary risk factor for transmission of HIV and other infectious diseases through injection routes as well as sexual behaviors (Page 1990; Singer 2006). New HIV/AIDS cases resulting from injection use increased 42 percent from 1998 to 2003 (United Nations Office on Drugs and Crime [UNODC] 2005 and 2007). Reported data by the Centers for Disease Control (CDC) show that injection-drug users accounted for approximately 19 percent of those living with HIV and 12 percent of all new HIV infections in 2006 (Centers for Disease Control and Prevention [CDC] 2010). Drug-related risk factors include years of use; frequency of use; receptive syringe sharing; distributive syringe sharing; and sharing of cookers, cotton, rinse water, cleaning syringes, and smoking equipment. Sexual risk behaviors include number of partners; multiple sex partners at one setting; engaging in sex while under the influence of drugs; unprotected sex; same gender sex partner; and an injecting-drug user sex partner (Maher 1997; Singer 1994)

The focus of much AIDS research in the United States has been on populations with known high risk for HIV transmission, such as men who have sex with men (Klitzman, Pope, and Hudson 2000; Ostrow 2000; Williams and Miller 2006), female sex workers (Blankenship and Koester 2002; Sterk 2000), and inner-city populations in economically depressed neighborhoods (Inciardi and Pottieger 1998; Singer 1994). The risk of drug-related AIDS transmission is greater among socially vulnerable populations, minority groups, and women (Inciardi 1995; Kwiatkowski and Booth 2003; Sterk 2000). Research shows that injection-risk behaviors among drug users are socially learned and influenced by the social context of drug use (Neaigus et al. 1994; Poundstone, Strathdee, and Celentano 2004; Schensul et al. 2002). Yet little is known about the social context of suburban drug users, specifically the suburban context of female methamphetamine injectors.

Studies on inner-city samples of drug users found that females in poor neighborhoods suffer from the normalized violence prevalent in their culture arising from social hierarchies and injustices (Sterk 1999; Taylor 1993). While poor urban neighborhoods have received much HIV- and drug-related research attention, and low-income rural areas are studied for drug-related health issues specific to isolated regions (Haight et al. 2005; Reding 2009; Sexton et al. 2008), the suburban social context has been viewed as a haven from such social problems. The symbolic and structural violence that researchers have found to pervade the lives of inner-city and rural drug users is, however, present but less visible in the social settings of suburban homes, trailer parks, and motels where methamphetamine use occurs.

WOMEN ON ICE: A SUMMARY

As Maggie's story illustrates, the lives of women who use methamphetamine are not quite like those depicted on television and in newspapers showing the "faces of meth." Neither are they like the life of the suburban marijuana-dealing housewife in the popular television show *Weeds*. Since they are a largely hidden population, little is known about suburban women who use ice. This book fills the gap in the literature with an in-depth analysis of women who use methamphetamine while living in the suburbs.

In this book I identify the complexity of drug-use patterns found among new and diverse social networks while employing the conceptual tool of drug use as a career and focusing on turning points and transitions in social roles throughout the life course (Becker 1963; Elder 1985; Laub and Sampson 1993; Rosenbaum 1981; Waldorf 1973). I question assumptions about suburbia as the idyllic social milieu for family life where young parents move to escape the violence and social pressures of the city. Moreover, I question the efficacy of the current stigmatization of women, particularly mothers, who use methamphetamine, and I propose solutions to address the conditions that lead to problematic use. I do this by providing a better understanding of how structural forces and seemingly arbitrary decisions made by those in power have far-reaching effects that can save or destroy countless human lives.

Within each chapter I weave classical and contemporary theories used to explain drug use and society's reaction to drug users. While I discuss a number of theories and concepts, no single theory explains all the situations and lives of the women in this study. Researchers on drug use employ different models drawn from psychological, sociological, anthropological, or medical disciplines. These theories can be used in combination for a broader understanding, or they can be used alone to focus on different aspects of methamphetamine use. More recent developments of these theories are enhanced by and expand on existing addiction discourse. The concepts and theories presented are used to view the women's stories from different perspectives, not necessarily to suggest that one is better than another.

In chapter 2, I describe the ethnographic methods I used. Many people ask me how I find drug users and get them to talk to me; here I answer these questions by explaining how ethnographic research on drug-using populations is conducted, using tangible and often graphic examples. A more academic explanation of the methodology is provided in appendix A.

The women in this book are presented anonymously. I gave each woman a pseudonym by applying names that were popular for babies born at least twenty years before or after the birth period calculated from the women's actual ages. Specifics regarding residence, employment, and other descriptors that are not essential to the analyses were changed from the original to protect anonymity. The women portrayed in these pages represent events and behaviors similar to those described by other women in the study, and their stories might sound familiar to anyone who knows a methamphetamine-using female. If a woman in this book appears to be someone you know by the same name, I can assure you the name and resemblance are coincidental.

In the remaining chapters, the stories of the women illustrate the theoretical perspectives discussed and help fill the gaps in our understanding of the gendered trajectories of methamphetamine use across time and place. To organize the women's lives analytically, I employed a typology of the drug-using career that illustrates nine phases found in the drug trajectory based on social roles and self-control (Boeri 2004). These include: (1) controlled occasional user; (2) weekend warrior; (3) habitué; (4) marginal user; (5) problem addict; (6) dealer/runner; (7) hustler/sex worker; (8) junkie; and (9) relapsing addict/junkie. These phases are described in more detail in chapter 2 and in appendix B.

The three women presented in chapter 1 were chosen to illustrate another primary organizing pattern I found among the women defined by social class and age: the suburban youth culture (SYC), the suburban working and middle class (SWMC), and suburban poor (SP). These organizing themes informed my analyses of the women's lives as I started to group the women by what I heard unfold in their stories up until the time of the last interview. Dee represents the suburban youth culture, Maggie represents the suburban working and middle class and Mia represents the suburban poor.

In this suburban sample, race and ethnicity were not found to be characteristics that separated categories of female methamphetamine users. The most obvious and interesting defining factor that emerged was age. The young people who used methamphetamine were more similar in how they used and why they used, regardless of class distinctions, than were older women. While no distinct age was identified as a cutoff point, generally those under age twenty-five had similar patterns and used drugs in similar contexts that were different from the women who were older. As I mentioned earlier in this chapter, they also expressed confidence that they would never become "meth junkies" like the women they saw who used for years. The younger females tried to avoid these women and sometimes spoke of the older female users in terms that were derogatory, perhaps because they feared becoming like them. The younger women typically started using methamphetamine with friends for recreational reasons and continued using because they liked the effect of having energy, being happy, and staying thin. They tried to avoid "bingeing" (using methamphetamine for days at a time without sleeping or eating), even though some had binged on methamphetamine in the past. Dee was an example of the younger generation of methamphetamine users who grew up in the suburbs. She will be seen again in this book.

The second category, the suburban working and middle class, included women who were similar in many ways despite differences in social capital and economic means. Their life histories showed that the invisible line between class distinctions was permeable. In the suburban communities, the working class and middle class had few differences in social norms. For example, a woman who was raised in a middle-class family often lived a working-class life as an adult married to a laborer. Conversely, a woman who was raised in a working-class family might acquire middle-class status through higher education, marriage, or business acumen. These were women who had already passed the age when drug use might be considered an occasional or youthful indulgence. The social capital inherent in suburban working- and middle-class norms and values influenced not only their drug-use patterns but also society's reaction to women who use drugs after they are no longer considered young. I note that although some of the women were born into or still had families who could be defined as upper class, none of the women were considered upper class at the time they were interviewed. The class status was always precarious, particularly after the Great Recession of 2008 (Grusky, Western, and Wimer 2011). The prolonged recession resulted in the loss of considerable working- and middle-class employment opportunities and the convergence of the "99 percent," to use twenty-first-century parlance. Maggie was one of the women who had been raised in a middle-class home but who stayed on the brink of the working class for most of her adult life.

The final category is a class distinction that emerged after I was introduced to a group of women who lived below the social and economic standards of the working class but typically remained outside the radar of the social services designed to keep these women and children from destitution. They lived in communities I call suburban enclaves of poverty. Many of the women had been raised in enclaves of poverty either in urban or rural areas. Some of these rural areas were now incorporated into the suburbs. Others who were raised in working-class, middle-class, and even upper-middle-class communities ended up in the suburban enclaves of poverty due to life circumstances. Mia is an example of this category, and her story will be explored more fully in the following pages. The failure of our social safety net to stop these women's descent into abject poverty resulted in some women being forced to engage in risky behaviors, including dealing drugs, prostitution, and reliance on men who had more resources than they did. I called this category the suburban poor.

The "vocabulary of poverty" has always been problematic (Katz 1989, 3). The "enclave" nomenclature aptly fit the social environment of these largely hidden and forgotten suburban communities (Bourgois 2003). The term "underclass," used to describe the urban underclass and the truly disadvantaged, and the more recent term "urban outcasts" (Wacquant 2009; Wilson 1987) are appropriate descriptors of the poor I found in the suburbs, but all these descriptors bring other connotations with them, so I use the simplest term—the poor.

The suburban poor were not a homogenous group, but at this time in their lives they had similar patterns of drug use. Typically in and out of homeless shelters, jails, and treatment facilities, these women learned various tricks of the trade to survive—generally not relying on social services but on their own wits and fading sexual attractiveness. Some said they had made bad choices at one point in their lives, but now they had few choices. Most were constrained by political and economic forces beyond their power to change. Contemporary structural inequalities and social inadequacies brought on by the Great Recession forced many into their current survival mode among the suburban poor. Their eyes reflected suffering and pain, and their voices often broke at some point in the interview. They were at the bottom of the social hierarchy and they knew it. And they used methamphetamine to forget.

CHAPTER 2

Ethnographic Research

EXPLORING METHAMPHETAMINE
USE IN THE SUBURBS

FIELDWORK

My research assistant and I had driven over fifty miles to a small college town southwest of the university offices where we had met earlier that morning. A recent contact had informed me that this town was full of meth users. Along the way we stopped at shopping strips and gas stations that looked like promising areas to hang our fliers. Once in town, we talked to coffee shop and bar servers to get a feel for the clientele, who appeared to be primarily college-age students and health-conscious folks who appreciated the town's crunchy granola ambience. It was hot and humid and the streets were deserted. The quiet was broken when a few older men with long gray ponytails made a noisy scene as their Harleys crossed the semi-deserted square. We went to the restaurant where the Harley riders stopped to eat to see if we could strike up a conversation, but as we drew closer I got the impression they were local college professors out for a ride. Dean, my research assistant, agreed, and we kept walking.

We did not have any leads to write about, but that was not unusual for our first day in a new area. Having canvassed the entire downtown on foot, we returned to my car and were driving around the outskirts of town looking for bars when I got a phone call. The male voice sounded full of energy—a good sign for a prospective interviewee. He said he had heard from a friend of a friend about my methamphetamine studies and wanted to know more. I briefly explained the study, my professor/researcher credentials, and the confidentiality safeguards before asking if he had any other questions. He had plenty, and his knowledge of methamphetamine norms indicated to me he was a user. After he seemed convinced that I could be trusted, he asked how many people I wanted to interview. I made an appointment to meet him and his friend later that afternoon before I discovered he was located about thirty miles northeast of the university we had left that morning—almost one hundred miles away from where we were now. I was used to such long travels. Ethnography in the suburbs entails a lot of driving.

We had arranged to meet at a public library, where I often met interviewees during the day. At night I usually met them in the local Waffle House or another all-night diner. I called the library ahead of time to reserve the only two private rooms available.

When I arrived in the town, I checked out the main street for field note purposes. Half the stores were empty; the rest were old and quaint, an indication that this was a dying commercial zone. The library was walking distance from the main street, with a parking lot twice the size of the library building. The lot was practically empty. There were only a few people in the library, and none that fit our caller's description. Dean waited inside while I waited outside to look for any male who drove up and seemed to be about thirty to forty years old, the age my caller said he was when I talked to him on the phone earlier. The few men who arrived were not my caller. I was about to suspect that he decided against it when I got another phone call from him.

"I'm here," I said, "Where are you?"

"I lost my ride," he replied. "But someone is coming to get me, and I will be there soon."

He didn't have a car—a frequent situation for methamphetamine users I interviewed. Most of them had to rely on others for transportation because they did not have a working car or their license had been suspended. I usually offered to pick up females who needed a ride, but I had never met this man, so I said I would wait. He said he would be there in half an hour. I went inside to avoid attracting attention in the parking lot, and after thirty minutes I went outside again. It was getting dark when I saw an old model car drive by with two women in it. One looked my way. They parked and walked toward the library. I smiled at them.

"By any chance, are you looking for Miriam?" I asked one.

They looked at me oddly.

"You the interview lady?" one of them asked.

"Yes, I do interviews. Why?"

"Tommy sent us," she said. "We came to do the interviews."

"How come Tommy couldn't come?" I inquired.

"He couldn't make it today. He said we should do them, and he will call you later."

This was not an unlikely story. But I asked if they could call Tommy so I could talk to him. Tommy made some excuse on the phone but assured me these women were okay to interview. I suspected that Tommy had sent these women to check me out first—which turned out to be the case. I was fine with having two more women to add to my sample. Women were harder to find for interviews, not necessarily because they used less but because they were more concerned about hiding their use.

I talked to the women in the privacy of the library room to make sure they were eligible for my research. After years of doing drug interviews, I knew the questions to ask for a screening. The women checked out. They knew the effects of methamphetamine, what it looked like, and how much it cost. They also knew a few ways to make methamphetamine that were local to the area, and other details only current users would know.

Tommy called me to set up a few interviews after this night, but each time he could not make it for one reason or another. He moved. His ride never showed up. He broke his leg and was in the emergency room. This raised suspicion, but I have heard the strangest stories from methamphetamine users and typically they were validated through ethnographic inquiry. For example, when I finally met Tommy, he limped toward me with his foot in a cast, a validation of his previous excuse for not showing up. I was able to conduct his interview by suggesting I come to where he was—at the time he was living in what appeared to be a boardinghouse located in the farthest county that was still considered a suburb of the metropolitan area. I took two research assistants with me since he said there were two more women who wanted to do the interview. The women were waiting at the house, along with Tommy on his crutches, and passed the eligibility screening.

Months later I met Tommy and one of the first women I had interviewed. They told me they were stopping methamphetamine use since they wanted to have children. I took them out to eat at a Mexican restaurant off the beaten track and we talked about their future. The woman was about ten years younger than Tommy; neither one of them had a job. I knew they both had children already; she had lost custody of hers, and he visited his children when he was near the state where they lived. I wished them luck. I had seen lives change before—why not theirs?

Tommy and his friends provide an example of the ethnographic methods used to recruit prospective participants in a study focused on illegal and stigmatized behaviors. Every person interviewed is recruited in a different way, but the common pattern is that I remain in the field and talk to anyone who shows interest. I give everyone my contact number on a card or a flier. Someone calls me. I meet them and they trust me. They refer more people who trust me based on their friend's word. I have learned how to look for indicators of when someone is not telling the truth about drug use. If something appears odd, I confer with my community consultants to get a better understanding. Ethnography is a flexible and reflexive activity that is difficult to explain or describe because it changes by setting, time, and actors involved (Charmaz 2005; Lofland et al. 2006; Page and Singer 2010).

I have been recruiting and interviewing drug users for more than ten years. People often ask me how I find the users and how I can trust them. The short answer is I go out and talk to everyone. Treating people with respect, of course, is needed, but beyond common civility, I am open and honest. Respect can appear deceitful when forced. My deference to their situation is real but at the same time I challenge what appears suspicious when the situation warrants it. I have heard that my sincere questions and my honest responses to their questions engendered trust. I am empathetic toward drug users' lives, having had a brother who used drugs all his life, and this probably shows in my interaction with others in similar situations.

When I can, I help those who need help in small ways. For example, I sometimes try to help the respondents find a job if they ask, although that has become almost impossible in the recession economy. I will look for doctors who will see them or homeless shelters that will take them. I bring them warm coats or buy a hot meal. I spend a lot of time driving them somewhere. I have to do this selectively, since funding does not pay for anything outside the research protocol, and helping them is not part of the Institutional Review Board (IRB)–approved study. It does help with recruitment, but I do this because I know about their situation, and I know that little acts of kindness establish my reputation as someone who can be trusted. I gain the trust of the people I interview to be a better ethnographer and because I do care, but I always am conscious of remaining a researcher and not becoming a social worker, which is not my role.

ETHNOGRAPHIC AND QUALITATIVE RESEARCH METHODS

The data for this book come from two ethnographic studies on methamphetamine use in the suburbs funded by the National Institute on Drug Abuse (NIDA), part of the National Institutes of Health (NIH). The objective of the first study was to gain an understanding of emerging trends among methamphetamine users in the suburbs, focusing on how they initiate, maintain, moderate, remit or resume use of methamphetamine over the life course of one hundred suburban dwellers. The goal of the second study was to gain a deeper understanding of gendered drug-use trajectories and risk-behavior patterns, focusing on risk awareness, risk behaviors, health care utilization, and accessibility to health care services among suburban women who used methamphetamine. Both studies used a qualitative research design.

Qualitative methods have been shown to be particularly applicable for studies among hard-to-reach and marginalized populations, specifically drug users (Lambert et al. 1995; Nichter et al. 2004). Qualitative methods allow researchers to identify a wide range of users, as well as to gain a better understanding of the meanings and motivation of use, specifically from the user's perspective (Denzin and Lincoln 1994; Lofland et al. 2006). The qualitative method used in the suburban studies involve ethnography, which is based on deep familiarity with the social setting from the perspective of those involved (Geertz 1973). This method of data collection requires the researcher to spend considerable time in the field, not only to become familiar with the environment of the study population but also to develop contacts and trust relationships (P. Adler 1993; Page and Singer 2010).

Three main types of data collection were used: ethnographic participant observations; drug history and life history matrices; and audio-recorded in-depth interviews. The second study included a follow-up interview and a focus group interview. These methods are further explained in appendix A.

I conducted the ethnographic fieldwork and interviews alone or with trained research assistants. Building a good team is an important part of research. The first research assistant I hired I met while in the field looking for potential interviews. My strategy that night was to approach anyone sitting in a certain public area, show them a little flier I had made, and explain that I was a professor conducting research. Since many of the people frequenting this suburban town square were students at the university or at least knew of the university, my role as a professor conducting research was not questioned. Typically I approached people who were alone or with a small group.

To be clear, I do not approach people and ask if they use methampheta-mine. My flier asks "Do you know someone who uses methampheta-mine?"—so I am not necessarily suggesting that the person I approach looks like a drug user. I find most people to be interested, and they usually ask more questions, such as what the study is about or if people in the study are given methamphetamine to use, which draws us into a conversation. After talking a few minutes, they might tell me that they know of someone to whom they will pass on the flier. I point out my phone number on the flier and remind them to tell the interested person to call me. I actually got a call one day from someone who got the flier from his friend who was a teller at a bank who I remember talking with as I withdrew money. The point is that I recruit all the time and anywhere I am in order to reach a diverse population.

On this night, I saw one young man sitting alone in a coffee shop patio. He looked as if he might be someone who could have connections to a diverse social network, judging from his long dreadlocks. While I try not to stereotype, I knew that not many people sported dreadlocks outside the city, and very few could be found in this conservative county known for its ultra-right-wing politics. In his case, my intuition was correct. I approached the young man and gave him a flier. He read it and said he did not know any-one. Since he seemed slightly defensive, I thanked him and moved on to a group of young women at a table across the patio. They were interested in my work, and I sat down to talk with them about the study. A few said they knew someone to give the flier to; then I moved on to an empty table to sit alone, reflect, and jot notes. The young man with the dreadlocks had watched my conversation with the women, and he came over to me. Still holding the flier in his hand, he mumbled that he might know someone. He sat down at the table and we talked about the study. I learned he was a student at the same school where I taught. His name was Dean. I invited him to come around to my office later in the week.

Dean came to my office a few days after this encounter. As I suspected, he had a large social network of friends and acquaintances who would qualify for the study. I asked Dean to go out on field research with me as a community consultant—a term applied to people who are familiar with the field. Within a few weeks, Dean was hired as a research assistant and started training to be an ethnographer. He was born, raised, and attended school in the suburbs, so his insights on suburban drug use were invaluable. He also had instant street credibility with everyone we met thanks to his demeanor and insider knowledge, and without his expertise the study would have taken much longer.

After training research assistants in fieldwork and interviewing, I tried to match interviewers with interviewees as much as possible by age, gender, or race. The insights provided by those with similar demographic backgrounds were usually helpful during the interview and especially during the coding of the interview data. Fieldwork was typically conducted in teams of two.

Our field of ethnographic research covered the suburbs and exurbs of a huge metropolitan statistical area (MSA). Canvassing this area with fliers, we visited bars, clubs, and coffee houses. Strip malls hosting tattoo shops, Laundromats, and pool halls were also popular. Trailer parks, motels, and all-night diners were added as we found them, or as we were referred to specific sites by a community consultant.

PARTICIPANT OBSERVATION

Participant observation can be categorized as overt or covert participant observation in public or private settings; the researcher may be an insider or outsider, and the participant can be more or less involved in the activity being studied (Lofland et al. 2006). Direct observation in drug research is needed to understand the social interactions of drug-using communities (Bourgois 1999). The type of observation used here was as a trusted outsider in both private and public spaces. I was not directly or knowingly involved in drug-use activities. For example, I often drove people to places they needed to go, but to my knowledge this was not for the purpose of buying or selling drugs. Typically, I learned more from the conversation we had while we were together in my car than I did in the interview.

I never hid the fact that I was carrying out research. I found that if I let people know immediately that I was conducting research, I was more likely to establish good rapport, since there would be no history of deceiving them. I did this in subtle ways that changed depending on the setting and the actors. For example, I did not flash our fliers in a bar but instead talked with people, usually the bartender.

Rapport building is the key to obtaining participants and gathering valid data for this type of study (Lambert et al. 1995). In addition, assuring the participants that their information is safe and will not be used against them is important. For this reason, I obtained a certificate of confidentiality from NIDA that protected our data and research team from court subpoena. I also allowed participants to use pseudonyms, and I did not ask for last names or exact birth dates. The trust and camaraderie engendered by being honest was also important. I answered every question a participant or potential participant asked about the research study and process, and there was nothing to hide except the identity of other participants. The participants and community consultants verified that they appreciated my candidness regarding the research process.

SUBURBAN ETHNOGRAPHY

Books of urban ethnography have provided a wealth of information on the ongoing changes in drug use in urban social contexts and how to conduct ethnographic research among hidden populations (Schensul et al. 1999; Bourgois 2003; Page and Singer 2010). In this book I apply the insights of urban ethnography to a new field that has been rarely studied—suburban landscapes.

While a geo-historical analysis of the suburban social ecology of the study site is beyond the scope of this book, the immediate historical context of our study's geographic ecology became important to the development of the research. At the time of the study, the most popular illegal drug (other than marijuana) used in the area was methamphetamine. Crack cocaine was used when available and in specific communities closer to the city. Prescriptions pills were becoming the primary drug for many suburban methamphetamine users as a result of the proliferation of pain pill clinics, called *pill mills*, in the area. Although there were a few small pockets of what might be considered open-air drug markets, the majority of drug dealing was in private.

The economic reality of the study site is also useful background data. Many of the women recounted stories of having lived relatively stable and comfortable lives in the suburbs, but they lost their economic security when they or their spouses or partners lost their jobs. After the Great Recession of 2008, fewer jobs and more job seekers made it difficult to find sustainable income. The loss of economic status in the suburbs typically forced the women to move from one community to another. For example, some women I interviewed went from home ownership to living in rental properties to working for a trailer park owner in exchange for a reduced rent on a mobile home. A few became homeless. Others resorted to small-time drug dealing or prostitution on a temporary basis.

The ecology of the study site and economic situation guided the methods. For example, I started recruitment in the relatively wealthy towns and college campuses in the suburbs; I ended in the poor enclave communities where more of the respondents now lived. Some of the women I interviewed had only recently moved to these communities as a result of economic hardship.

My first study on methamphetamine use in the suburbs, which was ongoing in 2008 when the recession began, produced unintended documentation of the effects of sudden unemployment on suburban residents, especially for women. The second study, starting in 2009, documented the unexpected changes in the women's social and economic condition and highlighted the lack of services in the suburbs for the marginalized. The effects of nationwide economic policies, suburban-specific structural inadequacies, and increasing criminal ramifications on drug use left entire families without any source of income unless they surrendered their family autonomy—a foundational feature of suburban life—to government bureaucrats. Many of the women chose not to do this and struggled in silence.

WRITING ETHNOGRAPHY

Protecting the confidentiality of the participants is complicated when writing ethnography. Using pseudonyms is a standard, and as explained in chapter 1, I made an extreme effort to choose names that were different from those used in the community. However, ethnographic writing can provide enough detail that friends or family of the participants might recognize the person. I try to avoid this by changing the minor details when possible. Since the patterns found in the lives of the women were often similar, one woman can easily be mistaken for another. Four or five women could have qualified as Maggie, described in the previous chapter, with few details changed.

The ethnographic works that have captured the hearts of the readers in recent years are those that tell the whole life story of its characters set in context, such as the crack dealers in El Barrio (Bourgois 2003) and the Hallway Hangers and Brothers in a northeastern housing project (MacLeod 1995). I attempt to keep the context and patterns of the women's lives intact enough so that you, the reader, can feel these are real people and not disembodied quotes. However, I have changed minor details throughout to provide further anonymity. These changes usually involve a personal aspect that might identify a woman when combined with her demographic description. For example, I might change the number of children she has, the type of employment, or the state and city where the women were born. When I have to do this, I choose a substitute that does not detract from the woman's life context.

For example, if she was a housecleaner (service work) I might say she was a server (service work). If she had five children, I might write she had six or four. I never mention the region's largest city by name, referring to it simply as "the city" to signify the metropolitan core of the study area. Suburban towns where I conducted research were not identified by name either. More than one town was called "the meth capital" by participants, so all references to a meth capital suburban town could be referring to one of four or five places.

Quotes are used throughout the book to paint a picture of the women's lives as well as to illustrate conceptual analysis. Each quote is verbatim. Ellipses, or three periods with spaces in the quote, indicate some unnecessary words that were repeated too many times ("you know," "uh," "um") were deleted, or sections of conversation were not included because they did not add to the flow of the conversation. Long pauses are indicated with [long pause] since they add to an understanding of the context. An em dash ([—]) indicates that the speaker interrupted her train of thought. Brackets [like this] are included when a slang word needs to be translated or when another word is substituted to ensure anonymity, such as a person's name, a place of work, or a specific location. When quotes are part of a conversation and set off in a block format, the questions asked by the interviewer are shown in italics.

LIMITATIONS

While the stories are not representative of all suburban women who use methamphetamine, they do provide a current insider view of the reality of methamphetamine use from a diverse sample of suburban women. For the sake of efficiency and readability, I often present the quotes without all the questions I asked or the broader context that provides further validity; however, most of the stories were corroborated throughout the data collection and analysis, and questionable data were not used in this book. Moreover, quotes and inferences regarding social services, health care, and law enforcement were confirmed. As a small convenience sample, the findings are not generalizable, but the norms, behaviors, and methamphetamine use patterns portrayed in this book through the voices of the women depict a panorama of methamphetamine use that can be found across the nation. The social situations that are common to the women and the interplay between structural constraints and women's agency are played out repeatedly in our postmodern society. This ethnography provides a few heartfelt snapshots of this contemporary scene.

24-HOUR ETHNOGRAPHY

The reason for using qualitative methods, particularly ethnographic fieldwork, was to obtain an in-depth insider view of the everyday reality of suburban female methamphetamine users and the effects of their use on their families and communities. To do this, a considerable amount of time was spent in the field interacting with the women in the study. The following account describes what actually occurred in a twenty-four-hour period during which I tried to help a homeless woman named Kat find a place to live. The account, taken from my field notes, provides a graphic glimpse of the methods that informed the data collection and what life is like for Kat and women in her situation. This account is only one day in my life as an ethnographer, but it sets the stage for the women's stories that follow in subsequent chapters.

May 22, 6:00 p.m.

I thought I would be home relatively early tonight. I left my university office and expected to take no more than an hour to deliver a resource list of social services to a recent participant in the study. She lived in one of the dilapidated trailer parks hidden from the view of the middle-class subdivisions and gated communities. We were about forty miles away from the edge of the city. The geography was ambiguous—between suburban and rural—yet the area was referred to as suburban. The women sent their children to suburban schools, but they were more rural than suburban in terms of their culture.

This particular network of women lived or associated in a poor suburban enclave. None of the women had steady employment. None had a car to find employment. Most were single or divorced. The county they lived in did not have public transportation. A convenience store at a gas station about a mile away, marginal walking distance, was their daily source of food and household supplies.

Most of the women I had interviewed who lived in the poor suburban enclaves had been abused by men. Some were molested as children, and all experienced domestic violence as adults. They used methamphetamine, the drug of choice in this area. Most were now using the latest drug of opportunity—pain pills. All the women said they were often depressed. Some had an official diagnosis. A few had been diagnosed with hepatitis C. None had continual medical, counseling, or psychiatric care.

Pat, the woman to whom I was bringing the resource list, needed help with rent for the trailer. She was constantly in fear of not making even the little she owed and not having anything left to pay the utilities. She was unemployed and probably unemployable due to her depression and stress-related health problems, which required medical care. During her interview she cried periodically whenever she talked about how her son had been sexually abused for years by a neighbor. This had happened over ten years ago, and although at the time she was not a drug user, she blamed herself for not knowing. She tried to commit suicide multiple times, which led to the ruin of her marriage. She said the main reason she started to use methamphetamine was because it took away her pain; she felt good as long as its effects lasted. Lately, methamphetamine was not as accessible as pain pills, since a pill clinic had opened near the trailer parks.

I pulled into the gravel and dirt in front of her trailer with my assistant, Debbie. We found Pat standing outside, sweating profusely. It was ninety-one degrees outside, according to my car's thermometer. It must have been over one hundred degrees inside that trailer with no air conditioning. I knew she had no transportation to go to the store, so I asked her if she wanted me to get some cold drinks, to which she agreed emphatically. Debbie and I drove to the nearby gas station store and bought some cold soft drinks. When we returned to the trailer, Pat told us Kat, another participant in the study, was now homeless.

Kat was one of the more stable women in this network. At the time of our first interview a few months earlier, she was living in a townhouse and had employment. She had recently left her abusive husband. Apparently, Kat was offered a trailer in this park for free if she cleaned it up. The trailer had been gutted and was inhabited by stray animals. It reeked of urine and excrement. We found Kat sitting dejectedly under the shade of a tree and offered her a cold drink. She told us she could not let her son stay there.

We offered to take Kat to a homeless shelter in a nearby suburban town, the only one in the area that took people unannounced at the door, if they had room. We called the shelter and were told that she would have to stay in the women's section and her teenage son in the men's section. She said she did not want to be separated from her son at a shelter. We called other social services and found no help anywhere. As the night drew near, I said I would pay for her and her son to stay in a hotel room tonight. Kat and her son joined us in the car and we headed to a hotel.

May 22, 7:00 p.m.

On the way to a hotel, I figured that one night was about $50 and extended stay for a week was about $200, so I might as well pay for a week. Before going to the hotel, I dropped Debbie off at the university where she had left her car so she could go home. The hotel was more expensive than I remembered. We were told the price for two people with taxes was $250 for the week. They also wanted photo ID from Kat. She said her only photo ID, her driver's license, had been stolen. The manager was adamant—she could not stay in the hotel without a photo ID.

Kat told me about a hotel where she had stayed recently when she still had an ID card and thought perhaps the owner would remember her. When we arrived at the hotel I saw it was extremely run-down. The reception area consisted of a tiny room with no chairs and a glass partition over a counter that separated the client from the reception area. This hotel was $50 cheaper than the first one, at \$200 for the week. I was about to pay, but the owner would not let Kat stay without an ID. Kat told me she had a birth certificate with some of her personal belongings she had left at a friend's trailer. We asked if a birth certificate was enough and his answer was a firm no. He said he was required to have a photo ID of all clients on record by law.

It was now nearly 10 p.m., and I realized we would be hard-pressed to find a hotel in the suburbs where Kat and her son could stay without an ID. I offered to take them back to the trailer where someone would let them stay. Realizing they had not eaten yet, I dropped Kat and her son off at a fast food restaurant, bought them dinner, and gave them money for a taxi back to the trailer park. I told Kat I would pick her up early in the morning so she could try to obtain an ID. I headed back to my home in the city about forty miles away.

May 23, 7:00 a.m.

We had a focus group with five women scheduled for today at noon. Kat was one of the five. I told Kat last night that I would pick her up early to take her to get an ID at the Department of Motor Vehicles (DMV) where her last driver's license had been issued. I expected to be back in time for the focus group. On the way to our meeting place I stopped at my university to leave the cash I had brought from home to pay for the hotel. I made a habit of not carrying a credit card, debit card, or more than fifty dollars with me when out in the field.

Kat was waiting for me at 8:00 a.m. at the house of another woman I had interviewed previously. She said she had not slept all night because she did not have an alarm clock and was afraid she would oversleep. I wondered if she had used methamphetamine to help her stay awake but did not ask since she would tell me later in the interview.

Kat told me that her birth certificate and social security card, which was required to get a photo ID, were stored at the place of a friend where she was keeping her belongings. I drove with Kat to a dead-end street in an unkempt subdivision about five miles from where I picked her up. I could not see the house from the street very well, but she said there was a doublewide trailer parked behind the fence on private property. It was uninhabited and locked, but she knew how to get in. She jumped out while I turned the car around, always careful to be in a position where I could pull out onto the road quickly if necessary. I looked around to assess my surroundings while I waited.

In a few minutes, Kat came back with a purse-size wallet stuffed with papers and cards. We drove towards the DMV while she searched through the many papers folded inside the wallet. She eventually found her social security card but not her birth certificate. She kept flipping through the papers over and over again, but it was not there. She expressed concern that perhaps the woman who let her keep her things in the trailer had stolen some of her son's belongings. I inquired what belongings, and she mentioned VCR movies and video games that belonged to her son. As she became more and more upset thinking that her son's videos and games were stolen, I told her those things she can buy again, but her ID is a serious theft. She did not seem to care as much about her birth certificate as her boy's belongings. She did not want to report the woman, however, which was a good decision since later the woman hired her for odd jobs—her only source of income.

I suggested we continue to the DMV and try to get her photo ID with only the social security card. After all, I thought, she already had her license on file there. We waited about an hour until the DMV clerk told her she could not get her license or even a photo ID used for voting purposes without the two pieces of documentation. I tried to convince the clerk and later her supervisor that Kat's photo and license were in the DMV files, and all she needed to do was to match her photo. We were told that a federal law does not allow them to look at anyone's records if they do not provide documents proving they are who they say they are. We were referred many times to a list posted on the wall of "acceptable documents." She needed two of these documents, and Kat had only one—her social security card. Kat was born in another state, so getting her birth certificate would be no simple process.

We went back in the car and I called all the places we had on our resources list (such as domestic violence shelter, homeless shelter, emergency help line) that should know how to obtain an emergency ID. Most were only recordings that said to leave a message with a number to call back; none returned my calls. Those with a live person who answered the phone only referred us out to other agencies I had already called. In the next week, I would talk to social service staff, domestic violence shelter personnel, and homeless directors who gave me the same directive: "She needs to get her birth certificate." None offered any help to get it, although they knew how hard it was to obtain this piece of paperwork, especially when homeless. Kat had no phone, no address, and no money. I dropped her off at the trailer park and told her we would work on the birth certificate after the interview.

May 23, 12:00 p.m.

I picked up the women at the trailer park and brought them to the university room we used for focus groups. We held the focus groups on a Saturday when few people were around. The ages of the women in this focus group ranged from twenty-one to fifty-one. Our coinvestigator, a nurse professor, led the focus group, accompanied by the two research assistants. The focus group interview was taped and I took notes as an observer.

By now, six months into the study, we knew that most of the women not only lacked access to resources but also that social services rules and regulations presented the greatest barriers. Our notes and a digital voice recorder captured their responses. Their major needs were employment, food, housing, legal aid, and medical care. The major barriers were lack of transportation, money, and paperwork obstacles, including lack of an acceptable ID. An additional problem was the fear of repercussion from the criminal justice system for those on probation or from the Department of Family and Children Services (DFCS), for those with children. Overwhelmed as we were by what we were hearing, I knew it would be difficult to get Kat's ID, and I was wondering how I would get her a hotel room without it.

May 23, 3:00 p.m.

One of our research assistants had picked up ninety pounds of food at a local food bank. When the focus group was finished, I took the food to the trailer park where the women split it between them. Meanwhile, Kat was looking for someone who would lend her an ID so she could get a hotel room. She came running up the dirt trail to tell me she found a woman who would do it.

Two rough-looking women came toward my car. I asked Kat if I could trust them and she said yes. Nevertheless, I told Kat to get in back with one of the women and let the other woman sit in front with me. I did not want two strangers sitting behind me while I was driving. Both women looked to be in their late thirties or early forties. One woman with dark hair wore a tight-fitting black tee shirt that accented her ample breasts. The other was a thin woman with bleached blond hair and colorful tattoos. The blonde woman said she would use her ID to get Kat a room. I was not sure if this would be accepted at the hotel and told them we had to be honest. They agreed. As we drove to a hotel, the women told me their stories and how they happened to be at the trailer park. I also learned that Kat had just met these women.

Apparently, they were both from another county and had come to a nearby neighborhood to party with friends. While they were sleeping, their car was stolen. They knew the person who stole it but did not want to report this person since he was a "friend." They were also afraid of the consequences if they called the police. This man had a record, perhaps an outstanding warrant, and he would be in deep trouble if they called the police. He was also a distant cousin of one of the women, so they decided to wait him out, hoping he would call them and return their car. They had been waiting for days. Meanwhile, their cell phones ran out of power and they did not have a charger. They had received no contact from the man who had taken their car. The women were now staying at the trailer park with a friend of Kat's abusive husband, so their social connection to Kat was through the husband Kat was escaping. I asked why they would use their ID to help a woman they hardly knew. They said they were helping her out because of the kid, and they knew what it was like to need help. I understood their motive and asked no more.

May 23, 4:00 p.m.

The women had not eaten a meal for a few days, so we stopped at a Waffle House and I bought them a hot meal. While they were there, I returned to my university to collect the money for the hotel bill. I looked in the back seat and saw that the women had left their large handbags in my car. The big bags were both opened wide and I noted there were no visible weapons (guns or knives)—which made me feel safer—but I also made a mental note that these women trusted me with their belongings.

I returned to the Waffle House and we started to look for a hotel, which was more difficult than I had imagined it would be. Kat wanted to stay in the area so she could be near the trailer park and the place where she kept her belongings. Every hotel gave us the same excuse—they would not let Kat stay without her own ID. The blonde woman came in with me. Most of the hotel managers (who may be the owners) were clearly foreign born. The blonde woman started yelling at one saying she was being discriminated against. She threatened to call the local television station to come out there and see how foreigners were discriminating against Americans, but her phone did not work and I would not let her use mine. I calmed her down.

Kat went into the next hotel by herself and came back to let us know the hotel manager said he would let her stay. I insisted we tell him what we were planning: the blonde lady was going to give her ID for the record; I was going to pay; Kat and her son would be staying in the room. I wanted to be sure that Kat would have the key.

The manager questioned the woman who gave her ID, asking her if she understood that if she gave her ID, the authorities would look for her if the room was trashed or a crime committed. She said she had nothing to lose. Then she asked for a discount with her military ID (her ex-husband was in the military). The manager said the military discount was only for the daily rate and not allowed for the weekly rate. This made her angry and she started to say something about the American men fighting in foreign countries, and he should go back to his own country (he seemed to be Indian). After the manager got the ID information he needed, I paid the bill in advance and led the woman, still arguing, out of the hotel before the manager changed his mind.

May 23, 5:00 p.m.

Kat got her hotel key and returned to my car, eager for me to take her back to the trailer park to pick up her son. We had been together almost all day. I offered to take her to the doublewide to get her personal belongings, but she insisted I had done enough already. She said now that she had some money from the focus group participation, she could pay someone gas money to take her over to the doublewide before they went to the hotel. I knew that unemployed or partially employed men who had cars often drove their neighbors for a small fee—usually less than a taxi would cost but more than gas money.

On the way, Kat's son called my cell to ask if his mother was coming. We had been gone a long time looking for a hotel. I heard her say "I love you" and her fifteen-year-old son said "I love you" back—a sweet and tender interaction between mother and son. My reverie was broken when suddenly, the blonde woman started to scream from the back seat, "My car! My car!" pointing to a car across the intersection.

Her car was at the four-way stop facing us. We were turning left, and her car turned right, so we ended up directly behind it. The women, both seated in the back now, became excited. They screamed, "Follow that car!" I phoned my assistant, Debbie, on my Bluetooth and kept her on the phone so she could hear us and know where I was—just in case.

Sometimes, fieldwork takes us into risky situations, and each decision must be made based on our experience and understanding of the situation. I felt safe in my car with the technology of a Bluetooth connection, and I was fairly certain the women meant no harm to me. What I did was on my own time. Since these women had helped Kat, I wanted to return their act of kindness. I also thought I might keep them as contacts or community consultants. I had already given them my card and was hoping to establish contact with a new network. More than this, I put myself in their shoes. They were homeless and helpless without their car. It was daylight, and I thought I had enough control of my car and the situation to keep following the car in front of us.

They were yelling so loudly, I was afraid that the person who was driving the car in front of us would hear them and turn around. If the driver saw the women in the back seat of my car we might have a high-speed chase, and I did not want to do that.

We came to a T in the road. The trailer park was on the right. The car in front of us turned left. "Hurry, turn left," the dark-haired woman screamed. "It's getting away."

Kat, sitting in the front seat, said she wanted to get back to her son. I suggested she jump out when I pulled up to the stop sign and head by foot toward the trailer park a few hundred feet away. I turned left to follow the car. The car was out of sight by this time due to turns in the winding road. The women were screaming to go faster. I knew that we were soon to come upon the railroad crossing around the bend, and I already heard the whistle of a train coming. I thought we might catch up before the crossing.

"What's your plan?" I asked.

"To get my car," was the immediate answer.

When we turned the bend, we saw the car was stopped in front of the train tracks. The crossing lights were blinking, signals ringing, and the guardrails were down. The sun was now setting. The sound of the train roaring, the deserted road, and only a lonely house nearby made the scene perfect for a movie set. But this was not a movie.

Both women jumped out of my car and ran to the car in front of us. The blonde opened the driver's door, and the dark-haired woman opened the passenger's front door on the other side. A young woman wearing a baseball cap got out of the driver's side of the car with her head low and went sheepishly to the back seat. The train was still passing in front of us. The blonde woman came back to my car to thank me and grab her purse. She returned to her car, slid into the driver's seat and pulled off as the railroad crossing guardrails lifted. I looked in the back seat to make sure they had not left anything in my car.

May 23, 6:00 p.m.

Debbie was still on the phone and asked me what had happened. I told her all was well and I was going home now. When I got home, I wrote my field notes. A few hours later, I had my first full meal of the day, and I went to bed. It had been a long and eventful twenty-four hours.

CHAPTER 3

The Gendered Drug Career

INITIATION AND PROGRESSION IN METHAMPHETAMINE USE

ISABELLA

I met Isabella at a conference I attended near the city and interviewed her in a hotel room. She had heard I was presenting a paper on methamphetamine users and self-identified as a former user. She was only twenty-seven years old at the time of the interview, and her use occurred when she was younger. Isabella was best defined by the suburban youth culture category. Like many of the young suburban users I interviewed, Isabella started using methamphetamine with friends. She was from a wealthy family, and both of her parents were professionals. Isabella spent her high school years in a boarding school, and her mother bought her a house in a guarded community while she attended a two-year college. After four years, her mother finally suspected that her daughter was on drugs and withdrew her support.

Isabella possessed social capital that gave her access to both conventional and nonconventional resources. Although her story revealed a weak bond with her family during her drug-using years, she appeared to effortlessly make new acquaintances with people from all walks of life. Her ability to connect across social barriers helped her to become part of a vast drug-using network that included dealers and producers. However, the detached way she talked about her life, including her friends, acquaintances, and boyfriends, indicated that her emotional bonds to these people were not strong. For example, she said early in the interview that she had a "step-sister, a brother, and a half-sister;" yet she never mentioned them again in her two-hour interview as she talked about intimate details of her life. In contrast, she described years of shifting from one social network to another. It was this ease of making connections that enabled her to associate with a variety of drug dealers, but it also helped her leave her old drug-using networks without looking back.

Isabella's drug trajectory started slowly. She was not part of a popular drug-using subculture in her juvenile years and described being an outsider in high school. When she was first introduced to marijuana at age fifteen, she did not like it. Instead, she said, she "loved" the effects of LSD and Ecstasy, "It was just a new experience . . . it was an escape from reality." When a friend introduced her to methamphetamine, she liked it immediately. The circumstances surrounding this incident provide more insight regarding her reasons for using this drug the first time. As she described it, her low self-esteem was made worse by an abusive boyfriend:

How was he abusing you? Physically?
Mm-hmm [yes]. And emotionally . . . If it wasn't physical, he said things to me. I think it's partially the reason I started using meth as well. I was just—he had convinced me that nobody else would want me. I was really, really overweight. I was almost three hundred and thirty pounds. And my self-esteem was just nothing. And I think it was a combination of just low self-esteem coming from myself and almost being afraid to leave. He had threatened to kill me, and I mean it was ugly.

How were you introduced to methamphetamine?
The meth? It was actually [a friend]. We were supposed to, all three of us were supposed to be going to a concert called Oz Fest, and it was the night before we were supposed to go up there to [Big City], and he got very physical with me and left bruises up and down my legs. I just called her and asked her if I could go ahead and come up there 'cause I left. And she just said she was going to get something, and she came back, and she had it [meth]. And I was just like what the heck. You know, I'll do it too . . . I was euphoric. I mean I just felt like nothing really mattered and I could relax for probably one of the first times in a long time.

Isabella said that her mother, who she described as a "psychology major," took her to the doctor because she suspected she had attention deficit disorder (ADD). She was diagnosed with ADD but appears not to have taken medication for it very long. However, when she described why she liked methamphetamine, she indicated effects similar to those of medication used for ADD:

What was it that you liked about meth?
It was almost like a self-medication type thing. With some people it has the cocaine type effect, but with me, I could sit down and write and focus . . . I really liked it. I just enjoyed the feeling that I got from it is the only way I can really describe the feeling that I had. It was just I liked it. I almost felt normal, as sick as that sounds.

Isabella, like many of the women I interviewed, appeared to have started using methamphetamine for functional purposes. Describing her trajectory by the typology of drug-career phases (see appendix B), she remained in a controlled occasional user (COU) phase for a short period of time. Although she used it every day, she did not binge in the beginning, as she would do later. She either smoked it in a pipe called a *chalet*, or sniffed it (snorted) when a pipe was not available. Further along in her drug career she injected it. This began her problem addict (PA) phase, indicated by her acquisition of a drug role and uncontrolled use for a short period of time. As she associated more with dealers and the drug-using culture, she dropped her salient student role and assumed a dealer role, which appeared to bring some control over her use for a short period of time. Her using dealer/runner (UDR) phase revealed how easily she could bridge to the upper-class echelon to interact with people from all levels of society. She described her home during this time:

> I was hardly ever alone. I had what they called a trap-house. It's where all the drug dealers would come and sort their stuff out and just kind of sit around and use the drug, and then they would go and deliver to other people. But, you know, they would bring it to my house and divvy it out.

At this time, she was living in the home her mother bought her, located in what she called a guarded community. This meant that not only was there a gate at the entrance that required a code number to enter, but a guard stood at the gate to allow or deny access to the community. I asked her to describe how she could deal drugs in such a closed community:

> It was a house by itself. It was in a guarded community . . . Well my mom just really wanted me to be successful. She wanted me to be in school. She had inclinations that I wasn't doing well in school. I actually did complete a degree but it took me four years to get a two-year degree. I come from a very wealthy family, and as long as I was trying to better myself, she didn't want me working. She wanted me to concentrate on school.

Isabella's story revealed the ubiquitous nature of methamphetamine in the suburbs regardless of class, yet class status did make a difference in her life. While she was not protected from being introduced to the drug, Isabella is an example of the social protection provided by membership in the upper class:

> *I was just wondering how you could live in a gated community and not have the neighbors suspicious if you have all these people over?*
>
> Oh, they were suspicious [laughs]. . . . The guards were too. I mean because you have to say where you're going when you come into the community. And I was probably from here to the other side of the hall away from the guard shack . . . you could see my driveway from the guard shack. So I mean everybody knew. And when I got clean, the detective that was talking to my mother, unbeknownst to me, told her that they had been watching my house. There were always six people at my house—five or six people.

Did you always know them?

Usually. I didn't really like people I didn't know coming over.

Did they sleep overnight, if they slept?

Yeah, sometimes. I had constant revolving door as far as roommates go. You know drug dealers.

What drugs were they dealing out of your house?

Meth.

Isabella's many connections led to her meeting the producers. She revealed that producers from rural areas as well as those in the city supply meth users living in suburban communities. For example, Isabella explained her connections:

I just had friends that knew people that made it out in the boonies. [Rural] County mostly.

Did you know any producers in [Big City]?

I knew people that made it in [Big City] . . . A friend of mine and I rode to [Big City] with one [producer]. I rode with him several times, but you know that's the time that I was introduced to all these people, was when he came to pick up something, and I was the one that drove him to [Big City] . . . it was actually in old warehouses that were turned into an apartment, and then they had all kinds of other stuff going on. Chop shops, everything . . . The place where I went was a string of them. There were several. It was like an old storage-unit type place. But you know people had them rented out, and had turned them into apartments. And there was a place around back that was like a chop shop. It was just like a criminal's mall.

Isabella appeared to be attracted to the excitement of dealing as much as the need to support her habit:

The guy that I went to [Big City] with had connections in the meth circle pretty high up, and he could get an ounce for between seven-fifty and eight hundred. And then if you came back to [Suburban Town], and then just kind of what they called quartered it out, you could make two thousand dollars. So I mean that was more than enough to get more drugs and support your habit.

Although Isabella was fully immersed in collaborating with methamphetamine dealers and law enforcement was watching her house, she never went to jail. Instead, the police used her situation to catch others. She described her last days with her drug-dealing associates, which indicated her weak bond with this network:

When did you notice that you had a problem?

Well, I lost everything. Everything nice that I had was stolen . . . 'cause there was just so—it was a constant flow of traffic in my house. Constant. And

I called and reported my car stolen about five or six times . . . I mean somebody would just take my car. You know, I'd let them use it for drugs, and then they wouldn't show up for two or three days later. The car was in my mother's name. I always got it back.

Usually when you report a car stolen the police come to your house. Don't you think they're going to recognize something's going on here?

Well, hindsight, yeah. [Laughs.]

I can't imagine a meth user calling the police with five or six people hanging out at your house.

Well, people would steal my stuff all the time, and I'd never call the police. You know, I wasn't going to call them and tell them somebody had stolen a TV. But whenever it was a car that was in my mother's name— it would be gone for days before I'd call. So I would normally have sobered up a little bit not having a means of transportation.

When the police came over, did they ask you what's going on here?

It got to a point where they were kind of laughing at me when they would come over, but it was—yeah, I would name off some major drug dealer that I just said I let borrow the car.

It just sounds funny that the police didn't catch on quicker.

They did. But, you know, there's so much investigation, they're not going to freak anybody out.

Were they waiting for the big dealer or something?

Well, they came to my house several times looking for specific people. And they would tell me that they knew that person had been there this week-end. And me being this little smart-aleck, "Well why didn't you get him this weekend?" . . . I think the only reason I never got in trouble is because I had so many people just coming out of my house. They would just watch my house and see who was coming there, and they would take note of that.

Isabella's experience of having her car stolen by people she knew in her drug network was similar to the two women described in the twenty-four-hour ethnographic account in chapter 2. But in contrast to the women from the trailer park, Isabella called the police. While Isabella does not credit her social status or the social influence her mother might have had for her relative safety and lack of an arrest, the fact that the house and car were in her mother's name was undoubtedly a protective factor. Unlike the women from the sub-urban enclave of poverty, who were afraid to call the police when their car was stolen in the trailer park, Isabella's car was stolen in a guarded commu-nity. Isabella, protected by social class and perhaps more than she knew by her mother's social capital, portrayed a nonchalant attitude about the legal repercussions on her own life and those of the people she allowed in her house. This was not the attitude of women from the suburban poor.

Isabella's story ended with successful rehabilitation, which will be recounted in more detail in a subsequent chapter. This comparison is not intended to criticize Isabella or women with her social status. On the contrary, I admire her ability to stop what appeared to be self-medicating drug use caused by low self-esteem and victimization at the hands of an older abusive boyfriend. Isabella not only turned her life around, but she also fulfilled a desire to "give back" by becoming a drug abuse counselor. However, Isabella was able to escape the legal repercussions that often destroy the lives of women whose families were already devastated by intergenerational poverty, as will be revealed in many more stories presented in this book. Isabella's successful recovery provides evidence of structural inequalities. Political economy theory suggests that policy change is needed to address the social inequity in drug-related legal consequences. Isabella, with her wealthy professional parents to protect her, was untouched by the single most destructive influence on the lives of the women who used illegal drugs—incarceration.

Isabella's cessation of drug use was relatively fast in terms of where she was in her drug-using phase. Having started as a controlled occasional user and progressing quickly to problem addict and then to becoming a using dealer/runner, she benefited from her family's social capital. At the time of her interview she was a former user who had been drug-free for more than two years.

Her story is illustrative of a young woman from an upper-middle-class family who has high bridging mechanisms for acquiring social capital in diverse networks. Like many of the women I interviewed who started using methamphetamine in their youth, Isabella indicated a fairly easy access to the drug once she was introduced. Her self-esteem concerns echo what I heard from other young women, as does her motivation to use methamphetamine to keep her weight in check. The young methamphetamine users, members of what I have categorized as a suburban youth culture, crossed all class divisions. While being young appeared to provide easier access and increased self-esteem through association with a large and extended network of users, the socializing and recreational aspects of methamphetamine use eventually became less attractive. But, unlike many of the young women, especially those from less wealthy families, Isabella returned to mainstream roles without a criminal record to constrain her future choices. She returned to college and obtained a certificate to be a substance abuse counselor. Her story, however, shows a trajectory similar to that of the majority of the youth culture. For example, she initiated methamphetamine with friends and was introduced to injection use very quickly. She entered effortlessly into a world of runners, dealers, and producers. Because of her age, she had few of the life course roles expected of older women who need to juggle work, family and drug roles.

LIFE COURSE AND DRUG CAREER TRAJECTORIES

Life course theory provides the general framework needed in this book to analyze changes over time in a drug-using trajectory, also known as the *drug career*. While *career* and *trajectory* are used interchangeably, the *career* terminology adds the characteristics of an occupation, or a work role, and incorporates the "problems peculiar to that occupation" (Becker 1953, 102). Drug careers are typically described as occurring in stages including the initiation, becoming, maintaining, off and on again, and a conversion when the user is abstinent, called "completely clean" (Rosenbaum 1981). I employ the drug career model to explain why women in this study start, continue, stop, or resume drug use, with a specific emphasis on social influences in the life of the user, as well as the problems associated with using drugs.

In the life course perspective, a trajectory is the pathway taken over time. In this chapter, the drug-use trajectory is the focus of analysis. A significant change in drug use or in social roles of the drug user may reflect important turning points in a trajectory (Teruya and Hser 2010). For example, incarceration might influence someone to stop using certain illegal drugs, and reentering society from prison might be related to using again. A more subtle transition in drug use might occur when a user begins a relationship with someone who does not use drugs and is motivated to cease using, or conversely use more intensely when a partner is a frequent drug user. In Isabella's case, the continued abuse by her boyfriend instigated her initiation into methamphetamine use. To examine the life course of the drug career for methamphetamine, I looked at the initiation and progression of this drug, specifically with whom the user started and why the user continued. Next, I focused on problematic use and turning points into uncontrolled use. The recovery and relapse phases of the trajectory are discussed in chapter 7.

Initiation routes for women included being introduced through partners (usually male), colleagues at work or school, with friends (usually female), and family members. After being introduced to methamphetamine, the women continued using it for various reasons or motivations that can be grouped into three main themes: for functional purposes (including the ability to function better or longer); for social purposes; and for aesthetic purposes (such as weight maintenance). As will be shown, these thematic categories often overlapped in the women's lives and were hard to disentangle. Although some women said they used methamphetamine because it was available, closer inspection of their accounts revealed that the underlying motivations fell into one of the preceding categories. For example, many women were diagnosed with clinical depression and did not like their prescription medication or could not afford to buy it without insurance. Therefore, even if they said they used methamphetamine because it was available, analysis of their lives showed it also relieved their depression, which is a functional reason to continue to use. Others felt they were depressed but never went to a doctor for a diagnosis. These women readily expressed the antidepressive effects of methamphetamine and how it directly relieved what would have otherwise been unbearable periods of despair.

The life course perspective is particularly helpful in this chapter because it focuses attention on specific transitions and turning points in the trajectory. Transitions are marker events in the life course that refer to distinct yet connected changes in social roles, such as from a novice to an amateur to a professional. Turning points are times or events that take a person in a radically different direction (Sampson and Laub 1993). Social roles may refer to both conventional roles and unconventional roles. To better locate transitions and turning points in the drug trajectory, I use the drug career typology to identify phases of the drug career, introduced briefly in chapter 1 and more thoroughly in appendix B.

Using the theoretically informed dimensions of social roles and self-control, the typology illustrates the diversity found in drug user career phases. The phases are identified by where the user is along a continuum of the dimensions of social roles and self-control. Every drug user follows a progression of phases in her life. The development and full description of the typology are discussed in appendix B; a brief description is provided here. The dimensions of social roles were identified as maintaining conventional roles, not maintaining conventional roles, or combining salient conventional and salient unconventional social roles. The property of control signified the control the drug user maintained over drug-use behavior so that it did not interfere with either a salient conventional or unconventional role. The three dimensions of control were identified as maintaining control, not maintaining control, or irregular periods of control and out of control. The result of every combination of social roles and self-control produced nine categories:

1. Controlled Occasional User (COU)
2. Weekend Warrior (WW)
3. Habitué (HAB)
4. Marginal User (MU)
5. Problem Addict (PA)
6. Using Dealer/Runner (UDR)
7. Using Hustler/Sex Worker (UHS)
8. Junkie (JNK)
9. Relapsing Addict/Junkie (RAJ)

The typology applies to active use phases, or current users. A former user in an inactive status is a category of its own. Phases are measured by three-month periods. Roles in the women's lives tended to change quickly, which is why I used a period over the past three months instead of a longer period of time.

I note that the UDR, UHS, and JNK phases are designated only when all conventional roles are no longer salient or are completely lost. Women who were able to maintain both conventional and unconventional social roles are not in a phase that indicated a loss of all mainstream social roles. Each phase except the UDR, UHS, and JNK phases depicts the women balancing a salient mainstream social role concurrently with a drug-using role.

Transitions and turning points can be identified at every phase of the drug-career typology, but the turning point into uncontrolled use is critical, since uncontrolled use is what describes the popular image of problematic methamphetamine use. For Isabella, whose trajectory progressed from controlled occasional user to problem addict to using dealer/runner to former user, we can identify a turning point into increased use when her mother supported her by providing a house, and a turning point into cessation when her mother implemented tough love and withdrew her support. This occurred around the time the police raided her house but she was not incarcerated, which implies that her mother may still have been involved while not directly supporting her daughter. Although tough love appears to have been effective in Isabella's case, it does not work for everyone. Other factors, most notably Isabella's considerably high social capital and her ability to return to college, were influential in maintaining her former user status.

A pattern of turning points into uncontrolled use can be categorized around four themes: dealing with family or work difficulties; experiencing emotional or psychological difficulties; having easier access to the drug; and involvement with the criminal justice system. Problematic use typically led to years of use and increased social setbacks (unemployment, police record, probation, divorce, homelessness) that made it more difficult to stop. Motivations for using mounted with each additional social problem. For some of the women, these same turning points into uncontrolled use triggered a turning point out of use as well. Some women who started using drugs with partners, friends, coworkers, or family took different turning points from others with the same initiation patterns. The turning points were dependent on their ability to choreograph the dance between structural constraints and personal agency. Some women handled their use better than others. Other women got fortunate breaks at the right time that seemed like luck, but on closer inspection were related to social capital.

Likewise, the women revealed multiple motivations to use. These motivations merged and changed over time. For example, we see in Isabella's story that she experienced emotional difficulties (overweight and an abusive boyfriend) that motivated her initial use, and she had easy access that led to her uncontrolled problem addict phase. Living a relatively carefree life thanks to her young age and her mother's financial support, she was not expected to have a job but instead to attend college full-time. This allowed her the freedom to associate with high-level drug dealers. Her own foray into deal-ing enabled her to control her use temporarily during her dealing phase. Ces-sation came when Isabella went to a private treatment center, and she eventually obtained a substance counselor certificate, a social role that put her back in a full-time mainstream role.

In contrast, suburban-poor Kat, introduced in chapter 2, was also moti-vated to use by an abusive situation, but her socioeconomic circumstances acted as a barrier to cessation. The stratification of society and the concomitant struc-tural injustice and symbolic violence experienced by the more vulnerable women like Kat emerged as the primary influence on the progression of the drug career. With increasing limits to agency, the free will of the women to influence their own lives was often revealed as a socially constructed deception.

The tools used in qualitative research, responsive primarily to the reality of human social life, expose these structural limitations on agency. A qualita-tive researcher is keenly aware that the reality of life does not fit neatly into categories. Thematic categories are not as mutually exclusive as demographic categories such as age, race, or gender. For example, an illustrative quote might easily fit two or more initiation patterns, as well as describe two or more reasons for continued use. It is difficult and sometimes impossible to completely disentangle one theme from others within the richness of the human language except to force it into predefined categories. I attempt to organize the women's stories by these various themes while acknowledging that reality is much more complex than can be described by categories alone.

The exploratory nature of qualitative research allows for existing theo-retically developed categories such as those found in the models and typolo-gies discussed here to be incorporated into the analysis. Moreover, new concepts and categories are allowed to emerge from analysis of the data. While conceptual models are practical for descriptive and analytical purposes, dissecting the women's lives into categorical groups is useful only if they help us better understand reality from their vantage points without imposing too many of our own assumptions. To guard against presumptions, I provide a number of diverse models and theories that examine the women's lives and their drug trajectories from different perspectives.

In this chapter, I present the lives of the women through quotes describ-ing initiation into methamphetamine and progression in the drug career. Analytical categories, including those from the models and typologies pre-sented in chapter 2 and in appendix B, are used to frame the context of use and provide a sense of what is going on in the women's lives under a socio-logical lens. Every attempt is made to weave the life stories and analytical explanation seamlessly. Some of these were lives of pain and suffering accom-panied by tears. The women's vulnerability was tangible. Their hopes and dreams, and for some despair and hopelessness, continued long after the interviews were over. The behaviors of these women, consumers of an illegal product, were already stigmatized. Yet, as sisters, daughters, wives, friends, mothers, and grandmothers, they are integral members of society. While I neither want to sanitize what is often ugly nor blame the victim, a subtle interplay between subjective and objective analysis is needed to identify the delicate dance between structure and agency that every woman in this book learned. It is this dance that I hope to present in the analytical descriptions woven between the illustrative quotes presented in each chapter.

INITIATION AND PROGRESSION OF METHAMPHETAMINE USE

Sophia was a twenty-three-year-old white former user when I interviewed her in 2007. She was part of the suburban youth culture and possessed high bridging social capital, which made it likely that her former status as a methamphetamine user would continue. When I asked her how she started her use, her response led to a discussion of how she continued using and why:

So, how did you get introduced to methamphetamine?
There was a girl that I hung out with and I went with her to this lady's house. Me and my parents always had problems, I mean, especially me and my dad. He used to be very verbally and emotionally abusive. He grew up with a horrible past which now he's, um, he's been through counseling and stuff and he's coming to terms with it and getting closure on it. But before there was no self-worth involved in his life. So, my mom was very standoffish, and, I think, just hurt because of all of the dysfunction in our family. And I felt like she withheld a lot of love from me. So my friend took me over to this lady's house. This lady became kind of my mom. Like, she wanted to adopt me.
Was she in a middle-class house?
Lower middle class. It was middle class, it wasn't as nice as my parent's house, but it was, she was going through a divorce, so she was there by herself. She was going through a divorce because her husband was cheatin' on her . . . and like a bunch of kids used to always go over there, I mean, we were all like her kids. We just stayed there with her and did drugs with her, but I was like her favorite. She wanted to adopt me. And, I guess, I don't know, it's like I was having problems with my family, and she kind of took me under her wing, but in a bad way.
And is that where you were doing methamphetamine?
Uh-huh [yes].
Why'd you continue using it?
I don't know.
Well, how'd you feel the first time?

The first time I did it? I felt great.

Great, like how?

Like, I felt powerful, I felt confident and energized and just—made me feel good.

And so why did you continue that?

Um, I guess, it became more of routine, like. I guess being in her house and staying with her, we were all like a family and that's just what we did, and I liked it. I liked the way it made me feel . . . because it made me feel confident. I had really low self-esteem, and whenever you're doing meth, it's always with a tight-knit circle of friends that you could almost call family. It's like all of ya'll, everybody is living in their own world. And everybody outside of that world doesn't get anything, and they're stupid. That's how it was. And it's like we were just all smart and we knew everything and, like I say, if I was still doing it, I would look at you like an outsider, like, you don't know anything. Like you were, you were shallow. Because crystal meth made me, and a lot of, everybody I knew, think about things really deeply. So you felt really intelligent and really smart.

This young woman from a solidly middle-class background, although she defined her suburban family as dysfunctional, revealed that she started methamphetamine with a friend and continued it for both self-medicating and social reasons. It made her feel more confident and energized. She indicated she had low self-esteem and that the methamphetamine addressed this issue for her. Moreover, it became part of her social life, setting her and her friends apart from others, and making them smarter than the outsiders who did not use methamphetamine. Such a tight-knit social bonding is attractive to most people of any age, but for young people seeking group membership beyond their family, it is an overwhelmingly positive feeling to be bonded to a social group. The methamphetamine use appeared to be social glue for her and her friends. This kind of bonding was beneficial for her at that time in her life, with the added benefit of helping her feel better about herself.

The importance of sociality for methamphetamine users in the youth culture cannot be overstated, which is one reason why I defined the suburban youth culture by age instead of social status. Among young women the dynamics of methamphetamine use appeared to be linked to having access as well as being with a social group. These motivations soon merged.

Rachel, a nineteen-year-old fully immersed in a suburban youth culture, started using methamphetamine at the age of sixteen, when she had scarce economic means to buy the drug. She explains how access and sociality became intertwined in her life:

After using that one time, were you able to continue having access to it?

Yeah. So when I was younger, one of my brother's best friends, um, I had like a really big crush on him when I was younger. And, like, I knew that he did it. 'Cause that's what the guy told me after I started doing it. And, um, so I called him—no, he called him to get me some. And I started gettin' it from him. Like I bought some from him, like, two or three times. And then I just started hangin' out with him. And I started hangin' out with anybody I knew that did meth. Like, I, like, went on a search. I'm gonna find people that do meth, so that I could do their dope . . . well, at first I got used for dope 'cause, that's, I mean, I did that to people, too. And then eventually, it was just like everybody always had dope. I hung out with other people that did meth. And I got as much meth as I possibly could.

Here we see that while Rachel sought people who used methamphetamine in the beginning of her career, eventually her entire social network consisted of meth users. This dynamic appeared to be part of the "everyone here does meth" syndrome, I heard so often, yet Rachel's seeking behaviors contributed to her being part of a meth-using network.

In contrast to Rachel, Beth was already a mother of three children when she tried her first hit of methamphetamine with her new partner. Her quiet life as a suburban working/middle-class housewife was shattered when her husband left her for a younger woman. Later, she lived with another man, who introduced her to methamphetamine:

Who did you try it with the first time?
With my current [long pause] . . . partner.
So with your current partner, he's the one who introduced you to it?
I guess, yeah.
And how did he do that?
Um, I think we were trying to get coke one night. We didn't have any kids. They were with their dad's family in another state. We were finishing a room in my basement, and somebody had come over to bring us the tools, and we were looking to get some coke, and they said they didn't have any. Well, I don't think I had even heard of crank, and they said, "Well, try a line of this." And I can remember I was snorting a little bit, and I gagged like I was going to throw up, but I'd be up for two days. I just thought that was the greatest thing in the world.
Why did you think it was so great to be up for two days?
Because I could get so much done. I could get, you know, we finished the basement and redid the floors in the kitchen and . . . I'd just lay down and go to sleep. But physically I had the energy that could last me forever.

As an older woman, Beth's involvement was less ritualistic than Sophia and Rachel's use pattern and not contingent on being part of a group. Sophia and Rachel took methamphetamine for the first time with friends but Beth did so with a partner. Sophia and Rachel continued using for primarily social reasons, but Beth used for functional reasons. Although all three women progressed through phases of controlled occasional user to problem addict and relapsing addict junkie before reaching their former-user status, Beth explained her motivation for using

How long would you stay up for? How many days?
The most? I stayed up for twenty-one days. I would peck [at the meth]. I would
   get my family at the dinner table, and I'd run to the store to get whatever
   I had to get, that way I could get it without having to shop with the kids.
   I was constantly running. I had one kid in swimming, one kid in judo, one
   kid that was just a social butterfly. I was constantly on the go. I did events
   at my daughter's school. Field trips. I had to be at every single one.
Did any of the teachers or other parents ever suspect?
I don't think so. I don't think so. My kid's homework was always done.
   Christmas time, all the school bus drivers got little baskets of cookies and
   homemade truffles, and I volunteered at every field trip.

While methamphetamine fueled her status as a supermom, eventually, Beth's uncontrolled use resulted in mounting social problems.

A family member, typically a sibling, introduced some of the women to methamphetamine. Such was the case for Nora, who started methamphetamine at age thirteen, and by age twenty was already in a relapsing addict/junkie phase. As a popular young woman with a young drug-using network, she had access to private pool houses and clubhouses throughout her middle-class suburban neighborhood—what she called "a privileged life." She described her initiation into methamphetamine by her sister:

She got introduced to it from one of her friends. And she, you know, her
   first thing was, "Look, I lost ten pounds in two days!" [laughs]. And she was
   like, "You know, you can stay up, and this and that." So, like any thirteen-
   year-old would be, I was like, okay . . . It was the summer before eighth
   grade. I had just turned thirteen. So I did it one night, and I liked it. And
   I didn't do it for a few months . . . and we started doing it together . . .
   my sister actually at the time lived in the guesthouse, at our house. And
   I'd go spend the night with her, and we would sit up and stay up all night.

Beyond siblings, intergenerational use of methamphetamine also was common among the women in this study. Julia, a twenty-two-year-old from a poor community, started using after a close family member offered it to her when she was fifteen:

It was with my step-grandmother. . . . she was just like here, try this or
   whatever, and she handed me some in my hand and she said eat it. And
   I did, and it kept me up for awhile . . . I stayed up for awhile. I mean
   yeah, I enjoyed it I guess, because I was around it so much. I was awake,
   and I just sat down with them—I mean my mom and my grandmother.

While younger women were typically introduced to methamphetamine by friends, family, or boyfriends, women who started later in life were often introduced to the drug by a partner or a colleague at work. This was especially true for working-class women. For example, Linda, who never used any drug except marijuana when she was in high school, was married and had children when she was offered methamphetamine at work:

> I worked with him . . . I worked at a plant, and I met him there. My sis, my stepsister, worked there too. And he worked. He was ten years older than me . . . and I didn't know what a drug problem was then

Linda continued to use methamphetamine from the first day she tried it, typically with friends and colleagues and eventually with her husband.

Although few women used alone, middle-class women who used mainly for functional reasons were less likely to use with a social network. Dolly was one of them. She recounted how she was raised in a town where she knew many adults who used crank, and she never wanted to be like one of them. She came from an upper-middle-class family and lived in a million-dollar house before her parents divorced. It was not until she was a housewife and mother that she decided to take some methamphetamine when it was offered to her at a party. She loved the way it made her feel, and used it occasionally. When she started to smoke ice, she continued using it almost daily, hiding her use from her husband. She said she used it alone:

I would do some in the morning when he went to work. For a long time there I didn't work. After I got married I was a housewife.
I'm just wondering why you want the high at home alone. What did it do for you?
Well it was wrong. It was strange [laughs]. . . . I just was—I wasn't miserable anymore.
What were you miserable about?
Well, we always had financial problems. We never had enough money.
You are saying that this methamphetamine made you feel better about your life?
Oh yeah. Definitely. Cause it would give me energy. Yeah, I'd get up, and clean the whole house up, and cook, have a big dinner ready, and felt happy. You know, that's the thing. That's the devil in methamphetamine—because it makes you happy. And you don't know why, and you don't really care. Personally I never associated it with being high. At that point I was not doing enough to get the high, high feeling. Just enough to, wow, I feel great. I feel good. Let's paint the house. (laughs)
The increased energy, was that a reason for doing it too?
Yeah, yeah. 'Cause I was depressed a lot, I think.
Were you ever diagnosed with depression?
Yeah. But then along came ice, and no more depression, and no more pills, no more feeling sleepy, and then feeling better tomorrow. You feel better now.

We see a convergence of motivations for Dolly to continue her use that had little to do with a social life. Although she had a diagnosed mental health condition she found that methamphetamine not only relieved her depression but also gave her energy. Her functional use of the drug helped her do the mundane household chores she felt unable to do when taking medication for her depression. Doing housework, and doing it well, was a gendered motivation mentioned by a majority of the women, even among the younger women who used methamphetamine as part of the youth culture. For example, Chloe, who at eighteen was the youngest participant in the study, was introduced to the drug by a member of her family. She indicated cleaning as part of the attraction for using methamphetamine:

What was the first high like?
I felt like cleaning my house. It was like [laughs] I did laundry actually, and then we just went and we got like a bunch of beers and stuff and just hung out the rest of the night. It wasn't like, oh my gosh, this is the best high ever.

The trajectory did not always follow a pattern of controlled to uncontrolled use to cessation or relapse. On the contrary, some women slid between controlled and uncontrolled phases. Emma was a twenty-six-year-old who had learned to control her use after a few years of being out of control. Introduced to methamphetamine by friends when she was very young, she used it with the youth culture. She explained that she really liked doing it to focus on her music. However, after periods of bingeing (days doing methamphetamine) and attempted suicide, her parents mortgaged their house to send her to a rehabilitation facility, where she stayed for eight months. She returned to using again a month after she got out, but now she used in a controlled manner. She explained her current use as:

Knowing the difference between responsibility and getting fucked up. Knowing when you can afford it. Knowing when you can afford to do it. Just physically.
So what makes you decide to use methamphetamine now?
Meth is a—it's one of my favorite releases. Like I can do meth, and write music, and be in my own zone, and clean my house, but I never have time to do it. I work too much to do that stuff now, you know. If I want to write music, I have to get days off to write it, and I can't necessarily afford to do meth just to write music. I'm a musician before I'm a methhead. So it's not like I need it to write music, but it's just, it helps. It helps to trigger of your imaginative side.
When do you take it?
Only on very extreme, rare occasions. I'm talking like once every six months.

While Emma learned to control her use, Danielle, a twenty-nine-year-old woman who had been using methamphetamine since young adulthood, never let her use get out of control. Having been raised by a controlling mother, she said she never wanted anyone or anything to control her again. As a current user in the habitué phase, she was one of the few who managed to use drugs in a controlled manner continuously. When asked how she learned to control her use, she replied

> Drugs? Well I would, like I said, I would give the last bit I had away, or whatever. Never to where I got to the point where I couldn't just smear, you know wipe off the line into the floor and it anger me. Or like, be greedy with it. Because when that happens, I mean, it's got control over me; I don't have control over it. Because it's controlling what I do. And I don't like to be controlled by anything, whether it's a person, a chemical—especially a chemical is not going to control me. I just have a control issue, you know, and it stems from how, you know, my childhood. I was controlled down to how I parted my hair, and I had to ask permission if I, you know, if I pick my outfits out the night before, ask my mom was it okay to wear. I just, you know, nobody's going to control me. Nothing is going to control me. I'm not going to let it, a chemical or a drug, get me.

Danielle said she was able to control her use by moving away from a suburban enclave environment where methamphetamine use was everywhere, and there was nothing to do. She identified a problem of social ennui in that community, and methamphetamine was the perfect drug for boredom. Not all women were able to move away from their situation.

RACE AND ETHNICITY

Based on this study data, it appears that in the suburbs there are few racial and ethnic differences among female methamphetamine users. One African American woman told me, "Once you're high it doesn't matter." With only two African American and four Latina women in the study, this finding is exploratory, however, and the social influences on drug-use patterns are likely to change if the current trend showing minority migration from the cities to the suburbs continues (Allard and Roth 2010).

In this study, the minority women show the same patterns of initiation and progression as the white women. The primary distinctions are related to social capital; women of color who used methamphetamine are women with white social networks. Both whites and minorities in the study confirmed this finding when asked specifically about racial aspects of using.

Tiffany was a twenty-five-year-old woman who lived in a suburban enclave of poverty near a bus line and therefore had access to a suburban city and employment opportunities. She had many reasons to use methamphetamine in a problematic manner, yet she never went beyond the marginal user phase. Her mother was Latina, and Tiffany lived with her father and stepmother, who she said was verbally abusive to her. When she was fourteen her father told her to leave the house because of the tension between her and her stepmother. Diagnosed with an addictive problem, Tiffany was sent to a rehabilitation center for alcoholism. After leaving the center, she moved in with a friend to finish high school on her own.

She was introduced to a form of methamphetamine called crystal meth by a roommate, but she always exhibited controlled use of the drug. At that time, Tiffany was a weekend warrior, a user who can confine drug use to weekends or periods that do not interfere with work and nonusing social life. Tiffany said her use "was mainly weekends, because I was so into trying to graduate from high school. Even throughout all this stupid-ass drug use and abusing myself and everything, I always had a goal and that was to finish school."

At one point Tiffany lived with her sister and her sister's boyfriend, who was running methamphetamine from another city. The drug was always available and in the best form—ice. She started to use more and was in a MU phase (in and out of control) when she had a fight with another woman that resulted in her arrest. While in jail she was given anger management classes and diagnosed with post-traumatic stress disorder. She used less often after leaving jail and eventually stopped using, with the help of a boyfriend.

While many of the women recounted multiple episodes of relapsing on their road to stable recovery, Tiffany was able to remain in a former user phase. Perhaps her status as one of the few Latina women who used methamphetamine in the suburbs acted as a barrier. Participants in our study told us that few Latina or African American females they knew used methamphetamine.

Lucy, an African American from a middle-class family in the Northwest, was introduced to all drugs, including methamphetamine, by her boyfriend, who was white and a drug dealer. She explained how she started methamphetamine when she came down south with him to meet his family:

His aunt, and cousins, and friends of theirs . . . a lot of them were using. . . . They would stay in these big houses, and on the outside it was like, gosh, it's a beautiful home, but then you get in there, and it's like a room for addicts. You know, just using. Just doing, and they'd be there for hours. And then I would have to sit and, you know, you sit there for a long time when you don't know anybody, and then that's how you get to know people, is you do what they're doing.

Is it unusual to see African Americans do methamphetamine?
I do think that it is, because I had not met other black women that did, and then he [boyfriend], we always did it in a hotel room where I was very secluded. So I didn't meet many people, except the people that he hung around with, and those were his aunts and his cousins, and *his* people. And those were the only people I knew.

I was curious if Lucy, having come from a northern city to the suburbs of a southern city, noted a difference in racial tension being the only African American among a white network:

So would you say there's prejudice down here against African Americans?
Oh yeah, hell yeah [laughs].
Well, I just wanted to know from your perspective how did you feel about being around all these white drug users when you are black?
Well, yeah. It's not as odd after awhile. It's not as odd. Only at the beginning, when you're sober and you're coherent. But when you're high, it doesn't really matter who it is as long as they have something for you, or you have something for them. And when you're under the influence, that doesn't matter that they're white or that I'm black. And then sometimes it would matter because I'm the only black person in the room, and maybe I have my own personal use or something but I have to share it for somebody to be nice to me while I'm here. He's left me, you know, somewhere for two or three days, and you know, you're sick, and you want to be high. And so you do whatever you have to do to get your next high. So, yes it's odd, but once you're high it doesn't matter that everybody around you is white.
So you said as long as you're not using drugs, when you're coherent, there is racism?
Absolutely.
But once you start using drugs there's not.
No. It's like a mutual respect for all the drug people in the room or something. It doesn't matter that you're black, if you're doing the same thing that they're doing. That doesn't matter that you're black. All that matters is that you're one of them. You know you're not black or white anymore; you're a drug user. So your race is drugs.

Other minority women in the study also had indicated that the methamphetamine networks they knew in the suburbs did not exhibit overt racial discrimination. Sensing good rapport between us, I approached Lucy with another question related to racial differences. Why did she think it was mostly whites using methamphetamine in the suburbs, when in the city, African American used primarily crack? Lucy responded with an unusual view based on her experience as an African American from a city and now living in the suburbs:

I've never used crack. But I've been around crack users and usually if you have one problem you don't want to pick up a worse one. And if you are a meth user, crack is a worse drug. And if you are a crack user, meth is a worse drug. You might be dumb for being addicted to the drug, but you have your common sense, and you have your sense of your surroundings. And you realize I already have one problem, what the hell am I going to do picking up another one. And so you try and stick with that drug. And then it's not as easy to get help. It's not as easy. You don't even know what you're fighting for. You're fighting for the crack; you're fighting for the meth; you're fighting for the cocaine; you're fighting for heroin. You know, you don't know what you're fighting for, and so you're like a dead man walking.

Lucy indicated that it was not the drug or its effects that attracted users of different races, but instead how they learned to view the drug.

When Lucy progressed through the phase of controlled occasional user to problem addict, her parents paid for her to attend an expensive treatment center in a distant state where she stayed for a year. Lucy was working and living on her own in an apartment with her two children, maintaining a working/middle-class status as a former user when I last saw her.

The only other African American in the study, Liz, was a forty-four-year-old woman who was part of the suburban poor. She was introduced to methamphetamine with white friends in another state. When she moved to this area, she developed connections with both cocaine and methamphetamine dealers. The suburban area where she lived changed from a white majority to a minority (African American and Hispanic) majority district, according to the recent census data. I asked her about the race of her dealers in this county:

Is it usually whites or blacks that are selling meth?
Whites. Mostly whites. You don't find too many black people selling meth because they don't know too many people that does meth, you know. And the drug of choice of most black people are cocaine. But I got in with the white crowd, and got affiliated with the whites, and that's how I got on meth. And I couldn't actually just let it go like that, because I have that urge every now and then I got to have something to arouse me.

Liz's motivation for using methamphetamine seemed similar to that of many of the women who expressed a desire for energy. And like many other women I interviewed who came from poor suburban enclaves, Liz was homeless and unemployed when I met her. By the last interview, she was living with an uncle in a boardinghouse and helping him with his part-time home repair work. A few months later, I lost contact with her.

Mercedes, the first Latina woman I interviewed, had been born in a northern state and put in foster care at age nine. She ran away at age fourteen and came to the suburbs of this southern city to find her biological parents. At this time she added methamphetamine use to her ongoing heroin habit. Although she started a catering business, she did not make enough to support herself. Using the legitimate business as a front, she was dealing methamphetamine to make the money she needed. Her producer's lab was in the suburbs, she said, "in a newly built subdivision. They even had teenage kids." Similar to the other women, Mercedes mentioned multiple reasons why she liked to use methamphetamine:

> A lot of times I would take it because I wanted to escape from reality. A lot of times I'd get overwhelmed by my emotions. And when I wanted to escape from reality and I had important things to do, like I used to take when I had to drive for long periods of time, I would take it and once I came down from the real intense rush part of it, I would be good to drive. And a lot of times if I had a real stressful, like, if I was driving to go make a trip to the border to pick up a large amount of drugs, it would kind of calm down my nerves in a weird way. It's like I could escape from reality and put on a poker face, and I could keep myself from being detected.

As one of the more risk-taking women in the study who spent a long time as a using dealer/runner (UDR), Mercedes went through multiple relapse phases (RAJ) before she was able to stop using for the sake of her teenage daughter. The last time I saw Mercedes, she had graduated from college, was employed, and was reunited with her grown daughter.

In contrast to Mercedes, Pam was a Latina woman who grew up in an upper-middle-class suburban neighborhood. At the age of twenty-six she was married and had already been drug-free for a few years when I interviewed her. She had used methamphetamine briefly in her adolescence. She said her social network was primarily white, and she had been introduced to methamphetamine by a white boyfriend. Having never entered a problematic phase, she stopped using when she became pregnant. As a beautiful young woman with substantial social capital, her firm standing in a middle-class status appeared to be the greatest influence on her quick trajectory to becoming a former user. Married with children and living in her own suburban home, Pam had only conventional roles when I interviewed her.

UNCONTROLLED USE OF METHAMPHETAMINE

While many of the women experienced a short period of uncontrolled use, and others stayed in an uncontrolled phase for years, some of the women eventually learned to control their use while maintaining a conventional social role. Other women, however, appeared to be stuck in a long-term and seemingly perpetual period of uncontrolled use with no hope for regaining control. These women had experienced traumatic events in their lives that resulted in severe emotional pain that they thought only methamphetamine could relieve.

One of the most tragic cases of problematic use was Nancy, a forty-four-year-old woman from a suburban working middle-class background.

A beautiful woman when she was younger, she married while still a teenager and was sheltered by her husband. She had been married for twenty years when she fell in love with a woman who worked in her remodeling business. At the age of forty, she left her husband to move in with the woman, who was a methamphetamine user, and she started using with her. She said she used for functional reasons—"to get things done." Their tumultuous relationship ended when her girlfriend left her on the day Nancy received a divorce from her husband:

> So the day my divorce was final is the same day that she moved out and moved in with another girl. So yeah, that day was very traumatic, but it wasn't because of the divorce; it was because she left.
> *What happened with the methamphetamine during this time? Were you using it regularly?*
> Very much. Very much, and bingeing, yeah.
> *When did you find out you had uncontrolled use?*
> After my auto accident.

After leaving her lover's house, she had a car accident that left her face terribly disfigured. The police report said she was on methamphetamine. She cannot find employment, and she believes her face repulses people. At the time of the interview she lived in an old trailer on her ex-husband's land, picking up scrap metal to make a few dollars, and still using methamphetamine daily. Having lived a middle-class suburban life, she was now a part of the suburban poor in a problem addict phase of drug use.

A traumatic event that affects the entire family can also trigger an increase in uncontrolled methamphetamine use, since by all accounts the drug makes users forget their problems and actually feel good no matter how horrible their situation. Such was the case for Nancy, as well as for Pia, a thirty-year-old white woman who recently moved to one of the poorest trailer park enclaves in the suburbs. Her husband and family lost the home they owned when he lost his job as a result of the recession. Her story gave little hope of ever achieving her former middle-class lifestyle.

Pia's initial use of methamphetamine was functional and social. She had three children at a young age with a man who never married her and eventually left her with no financial support. Soon after he left, their oldest son was diagnosed with a chronic health condition. She lived alone as a single mother with her children for years.

A friend came over with methamphetamine one day, and she tried it. It made her feel better and she liked the company. Soon she had meth-using friends coming in and out of her house. A neighbor reported her to the authorities, and the Department of Family and Children Services (DFCS) came by with the police. Pia was tested for drugs and meth was found in her system;

CHAPTER 4

Gendered Lives

Combining Work and Family with Drug-Using Roles

Mia

Mia was a fifty-year-old woman who remained in a relapsing addict/junkie (RAJ) phase throughout the three interviews we conducted. Although she was decidedly one of the most despondent of the suburban poor when I met her, she had been raised in a middle-class neighborhood until her parents divorced. Her father wanted to keep her, but her mother fought for custody and won. Mia sighed when she told me this, adding that she wished she could have been raised with her paternal grandparents, who had fought for custody and lost. Mia moved to a poor suburban neighborhood with her mother, a depressed alcoholic who was sexually promiscuous. She recounted an incident that occurred when she was nine years old:

> My mother was just full blown alcoholic. Um, men in the house all the time . . . I remember one time—my mother was always drunk but she got drunk this one particular time—took off all of her clothes. Put on a short fur coat that just covered herself. Got in her '65 Mustang and drove off naked and drunk. And she would tell me stories even back then that she would sleep with the policemen to get out of tickets and DUIs. You know, back then weren't like they are now. You know, I really was disgusted with her.

When Mia was older and her father remarried, she lived with his new family during the summer. He led a considerably higher-status life and she noticed the difference, secretly wishing to live with him instead. She did not tell her mother:

> I felt real guilty because my mother would always be so dramatic. Very jealous of my relationship with that whole family—my father, my

stepmother, my half sisters, and brother. I mean she would be, she would torment me with jealousy over that. So I had to balance the feelings and try to take care of her feelings. And I'm a child just trying to live my life. Wanting to be more like my father but [sighs], you know, she would be drunk and crying and "you're all I've got." . . . And if I came home and said something that was good about my stepmother she would be enraged.

Torn by the emotional turmoil in her daughter role, when she was fifteen Mia started to inject Preludin, what she called prescription speed in a pill form, with a boyfriend. At sixteen she ran away with him. She experimented with different drugs while they were living with his mother, who she described as the "biggest Dilaudid dealer in the area." Mia and her boyfriend became physically addicted to pain pills, and he coerced her to help him make enough to maintain his habit. She explained, "And that's when the crime started. He put it to me in a way that you're going to help me burglarize these houses and apartments because if you're going to be strung out on my bill, um, you're going to have to help."

Her crime spree came to a halt when she was arrested and incarcerated for burglary. She went deeper into the drug world and acquired more unconventional roles after she was released:

Actually when I started dancing I was twenty. But I was still with him—the dope dealer. And I actually went from that dope dealer, from him, to the dope dealer that was bigger than him. And the second dope dealer introduced me to dancing. And I had no idea what I was—you know. He took me downtown to the [City Hotel] and said well you're going to do this. And I'm like, what am I doing. But I, I was not a prostitute at that time, but I had slept with men for money—not really for money but I guess for drugs. I would sleep with anybody for drugs at that time. When I started dancing, the prostitution came in. Just to support my drug habit.

As it did for too many of the women in this study, Mia's time in jail did little more than increase her involvement in the criminal world when she got out. By the time she was twenty-one, she says, "I wasn't working in the clubs. I'd be walking the street. I got arrested for prostitution at that time."

After spending time in jail, she found a regular client she called a "sugar daddy," who supported her in her own apartment. Mia now had the time to attend a technical school and obtained training as a dental technician, graduating with a certificate that led to her first conventional work role. Moving to another town, she worked in an office and used drugs recreationally for a few years in a controlled-occasional-user phase. When her drug use got out of control, her employee health insurance allowed her to attend a private residential treatment facility. Each rehab success lasted about six months before she relapsed, yet the cycle of white-collar conventional work and rehab protected her from occupying unconventional and illegal roles associated with drug use for many years.

Mia's first steady partner was the woman who introduced her to methamphetamine. She lost her job and her partner around the same time. The loss of her partner was particularly devastating to her emotionally, and her drug use increased. Her family members eventually stopped aiding her. She lost her certificate to work in a dental office and took temporary low-paid employment with no health insurance. She explained that she was forced to engage in unconventional roles, such as sex work, during this time to supplement her income.

Mia had no teeth in her mouth when I met her, and she was living in a shelter. She said she was on a list to get dentures from a social service provider who gave free dental care to the women at a treatment facility. She still did not have them at her last interview two years later, and having moved out of the county, she was no longer eligible for their services. During the first interview I noticed the scar tissue visible on her arms, which I thought might be track marks. She explained: "That's a cut. Scars. From cutting. From suicide. The shooting dope scars are here, here, on my ankles. And these are old scars. There's a—somewhere where I missed some barbiturates and it never went down. You know, I mean I could usually only get off in my hands. I bruise up here and stuff." Mia was fortunate to have a bed in the crowded local homeless shelter, and she recently found a part-time telemarketing job within walking distance. However within a few days, she was ejected from the shelter when she failed to pass the Breathalyzer test. The next time I saw Mia, she was walking the highway looking for sex clients and living in a motel room. She called to ask me if I could drive her to pick up a paycheck still owed to her.

Meeting Mia at a gas station on the busy highway, I saw she was intoxicated, so I took her for something to eat while she sobered up enough to make sense. Mia described her afternoon: "Remember when I called you and I said I'm going to walk. I'm walking, and he pulls up, and I'm like, you know—I probably said it. He stopped, and I said, can you please give me a ride half a mile down the road. And during that process, during a half a mile, I figured out that he was old, married, needy, wanting just a five-minute." Mia got thirty dollars for that five minutes and did not use a condom. I asked her how she had gotten into this situation again. Mia recounted how a homeless man with a car, Frank, was nice to her and they became friends. One day while she was waiting for the homeless shelter to open she was sitting in Frank's car, where he lived, when he offered her a drink from his bottle. She took it, more to be friendly than because she craved alcohol. She was denied entry to the homeless shelter that night when she failed the Breathalyzer test, and she was put on the no-entry list for six months. Mia still had her job, so she could pay for an inexpensive hotel room for a few nights. Frank, her only friend, drove her from the shelter to the motel. She recounted the chain of events:

> And it was payday. And he's like . . . he was helping me. He helped me move from where I was to where I am now. And I gave him like twenty bucks. It wasn't thirty minutes later he was in my room with a twenty-dollar rock [crack]. I said get out of this room. . . Frank put it in my face. He said, "Let's do some." And I said [snaps fingers], that quick, I said ok. That's all—and that's all it took. But I—I don't know if you know from ever doing it, you probably know from doing what you do with other drug addicts, that once you take that first hit—I spent at least three hundred dollars in that night. And I couldn't go to work for the next two days because of it. And I hated him for it. And he tried to put it in my face again a week later, and I said get away from me.

I asked Mia why she thinks she befriended Frank. She started to cry, and I turned the recorder off as we sat in silence in my car parked in front of a fast food restaurant along the highway. Mia tapped on the Styrofoam take-out box where she had put the rest of her food, which she would eat later in the motel room, silent tears streaming down her face: "Men are creeps," she said. "If he knew how much I care for him." She continued to cry.

SOCIAL CAPITAL AND SOCIAL ROLES

Mia's story highlights the distinguishing feature of social roles and the difference between mainstream conventional roles and unconventional roles linked to the drug-using world. Mia's life shows that she started her young adulthood occupying unconventional roles as a sex worker and successfully transitioned to a very conventional role as a dental assistant. She had to control her drug use during the years she was studying for the dental assistant certificate. As a result of increased drug use, she lost her conventional work role and became homeless and involved in sex work again by the time of her interview. Her acquired mainstream social capital provided more bridges for Mia than for many of the women in this study, yet her lack of bonding to her mother and father, as expressed in her childhood story, left Mia emotionally and socially devoid of the family roles that often sustain women when they are in need.

Social capital is defined as the social resources available to individuals within their communities and across social networks that facilitate achieving individual goals through shared enterprise (Bourdieu 1984; Coleman 1990; Putnam 2000). The emphasis is on the relational aspect of social capital that occurs between and among individuals and their social networks (Schuller 2007). Social capital that results from relationships between individuals in the same community or network is called "bonding" social capital; "bridging" social capital results from relationships across social divisions such as race and class (Lockhart 2005).

Social roles are the primary mechanism for accumulating social capital. While mainstream social roles are known to strengthen bonds with the community, substance abuse has been shown to be incompatible with maintaining legitimate and conventional social roles. However, the social bonding that occurs within drug-using networks can increase the social capital of drug users. For example, acquisition of drug-user roles, such as dealing drugs, increases social capital within the drug-using world.

Social capital can be negative as well as positive (Wacquant 1998). An increase in drug-related social capital and social bonding to marginalized networks decreases the opportunities for social capital bridging to mainstream society. Members of marginalized communities are also challenged by negative social capital, which operates to keep marginalized populations in their dependent states. For a woman, the social capital associated with mainstream social roles is crucial to recovery from drug dependence.

Women's roles are affected differently from men's roles by society's reaction to and the social consequences of illegal drug use. Being a good mother and being a drug user are likely to cause role strain among women to an extent that is much less likely to be experienced by male drug users who are fathers. Moreover, women are more stigmatized than men are when drug use is discovered. While both men and women lose children, employment, friends, and family, suburban women who use methamphetamine also lose their cherished reputation as superwoman or supermom. Society tends to be harsher toward women who do not perform to high standards of motherhood than toward men who fail at fatherhood.

Few of the women in this book used methamphetamine for purely recreational reasons. One of the primary reasons women use ice is to maintain the many roles they occupy in postmodern life. Methamphetamine helps them do this or do it better. Accumulated social capital provides women with resources that can be accessed to help control their use or to delay the debilitating physical effects of the drug. Those with less access to resources become entrapped in a world that quickly spins out of control.

With depleted social capital and facing barriers to social service aid, the women engage in unconventional roles to survive. While engagement in these unconventional roles of drug dealing, sex work, or hustling makes the women more vulnerable to the risk of arrest and becoming victims of crime themselves, they appear to have no other choice. Mia's story illustrates this: after she was rejected by the homeless shelter and lost her employment, she engaged in sex work so she could afford a motel and avoid living in the woods or on the street, exposed to innumerable risks to her safety.

For most women, the drug roles eventually take more and more time. Some women were able to maintain the drug-using roles along with their mainstream roles without much trouble, and it appears they might have continued to do so if their drug-using role had not been discovered. Mia was able to maintain her drug use and conventional roles for years based on her increased social capital by first attending school and earning a certificate, and next by holding a semiprofessional job with insurance that paid for treatment. However, after a few times in treatment, and relapsing, she lost her strongest hold to a mainstream role—her legal job.

For the women in this study, occupying illegal roles typically resulted in being arrested, charged, and incarcerated. If the women had small children, a drug charge often meant losing their children. For both men and women, a drug felony conviction made it difficult to find employment. Mia was one of the few women with a criminal record who avoided a drug charge. Most of her record involved charges related to prostitution, but her value in this line of work depreciated with age.

Opportunities to increase social capital in both the mainstream and drug-using worlds decrease more rapidly for women as they age than for men. The types of roles acquired by females in the drug-using world are typically the most degrading and least desirable. Whereas male drug users acquire roles that place them at the top of the drug-world hierarchy, such as high-level dealers, bank robbers, and pimps, female drug users typically resort to low-ranking roles in the drug community, such as low-level dealers, runners [delivering drugs], boosters [stealing in stores], and prostitutes. Even among the prostitute social hierarchy, drug users fall quickly to the bottom and tend to be street sex workers in drug-infested neighborhoods or sex workers who exchange sex for drugs. For younger women, higher-ranking drug roles were easier to achieve and maintain until they aged. We see this play out in Mia's life. Fully supported by a sugar daddy when young, she was valued at thirty dollars by age fifty.

Loss of conventional social roles is devastating. Some women in this study, such as Isabella, were able to regain social roles after years of recovery, but they were the exception. Isabella avoided legal repercussions because of her social capital. For others, the result of incarceration was usually a loss of social capital in mainstream society. In most cases, legal and social sanctions on methamphetamine use by women left the women socially scarred for life and increased their marginalization, victimization, and problematic drug use.

In this chapter, the social roles of the women in this study are examined and organized by categories of conventional roles and unconventional roles. The choices they made concerning which roles they could occupy were constrained or facilitated by whether they were part of the suburban youth culture, suburban working middle class, or suburban poor.

GENDERED CONVENTIONAL ROLES:
FAMILY AND WORK

Family

The most important role for most of the women was the mother role; this was often entangled with other family roles, such as wife or daughter, however. Children of many of the young women often lived with the grandparents. This made the daughter role of the young mother either strained or stronger.

Tammy was born and raised in one of the poor enclaves of the suburbs. Marginalized for most of her childhood, and without a strong bond to her mother or the community, she had no one to turn to when her mother's boyfriend molested her. The abuse continued for years. When she eventually told her mother, her mother did not believe her, indicating a severely broken daughter-mother relationship.

Although the mother role was very important for Tammy, she lost her children when she became involved with drugs. At thirty-five, she again had no one to turn to for help. When I asked her what she liked about methamphetamine, her answer identified not only the reason but also the effect of her cherished lost roles:

> Nothing, nothing. It's just, like I've always said, even the methamphetamine, it's a rich man's high and a poor man's dream. And it is. I mean look where it's got me today. I have no home. I'm living out on the streets. I don't have my children. I've got a son that's almost eighteen years old. I mean, life just ain't the same no more.

Tammy's sister was awarded custody of her children, and she was only allowed visiting rights occasionally. When I spoke to her, the last time she had seen her younger children was on Christmas, more than two months earlier. Her description of past times with her children provided insight into how she felt:

> It hurt because I could remember all the good times that we used to have. I mean, because basically I was, you know, I tried to be the stay-at-home mom, but I was working around the trailer park too, and all that. But just to wake up in the morning and get up and take care of my kids, and get them off to school, and then have to sit there, and wait on them to come home, you know. Me and my kids—we was inseparable. But my sister, she told me, she says if you don't stop what you're doing, she says I'm going to take your kids.

Although Tammy's painful daughter relationship with her mother and the emotional confusion of her childhood abuse was a reason for her methamphetamine use, the harshest consequence was losing her own children.

In contrast to Tammy, Uma remembered a strong and loving mother-daughter connection. Uma's cherished relationship with her mother came to an abrupt end when her mother died and she was sent to a series of foster homes. She recounted numerous stories of neglect in foster care before she indicated a positive relational bond with a foster care worker:

> [Suburban County] was actually, it was a turning point in my life as far as the way I was treated and as far as trusting adults. I had one, Annie Hall, oh, she was the best caseworker ever, here in [Suburban County]. And she really loved me. And she used to worry about me. And she would come on her own time and get me and . . . because I was just a little girl out there in a big old world. And she just, she truly cared for me.

We see in Uma's childhood story that after her mother's death resulted in a lost role, her need for a social bond led to a relationship with a surrogate mother, who was part of her life for only a few months. When she lost this relationship too, she ran away from foster care with a boyfriend.

The daughter role was often strained when young women chose to live with drug-using boyfriends against their parents' wishes. A new mother role often motivated younger women to reconnect with their own mothers. For example, Sophia, at the age of only twenty-three, stopped all drug use because, as she said, "I knew if we were gonna have a baby I had to quit. So I quit and that's when my life straightened up." When she discovered her boyfriend, the father of the baby, was still taking drugs, she left him to protect herself and her mother role. As she explained, "I'm not gonna put me or my child in this situation." Sophia was able to return to her parents' house, and with their help obtained the resources she needed for the new life she desired.

Most parents tried to help their daughters when they returned home, typically by paying for private treatment programs or helping to care for their grandchildren. If intergenerational drug use was present, it was problematic for maintaining a conventional mother-daughter role.

Julia is an example of a young woman whose family role was affected by intergenerational drug use. Raised in a poor suburban community by a mother who used drugs openly in the home, she became accustomed to seeing her mother overdose:

> Yeah, my mom had an overdose of cocaine when I stayed with her, and I was like twenty, I think I was nineteen, and she overdosed on cocaine she shot it up. And I've watched my mom actually hit [inject] this stuff over and over again, on the bathroom floor, puddles of blood. I mean my mom's, she hit herself, and her veins are so like dried up, like, you know, that they're calloused. She would just stick herself anywhere and

just try and hit herself, and I guess she was addicted to getting herself off and so she would not let me do it. I mean I've seen my mom shoot up a lot of drugs—crack, cocaine, and meth. I used crack with her one time. I think I was like nineteen, and me and my boyfriend stayed with her and she was doing cocaine. And we told her it was too much. Cocaine will kill you quick. And she tried to do it anyway, and she died on my floor, and we had to resuscitate her. And that was, I mean she had overdoses before that, but she didn't die.

Julia appeared to be both disgusted with her mother's use and worried for her safety. Although she saw the direct and immediate effects of risky and unsupervised injection, this did not stop Julia from eventually injecting methamphetamine herself.

Intergenerational drug use occurred in middle-class homes as well. Typically, the exposure was very different. Stella, a young woman with trendy clothes and a youthful hairstyle, looked like a typical modern suburban young woman except for her slightly emaciated appearance. Speaking of methamphetamine use as a normalized behavior, she justified her own use by retorting, "I mean, my mother does it, and she's a very successful mom now. She married a rich guy and then got half the business, and she smokes meth every day." Stella appeared to imply that if her mother could do so well—and by this she meant become wealthy—and her mother used methamphetamine, then she could use it too without adverse effect to her social life.

Lea, at age twenty-five, had already transitioned to an adult role as a mother, but as a result of her previous dealing days and a criminal record, she and her child were living at home with her parents. She acknowledged that her daughter role was strained when she was using methamphetamine. She did not blame her parents for her wild years; on the contrary, she explained that she knew how to manipulate her mother:

And see this is funny, because when I was put on probation I was given an eleven o'clock curfew that my mom did not enforce. She tried to and I manipulated my way out of it. She was a pushover. She did not discipline me at all. She wanted to, but she couldn't. I just told her—you know, I wasn't defiant, I was very good with my words. I talked her out of it and said please, please, please. She never told me no, even when I was a child . . . she gave me what I wanted. She didn't make me finish school projects until the very last night . . . she spoiled me. She just wanted me to be happy. And she wasn't like trying to be my friend, but she wanted me to be happy. And she wanted the best for me. And she wanted to give me everything I wanted. And she felt guilty a lot, very easily if I made her feel guilty for not letting me do something. And so it was very hard for her to say no. And I feel so bad that I did that to her now.

Another family role often mentioned was the wife role, although usually in the past tense. Not many of the women were currently married. For example, Flo, still a beautiful woman at fifty, had been married three times. Although she appeared nonchalant that she was single again, the fact that she kept trying to find a new husband indicated she believed in the institution of marriage. She said she tried to be the perfect wife during her last marriage, "He just wasn't being a husband to me, and I wanted to be a wife. And, you know, I didn't know what to do. So I said, piss on it."

Some women stayed with their husbands through years of abuse. Bev's wife role had been strained for years before she was put in jail for presumed drug distribution. Her husband abused her and cheated on her. Yet she excused him: "I mean I blame it on the—he's really a decent person. I know that sounds funny. But meth changed him." After she was released from prison, he stayed with her for a few weeks and then deserted her.

Work

Emma, mentioned in the preceding chapter, was typical of the suburban youth culture. She came from a middle-class family that moved often because of her father's military job. Although she said her parents were alcoholics, she loved them and described them as awesome. Emma attributed methamphetamine use to coping with her emotions after losing a close family member to suicide. Her parents sent Emma to a rehabilitation center where she stopped using methamphetamine, but she relapsed and began to use in a manageable controlled occasional user pattern. Today her most salient role is a conventional work role as a concert promoter. She still uses occasionally but for functional reasons, such as to stay awake when working. She considers herself a very controlled user whose drug use plays a minor role in her life. At age twenty-six, she appears to have passed the age-dependent transition to adulthood and says she is serious about her career as a promoter. While Emma is still relatively young, and another relapse into uncontrolled use is possible, she benefits from the fact that her parents helped her through her problematic drug use period. She was able to start an adult conventional career without a criminal record as a barrier to employment.

For Flo, acquiring a conventional work role with her long prison record was not so easy. Just out of prison boot camp, she was homeless at the time of our first interview. By our second interview, I learned that Flo was living with other formerly homeless women in the home of an older man who hired them for odd jobs in his cleaning business. Flo explained:

> I just got blessed. I knew the man—he was trying to help other people out through [the homeless shelter] and stuff. I met him a long time ago and I told him I didn't have nowhere to go. He says, "Well come on."

He says, "I won't mess with you or nothing." I said yeah right. I said I don't know but I need a job. And I had my own room. See it was going to work out where I work—basically working for my rent and then a little money on the side. The work kind of slowed down a little bit, but he never not one time says get out or anything like that. I get my food stamps so I eat. And he doesn't bother me.

I was skeptical at first, but after I met Buddy, the older man who helped some of the homeless women, it appeared he was engaged in a rational exchange; the women needed a place to stay and he could use their help with his home-cleaning business. Buddy gave them rooms in a nice suburban home and conventional work roles. The pay was not much, but it offered a bridge to mainstream society. He helped a few of the women I knew among the homeless networks. Flo eventually moved on to live with a new boyfriend she met in a church twelve-step group, but the time she had at Buddy's home gave her respite from living on the street. Without his help, she might have assumed another unconventional role, as she had in the past.

GENDERED UNCONVENTIONAL ROLES: DEALING, HUSTLING, AND SEX WORK

Dealing

For Lisa, a thirty-year-old woman with a working-class background, dealing was a normalized activity in her community. She was a mother at fifteen. She kept her pregnancy hidden from her family until a few weeks before the baby was due. After the baby was born, her mother helped watch the baby so she could continue school. When her mother became sick, she quit high school and went to work. Her work roles at the time consisted of only low-paid service employment. At age twenty she began to use methamphetamine and then started selling it so she did not have to pay for her habit. As she explained, "I'd just buy more and then sell it to like family, people that done it, and people at work, and then it became bunches of people comin' over and buyin' it, and it was just easy money really."

Her dealing role was not unusual, she said, since everyone in this community used methamphetamine: "You can ride up down this road and just about every other house at least is somebody that we can say, hey we know he does dope."

Lisa's using and dealing roles created conflict with her mother role when neighbors called the authorities and the Department of Family and Children Services (DFCS) showed up at her door. She recounted her ordeal: "So they came out and made me take a drug test and I failed. They took my kids for three weeks. I got 'em back, and then a couple years ago, they came back out because somebody turned us in, and they took my kids again. I had to sign them up to my aunt and my grandmother for two years." Her husband was in jail and could not support their family. His crime was leaving the state while on probation to seek construction work in another city. Since she had a low-paid service job, she was dealing to supplement her household income. Social support services failed her. Instead of providing training to find a better job, they took away her children. Alone and despondent, Lisa increased her drug use and her involvement in unconventional roles, eventually spending time in jail.

While allowing children to live in homes where methamphetamine is used or produced presents a potential danger, and the goal of DFCS is to protect the children, the agency's purported aim is also to try to keep the parents and children together. Instead, my data show that no effort was made by social services to find residential treatment for women with children. Their first action was to take the children away, and as shown in every story told by women who needed a living-wage job, little effort was made by social services to address the underlying problem of their drug use or drug dealing. Ironically, the only women who obtained low-cost public treatment did so by being arrested because they lived in counties that mandated treatment or offered drug court for women with drug offenses.

Lea, a young mother, stopped all drug use while she was pregnant: "I worked through my whole pregnancy. On my feet, every day—forty hours a week. And I stopped doing everything. I didn't drink. I did smoke cigarettes, but I didn't drink. I didn't do any kind of drugs or anything."

Her mother role was not enough to stop her from returning to drugs and acquiring a drug role, however. She became a runner for her boyfriend, a drug dealer, and made more money than she ever imagined. When the police caught them, her rich boyfriend did not pay for her lawyer. Instead, her mother paid for a lawyer so she could come home on probation; she now held another unconventional social role as an ex-convict. Lea was court mandated to attend a treatment program, and she participated in a twelve-step fellowship. At only twenty-five, Lea was already a recovering methamphetamine addict, to use the lingo of her support group. She had no car, little education, and a child to support. She lived with her parents, and since her father out of work, she was trying to rely less on her parents for financial help.

Lea avoided a long prison sentence because her mother intervened. She was relatively young, and her parents were still alive and working. But as the women in this study aged, they had to rely more on their own wits and accumulated social capital when drug use led to involvement with the criminal justice system.

Bev was a forty-year-old woman with a criminal record. Although she was raised in a middle-class family, her childhood, like those of most of the women in the study, was not exactly conventional. Bev married early and had a child who was left in the care of her mother. She was using methamphetamine with her husband, and they were both dealing as well. She explained that she was good at the business: "You realize that you have a good business sense—well, if you're going to make it you've got to have a good business sense. And I made it. I mean, I'm not proud of it, but I sold it for seven, eight years and made very good money. I mean, lots and lots of money. But I took a lot of risks too."

Another dealer with a good business sense was Mercedes, who was also one of the few women in the sample who achieved a high-ranking position in the drug-dealing hierarchy. Being Latina and able to speak Spanish, she was buying methamphetamine for her own use when she heard her dealer speaking Spanish and she asked for it wholesale—in perfect Spanish. Mercedes was connected to the network and soon had dealing contacts everywhere. Wholesale dealers were of every race, but all were men; she was the only woman at that level. Her wholesale contacts typically lived in middle-class family neighborhoods in the suburbs—husband, wife, and kids—nothing looked suspicious. Her suburban clients came from all walks of life: a doctor, a plastic surgeon, a paralegal, an accountant. Mercedes invested her money wisely. Capitalizing on bank foreclosures, she paid cash for two houses and started a legitimate rental business on the side.

Hustling

Hustling is an unconventional role that provides money—typically the process involves doing something illegal. Not many of the women in the study engaged in hustling, since dealing and sex work provided more money. However, some engaged in burglary or shoplifting in order to survive. Ida had an expensive methamphetamine habit, and when her husband was in prison, she managed by hustling:

> Any way and every way . . . well, I mean, like anything, like opportunities came up. Somebody, say, you go get twenty cartons of cigarettes from Walmart. Okay. Like say two guys, they want to go to a construction site and steal a bunch of tools, and then you go to a Mexican apartment complex and you sell them all. That's three hundred dollars. Boom! You know, you go back again. You do it again, you do it again. . . I wasn't a hoe [prostitute]. I didn't like the hoe thing. I did criminal type things. Which wasn't good. I don't do them now but I'm saying, back in the day when I was younger, and more out of my head on drugs, I used to do those things to support my habit. . . Sometimes I would do day labor when I couldn't boost [steal] or do anything else for my drugs. There were several times guys would stop me and ask me for sexual favors, and I just wasn't into it. I would panhandle. I would steal. I would probably

beg somebody. Beg churches for help. Just different things. But I never wanted to do the hoe thing.

Ida had a child and was trying to fill a few incongruent roles simultaneously—wife, mother, criminal—until role strain forced her to give up one role, the mother role, when her mother took her daughter. Ida explained that she was so busy trying to make money for her habit that she never contacted her mother or child.

Sex Work

In recent years, sex work has been called "prostituted sex" to call attention to the sexual exploitation of women and the power differential between the women (generally young) who are prostituted and those who exploit them (generally men). Here I discuss exchanging sex for drugs or for money. Among these women, the latter was typically for survival. The abusive and violent nature of prostituted sex is discussed in chapter 6.

One of the primary differences found among suburban women who used methamphetamine was their attitude toward sex work. Contemporary younger women in the study emphatically claimed they did not engage in this role at all—and never would. Yet they talked of having sex almost indiscriminately with males during shared methamphetamine use to obtain drugs or with serial boyfriends who provided them with drugs. Many of the older women recounted prior engagement in sex work when they were younger. However, the majority described situations where sex was in exchange for drugs—for them or for their partners. For example, Sue explained matter-of-factly that she could get methamphetamine for free for both herself and her husband:

Okay, when did you have sex with the dealer?
Oh, um . . . for years. Um, I guess that's why I guess I didn't consider it—I mean, it never—I'd known him for a long, long time, and then once me and Bubba got married, like I'd said, people's not going to give Bubba dope for free. But they'd give it to me.
So your husband didn't mind?
Well, he didn't really know. I still say he knew, but he didn't want to know that type of thing.
Yeah, because he was getting free meth.
Right. Exactly.

In this exchange we see that Sue was not actually forthright regarding her sex exchange for drugs.

Another type of sex work role was escort service. Previous work in an escort service was mentioned not as sex work necessarily, but as a way of survival. The fact that this type of work needed to be excused indicated that the

women felt it was undesirable in some way. Liz, a single mother, explained
that she engaged in escort services instead of the usual low-wage employment because of the flexible hours:

> I worked for an escort service but that was to support me and my two
> kids that I had, because she [mother] wasn't going to support me. So I
> started working with an escort service. It didn't have anything to do with
> sex or anything. I was just an escort. I was making over $1,000 a night.
> No sex. . . It was a drug cartel that had the company and they could
> afford to pay it. And they get a percentage of it but of course, for getting
> the dates for you, and I was making pretty good. Because I drew two or
> three escorts a night . . . just to sit there and watch them smoke and to
> be naked while they're doing it. And jack themselves off, and smoke the
> dope. . . We'd go get a motel room. Not cheap, but they would already
> have their motel already set up. And you know I'd walk in with them as
> if I was just their girlfriend or whatever. I knew the people that was sell-
> ing drugs, so I could just call them and tell them they meet me in the
> lobby. They would get their drugs or whatever, and I'd let them know
> up front, I don't do oral sex, and if you want sex, it's going to cost you
> more than what you paid my company, and that is mine.

Liz was engaged in this work when she was much younger. By the time
I met her she was forty-four years old and living from couch to couch or
sleeping under a stairwell in a rundown apartment building.

The majority of sex work was more as Mia described it, walking the suburban streets and highways. As Uma explained, "Honey, you can just come
outside and walk down the road and you got these—well you know, you
learn how to—they'll be like, 'you need a ride?' And you get in, and they're
looking for sex."

Like many of the women who engaged in sex work, Uma had been sexually molested as a child, neglected by foster care services, and physically
abused by her husband. After she left him, she supported herself and her
increasing drug habit by prostitution. She did not enjoy sex and described
her sex work as if it were a job:

Did you like having sex on meth?
I don't like having—no. I got some issues with that too because I ended up
    getting into prostitution, that whole kind of stuff. I don't like sex period.
    No, I didn't like—when I was high I guess I thought I did at the time,
    but in all honesty I don't even [makes disgusted sound] I don't even like
    sex no more.
Did it [prostitution] have anything to do with drugs?
Oh absolutely! That's exactly why, because I needed money to support my
    drug habit. And so it would start out—it started out at first as just like,

give me some sex, and I'll give you dope. And that was ok too, but then I needed money to just survive. And the next thing you know I'm wide open out in the streets, and that's what I did was sell my body and do dope.

How much do you get?

Well, I've gotten as low as twenty dollars and I've gotten as much as two thousand dollars. It just depends.

Addict Role

Many of the women identified an addict role as a salient role in their lives. "I am an addict" they said, to make sense of their chaotic situation, but they rarely acknowledged the amorphous nature of this role, and few could define what it meant.

When I asked Uma about her polydrug use, she referred to the popular understanding of an addict role as an individual character flaw:

I did crack. I did meth. I did pills. I did whatever. I'm cross-addicted. I mean I'll—I can abuse food. Ok, I mean I've got—I'm very—I've got a very addictive personality. Very addictive. It's easy for me to get stuck.

And you learned this in treatment?

Yeah. I went there, and I ended up staying eighteen months. And that's when I learned that what I was doing—these drugs and stuff that I was doing, there was a title to it, and it was called addiction. That's when I was got introduced to the rooms of Alcoholics Anonymous, AA, all that old crap. And I've been battling it ever since . . . I remember I went to this club with a friend of mine and I started drinking margaritas. And when I get drunk I end up wanting to do meth. You know what I'm saying? I want to do something harder. So I've come to terms now that I can't even drink, man. I can't, I can't do nothing . . . and I can't blame it all on men. I don't need a reason to get high. I just might wake up one day and my brain says, you know the urge and the craving is so strong and I just get tired of fighting it, and I give in and I go get loaded. But I'm one of them people that once I start I can almost guarantee you it's going to end in a jail.

Can you just take one drink or two drinks and then stop?

Hell no!

Why not?

Because I'm a drug addict and alcoholic. One is too many. I can't . . . I've tried that. Been at it for twenty years. It don't work. I've tried controlled drinking. Controlled using. Using on the weekends. Change the brand. Leave the hard [stutters]. I'm not putting anything in my body except for what's supposed to be and that's my mental health medication.

There may be some people who should never take a drink of alcohol again; however, the preceding conversation reveals how pervasive and ingrained the addiction discourse was in lives of the women interviewed. Being an addict requires individuals to believe that they have some sort of pathological inability to manage themselves properly and that they are incapable of decision making when it involves using drugs (Hammersley and Reid 2002). Uma, like Mia and many others, accepted an addict role that had been socially constructed by contemporary addiction discourse, which defines the nature of addiction as an individual root cause and not as a result of social influence or structural inequalities.

Many years ago, William I. Thomas (1966 [1918]) proposed that human action cannot be understood apart from the subjective interpretations given to situations. The now famous Thomas theorem states that if people define situations as real, they are real in their consequences. In other words, how an individual defines a situation has real consequences for that individual, whether or not the definition is validated with objective reality. Perhaps nowhere is this theorem better seen in the women's lives than in their acceptance of their inescapable path of addiction. Uma's last sentence implies that addiction was a consequence of a different problem—her mental health status, which she is now controlling with medication.

SUMMARY OF GENDERED SOCIAL ROLES

A number of patterns emerged in the analysis of the women's social roles. First, the mother role was very important to all the women with children. However, when their children were taken away by DFCS or legal custody was given to relatives, the women with more resources were able to navigate the paperwork and drug treatment requirements better than those without resources. This is not indicative of middle-class women being better mothers or caring more, but it is a sad commentary on an unjust system that requires seemingly senseless bureaucratic regulations and processes to be meticulously followed by women who are already suffering emotionally and have few resources. When these women were caught self-medicating with illegal drugs, the process for regaining custody of their children became not only more difficult but also self-defeating, and some women accepted their motherless status. Many had such a hard time navigating social service paperwork and requirements that they gave up. Those women who still had the support of family fared much better.

Second, a pattern of abuse and/or intergenerational drug use affected the poor, the working class, and the middle class alike. Once again, the middle-class women and some of the working-class women had access to resources through social capital that often mitigated earlier negative experiences. The poor had few resources in their community and no bridges out of it.

Third, mainstream work roles appeared to provide some protection from immediate descent into a junkie phase of uncontrolled drug use, but for women who occupied low-paid work positions without benefits, this advantage was short-lived. Even those with health insurance benefits discovered their health plans were discriminatory toward addiction issues and limited the amount of treatment covered by insurance. While addiction professionals use the widely accepted model of addiction as a chronic disease, a medical diagnosis of being dependent on drugs does not receive the same insurance benefits as other chronic diseases.

Finally, methamphetamine was often used to numb what was later diagnosed as depression. Very few of the women received continued help in the form of treatment, although many were told they needed treatment to return to a conventional role. Once in jail or treatment, finding a conventional work role became more difficult, and as more mainstream roles were lost, control over drug use decreased. The women who were still young often had help from parents. Older women who lost mainstream roles became more involved in illegal and unconventional roles. If they were working- and middle-class women, some were able to use their accumulated social capital to regain mainstream roles and control their drug use. The women from the suburban poor, however, had less social capital, fewer opportunities for acquiring mainstream roles, and far fewer options for transitioning out of problematic drug use.

CHAPTER 5

Gendered Risks

HEALTH AND INFECTIOUS DISEASES

DOT

I was waiting for Dot at the library. She was about an hour late for our appointment, but I was aware of her situation. She did not have gas money for her car and had to call someone to bring her a few dollars just to get here. I had offered to pick her up, but she said she would meet me. Perhaps she did not want me to know where she lived. A former methamphetamine user, she had started using opioid pills and had been on methadone for the last few months but could no longer afford the daily dosage. She was dependent on friends who would share their take-home methadone or other pain pills with her, and just about any other drug she could get to help ease her withdrawal symptoms. With little or no income, she could not afford private methadone clinics, and fully funded methadone treatment for the poor was not available without Medicaid. I was interested in the phenomenon of switching from methamphetamine (a stimulant) to pain pills and methadone (depressants), a pattern of use I was finding among many of the women. Dot was a good subject for this inquiry. She also needed help obtaining health and social services, and my study was designed to track this process.

Born and raised in the two neighboring counties that made up the outer eastern suburbs of the metropolitan area, Dot moved often within these suburban counties when she was young. As she explained, "I've been to about every school in this county [laughs]. Yeah, moving around a lot. Maybe had a handful of homes on my own. We always lived with somebody. Always. So it was pretty rough." She was an only child and spent time with both parents after they divorced. When I asked how that affected her, she responded,

> Horribly, because the two options I had wasn't all that great. My dad was an alcoholic and my mom was bipolar. Diagnosed bipolar. She was also epileptic. It was always, she always came first. Her issues always came first. And she didn't bond—she still don't bond with children. So she

didn't bond with me. My dad did. And I was a dad's girl. Usually if I was at home with her it was because I had to be not because I wanted to be.

The effect of growing up with a mother who had untreated bipolar disorder weighed heavily on Dot as an adolescent. She dropped out of school when she was sixteen because she was pregnant. She married the child's father, whom she loved, and had four children with him. While she was faithful to him, he was not faithful to her:

> Me and him were separated. And we had been separated a couple years because he had to go sow his oats. You know, he had to go out and be wild and fool around, and so we ended up splitting up. And I had got this little bitty junky house. And was trying to work as a waitress, at fact it was at the diner. And we get in this house, and my mother-in-law, his mother, was really good to me. She had brought me some new carpet— not new but some she had gotten somewhere—to lay. And the house hadn't been put together yet and I was working, and the kids needed dinner and homework needed to be done, and I was just totally exhausted. And, um, a girl I had met from down the street come in with this little baggie and she said here chew this. And I'm like what is it? She said, don't worry about it. Just chew it.

This was Dot's first introduction to methamphetamine, at the age of twenty-eight. As other women who had children and worked told me, she liked it because it gave her energy:

> And I chewed the baggie. And before I went to work the next day I'd laid the carpet, cooked dinner, all the kids were bathed, the homework was done, and I still had energy [laughs]. . . . And I came home, and I was like where can we get more? And that was it. I mean, I don't think I went another week without it for five years. I sure didn't. I really wanted it. Really! But what people don't understand though is, like, you get to the point where you can't function without it. You can't get out of bed without it. You don't want to get up and get those kids off to school without it. And things fall apart. As quick as you put them together they fall apart with that stuff.

After five years of using methamphetamine almost daily, Dot's body began to show the signs of its physical effect. Her teeth were seriously decayed, and she could not afford a dentist. She was becoming paranoid about everything and was anxious. Her friends informed her that a few pain pills would make her feel better: "I had started out on Lorcet . . . meth'll give you like this wired, paranoid feeling. And with the pills, it kinda took that away. And it would also kind of boost the meth."

The Department of Family and Children Services (DFCS) came to the house because Dot's daughter was having problems at school. The DFCS social worker wanted her parents to be tested for drugs. Dot tested positive for methamphetamine and opiates and her husband for methamphetamine and marijuana. The children were removed and put in foster homes.

Dot believes she inherited addiction from her father's family:

Addiction's in my blueprint. The side where I have a bunch of family. Everybody's on something. Whether it be crack, alcohol, I mean, something.

Dot eventually left her husband because of his continued unfaithfulness, but she never obtained a divorce because she could not afford the legal fees to get one. Living with a boyfriend, she was free of drugs for enough time to have her children returned. Her boyfriend was not a drug user and took good care of her children.

Soon after her children were returned to her, Dot had a car wreck that left her with pinched nerves in her back and neck. The doctor gave her a prescription for Percocet 10 and Xanax, and she soon became addicted to the pain pills. This led to years of pain pill addiction.

Dot was also diagnosed with attention deficit disorder (ADD) after she saw a doctor about her lack of focus:

I asked her what in the world is wrong with me? I can't—do anything, you know, I plan to do. I can't do any—I can like, these forms. I don't have the will to complete anything. I get very frustrated. I lose interest. And I mean, it—it seems like I'm weak. Because I just can't do it. I just can't!

The doctor prescribed Adderall, which helped Dot avoid feeling the need for methamphetamine, although she was still taking pain pills. On Adderall, she could watch the children, clean the house, and still have energy. However, when her last child was taken away by DFCS again because of her pain pill addiction, she lost her Medicaid and could not afford any medication. To counter the effect of the pain pills she took to keep from being sick, she returned to methamphetamine use for energy. Her boyfriend finally told her she had to leave the house with her children. He could not put up with her addiction any longer. She was devastated:

This time, we got without a place to go. . . . I had really bad panic attacks. So everything is like way more serious to me than it used to be. I just walked right into DFCS and I said, I need help. I can't do it no more.

DFCS response to Dot's pleas for help was to put her younger daughter in foster care. The older children, now adults, went their separate ways.

In order to regain custody of her child, DFCS required Dot to see a counselor who could recommend her to treatment. Dot tried unsuccessfully to meet her counselor so she could get a recommendation for treatment:

> They [DFCS] are telling me that they're not going to send me to treatment. I had to earn that privilege. Of course I'm not going to miss any appointments with my child or visits. They had assigned me with a counselor. We didn't hit it off too well . . . you know, we kinda like speak two different languages. They've assigned me another one, but I haven't met with her yet. But there is a counselor I meet after I see my child every Wednesday. And she's kinda like a drug counselor and we talk. I haven't missed any appointments with her so I'm hoping—I don't know how many of these appointments I have to do to actually earn the right to go to treatment. I really don't understand how I'm supposed earn a right.

Dot was still addicted to opioids and needed to stop her withdrawal symptoms or she would be too sick to drive to her appointments. She typically obtained just enough methadone or pain pills from people she knew who felt sorry for her. She was also involved in "running" pills:

> I know enough pill heads in this county that—and I know people. When people run out, I can—I earn them. I don't have money to spend on them. I earn a couple going and getting so and so some. And then I do have a friend that when she gets hers, she will call me over every day and dose me pretty much. And I can get my twenty milligrams of methadone a day. Twenty milligrams. And, it ain't—it don't make me the most unsick, but it makes me to where I can cope. And that's sad you know, I can't even—it's hard.

However, her friends were getting tired of helping her. Every time I talked to her over the next few weeks she was in terrible withdrawal pain and asked if I could find her a detoxification facility. Somehow she always found enough pills from somewhere to keep her going. One day she drank cough medicine with codeine to keep from being sick.

Knowing that she must be paying something for her street drugs, I asked her why she doesn't go back to the methadone clinic, "Well, if I could afford it then I would do that. I would, but I can't afford that twelve dollars a day." I commiserated about the lack of employment opportunity. She had tried to find work, but at this point she was hopeless, "And I don't know, half the time I don't have the energy. Right now I'm dealing with depression."

Dot usually called me in the middle of the night and left a message, "Miriam, help me. I'm so sick. Please can you call me?" When I called back there was no answer. I would lose her for days and then she would call again.

My assistants and I tried to find a treatment facility for her, but to no avail. We called every number on the government list of treatment programs. If we found a bed, she lived in the wrong county. Unless she could pay for a bed in a private residential center, we were told there was no room. I suggested she go to an emergency room (ER).

Ten years ago, when I first started conducting ethnographic research among drug users, I knew that hospital ERs took heroin addicts who were withdrawing. They stabilized them until a bed opened in the public detoxification unit (detox). By 2010, the ERs were not admitting drug addicts indiscriminately. Some of the women in this study learned that you had to tell the ER you were suicidal and withdrawing from Xanax (one or the other or both) in order to be admitted. I learned later that much also depended on specific hospitals and the staff on duty. For example, one of the women in our study was rejected at her local suburban hospital but accepted in the city.

Dot should have received care if she showed up at the ER. She was withdrawing from methadone, Xanax, and Percocet. She had high blood pressure, had lost a gall bladder, and her liver was infected by hepatitis C. She was having panic attacks and her "restless leg syndrome" a recently diagnosed disorder, was bothering her. She also had been diagnosed with depression, which left untreated could be suicidal. Any one of these illnesses and symptoms were enough for a bed at the hospital while she waited for an opening in detox.

Dot called me the next day. She had driven herself to the ER in the middle of the night and been discharged in the morning. I called the ER and a staff member told me that a medically stabilized patient could be discharged. I asked to talk to a head nurse. The nurse told me that the ER did not want to help drug addicts and did not need to do so.

Dot's story illustrates many health-related themes, yet her need for medical treatment remained unmet by the scarcity of services available for the poor. As the head ER nurse insinuated, drug users are at the bottom of the list for emergency help. The ER staff was tired of seeing them come through the revolving door, literally as well as figuratively.

Dot's drug career from methamphetamine to prescription drugs was a common pattern I found among poor suburban women who became physically addicted to pain pills while also needing the energy supplied by methamphetamine. The withdrawal from opiates usually supersedes all other needs, and stopping withdrawal pain soon becomes the single focus every morning when they wake up sick. At the close of my study, many of the poor suburban women like Dot who were using methamphetamine were now addicted to pain pills. Pill mills were popping up everywhere. While methamphetamine was still one of the most popular drugs among this population, prescription pain medications were being used simultaneously.

POLITICAL ECONOMY

Political economy theory has been used to explain social, economic, and political realities at both the macro and micro level of analysis, typically with a focus on social justice (Habermas 1985; Romero-Daza, Weeks, and Singer 2003). Looking at the women's methamphetamine-related health issues under a political economy lens focuses attention on the variations in individual agency and the constraints and opportunities caused by structural inequalities. These women's agency, or the ability to direct their own actions, varied widely by their access to resources and health care. A focus on agency would indicate they made choices in their lives that influenced this trajectory. A focus on structure would reveal they had limited choices in their social environment and numerous economic barriers. The interplay between social constraints and agency is one of the most basic and long-standing debates in sociology. The women in this book made choices constrained by barriers that limited their access to basic human needs, such as food, health care, housing, and security.

The health care needs of women from the suburban poor group often were unmet by public health services; therefore, their lives continued within the cycle of disease, illness, injury, pain, despair, and self-medication. Drugs were not a choice at the beginning of this cycle. Drug use was often the consequence of poor health and chronic disease.

Using a political economy perspective also focuses attention on the everyday violence experienced by female drug users and aids in our understanding of why women engage in risk behaviors (Bourdieu 2001). Women in this study, especially those who were more vulnerable due to poverty and age (very young or relatively old) appeared to resign themselves to a subordinate health status to the point of appearing fatalistic. For example, some of the women in the study seemed to accept the inevitability of contracting hepatitis C infection and did not attempt to overcome the barriers to access to health care after they discovered their status.

Looking at the health of inner-city drug users, Merrill Singer (2006) used a political economy framework to identify what he called "syndemics," two or more endemics that occur in clusters in society and are linked to causative structural and social conditions. Syndemics of diseases associated with drug use are hepatitis C (HCV), HIV, and liver disease. Not surprisingly, syndemics were found in the suburban poverty enclaves. Poverty and mental health issues intertwined with physical disease and drug use as both cause and effect. Moreover, suburban women of all classes, stigmatized by illegal drug use, were often ashamed or fearful to seek help for health problems that might expose them as methamphetamine users. Some of the women who began using methamphetamine to maintain their middle-class status ended up living among the most vulnerable populations in marginalized suburban enclaves of poverty as their multiple chronic diseases progressed with little medical attention.

Risk behaviors associated with methamphetamine use were prevalent in the women's stories. Females who use methamphetamine, especially those who inject drugs, are a population vulnerable to transmission of infectious diseases. Physical and sexual abuse and violence, exacerbated by methamphetamine use, also put females at high risk for contracting HIV, HCV, and other infections and were the cause of many unintended injuries.

This chapter takes a closer look at the health issues faced by suburban women who use methamphetamine and other drugs. The issues are categorized by three main themes: physical health, mental health, and social health. The last category includes infectious diseases related to drug use and transmissible throughout a community of both users and nonusers, making it a public health concern.

Physical Health

Physical health effects of methamphetamine use discussed by the women included weight loss, tooth decay and loss, organ damage, and health issues related to withdrawal. Sleep deprivation from bingeing on methamphetamine was also discussed in terms of the associated accidents and injuries that resulted in severe disability.

Weight Loss

Weight loss was the most immediate effect noted by the women, although often it was also considered a benefit. For example, Isabella recalled being pleased with the pounds she lost: "I weighed close to 330. Well, by the time I got clean I was about 165." While many women said they used methamphetamine expressly to lose weight, the drastic weight loss that most women experienced after continued use was not what they desired. Linda, a former user, described how she looked when she had spent years bingeing on methamphetamine: "I weighed 83 pounds at the time. My face, around my eyes was sunk in. . . . I remember a few people seein' me and I can remember them goin' 'Damn, you look like a walking skeleton.' And I did. I didn't realize it. I do remember when I would sit down my hip bones would stick into the—and it hurt." Unfortunately, being thin at every age is the ideal for contemporary women in our culture, and the women I spoke to expressed an almost neurotic need to remain thin, even after motherhood. Beth explained how she used methamphetamine to keep her husband's attention after having four children:

> I started doing the ice a day I remember calling the dope man driving home from the hospital after I had my [fourth child]. I wanted to lose weight. With each one of my kids I weighed 214 pounds when I delivered. But I can honestly say that I never had a problem losing the weight afterward. . . . Although in my mind, when I started using ice, now mind you I was thirty-six, this skinny little bitch that lived across the street

that was so cute and teeny and I was, in my mind I guess I thought I was inferior compared to her. Thirty-six, I had another kid. I'm with a guy that just left his wife that could get any twenty-four-year-old. I don't know why I thought that. I think—my husband tells me that I went into depression after I had the baby.

Here the motivation of adhering to the standard of society's ideal trim figure as well as suffering from what appears to be postpartum depression resulted in Beth using methamphetamine and continuing to do so for years.

Older women with years of use gained weight rather than losing it. For example, Dot believed that her body changed after she used methamphetamine continually:

I guess after about five years. I mean, because you push your body so hard. You really do when you're on it. I mean trying to do everything I was trying to get done. . . . Actually I gained weight. Which is kind of weird, I know. But, it—on the days I, when you're coming off of it. I couldn't get enough to eat. My body would crave something.

Weight loss was not Dot's primary health concern, nor was it for many other women who continued using methamphetamine.

Tooth Decay

Tooth decay and gum disease, often called "meth mouth" by the media, is a well-publicized effect of methamphetamine. The women usually did not notice it, however, until after years of methamphetamine use. Moreover, middle-class women who had the economic means to afford a dentist indicated that dental hygiene, or the lack of it, was the main reason for tooth decay. For example, Joy, at thirty-two, had few of the visible signs of long-term methamphetamine use, but she reported that her teeth were rotted. I asked if she thought that was the effect of using:

I don't know if it's as much an effect of methamphetamines. I think it is something to do with meth. Or just the not eating right and not taking care of myself that came along with that. But I would grind my—a lot of people when they're on meth will grind their teeth. I would do that in my sleep. So I wasn't aware that I was doing it to make myself stop. . . . I think it's more so the hygiene.

Dolly, a thirty-seven-year-old woman, said she started injecting methamphetamine to avoid further tooth decay that she attributed to smoking methamphetamine:

But you asked me why I started shooting. That was probably one of [the reasons] right there. It's what it was doing to my teeth. My teeth were falling apart. And I've always had good strong teeth. They survived through pregnancy after pregnancy you know. And then when I was smoking that stuff, ooh. My teeth would just hurt. And they started disintegrating.

Pam, one of the young Latina women in the study, seemed to confirm the assertion that good dental hygiene was a factor in the extent of tooth decay, which is true regardless of how one uses methamphetamine. She had beautiful teeth although she had used methamphetamine for a number of years to about the same extent as another woman in the study of the same age, whose teeth were riddled with visible black and brown holes. As Pam explained:

> I snorted it, and then I got to the point where because my nose was so like messed up from it I would either get, buy pills or something and empty out capsules and I'd put it in there and swallow it because my—I couldn't take it in my nose anymore/ . . . I smoked it a few times . . . like ever since I was—you know, got my teeth, I—my mom's always took me to the dentist. She works for an oral surgeon. . . . I take care of my teeth, but even like doing meth just snorting it, I mean, can ruin your teeth. I've got like, good dental genetics in my family . . . but even just by snorting it, like I mean I had cavities. I had to get one pulled out because it broke while I was pregnant with my second child and I couldn't get it filled, and they had to pull it out. And I don't, you know, have meth mouth or anything like that. It was just a cavity. And it wasn't like turning black. My teeth weren't turning black or anything. It just got so weak that it just broke.

As Pam shows, good dental hygiene appears to counteract the damage caused by using methamphetamine.

Zoe was a forty-seven-year-old woman who started use relatively late in life. Aware of the highly publicized effects of methamphetamine, she described the dental hygiene routine she followed to avoid meth mouth:

> When I clean my mouth, I floss my teeth, I brush my gums, I brush my tongue, I brush under my tongue, I brush the jaws. I brush as far back as far as I can get 'cause I know how that forms on stuff. And then I use that Listerine, you know, the most potent kind I can get and I'll take a wash rag and wash my tongue, and wash everywhere in there.

From my observation, Zoe's teeth were exceptionally healthy considering the amount of methamphetamine she used, having a husband who produced it.

The greatest influence on tooth decay, based on the women's stories, was having access to a dentist. Meth mouth, like almost every other health issue related to drug use, was highly dependent on social and economic status.

Organ Damage

Since methamphetamine increases both heart rate and blood pressure, it is not surprising that many women expressed concern over its effects on their heart. Other organs that can be damaged due to the toxins used to make methamphetamine and the effects of its use include the lungs, kidney, and liver.

Rachel was a nineteen-year-old young woman who learned while she was in rehab that she had a heart condition, but she was not sure of the name. She described a few scenarios in detail:

I mean I had had like real bad heart problems whenever I was using, but I just assumed like meth-related. I'm not going to the doctor, or I'm going to jail. Like my heart would be like [makes a trilling sound] and then it'd like stop for a couple of seconds. Then it'd like beat, you know how your heart goes bup—bup—bup—bup . . . and I kept like passing out.

And you never went to the hospital for it?

No. I'd been to jail. I didn't want to go again. But in rehab, um, I'd been clean like a month maybe and my whole left arm went completely numb. And it just like it was numb, but it hurt. And my heart was [makes a trilling sound]. And I can remember walking in and my roommates at my rehab were like, "You're like green." And I just went down. And one of my roommates was a registered nurse. And she took my heart pressure and she was like, "We're calling 911. We're calling 911!" I was like, "No, no, no, no, no! I'm not going to jail! I'm not going to jail!" And they were like, "You're not getting fucked up." And I was like, "Oh. OK, let's go!"

Rachel was no longer using methamphetamine when we met her but she was not receiving any medical attention either. She said, "It hurts sometimes. Sometimes it messes up, and I just kind of pull through it. I can't afford to go to the hospital, though." Rachel, a nineteen-year-old woman, did not go to the hospital for fear of being sent to jail for methamphetamine use, and when she stopped using drugs, she could not get medical attention because she had no health insurance. This situation was typical among women of all ages in this study.

Ely, a fifty-one-year-old who had been a heavy user of methamphetamine, cocaine, and pain pills, described a series of adverse health effects after years of daily methamphetamine use:

You know what reality check was on me? I was speed balling [here referring to using methamphetamine and pain pills concurrently]. That's what I call it. Well, my kidneys locked. My kidneys went down on me. Then my lungs tried to shut down on me. . . . I couldn't pee. It wasn't no pee in it. I'd go days and days and wouldn't pee. And I'd hurt so bad

I couldn't hardly get up. Oh my God. Then my lungs, then my lungs—
because I got bad lungs anyway.

Ely, as was typical in her poor community, had no insurance and could not
receive emergency care since her condition was considered chronic.

Gall bladder disease emerged as a common health issue among the
women who were using a homegrown type of methamphetamine they called
cold cook meth (Boeri, Gibson, and Harbry 2009). Two of the women in
this small user network had their gall bladders removed. Hearing how the
cold cook meth was made, I suspected this health effect was linked to the
particularly toxic ingredients used to make this type of methamphetamine,
which included dangerous levels of heavy metals.

We know that methamphetamine production involves mixing a number
of flammable and toxic ingredients that have a high potential for explosions
(Hannan 2005). Recipes used in the local area, however, had less risk of
explosion, such as the cold cook method, discussed in more detail in chapter 6.
Some women said it was the best ice around; others claimed it was poison.
One woman observed, "I think a lot of people want to make it and don't
really know how to make it that much, and might put too much of something. You know, too much of one poison in there. " One woman attributed her daughter's recent medical issues to the toxic ingredients used in the
local product. When I first interviewed her twenty-one-year-old daughter,
Kathy, she was already losing patches of her hair, and large bald spots of scalp
were visible. Kathy claimed to be using only cold cook methamphetamine,
which contained selenium, a trace mineral that can cause hair loss at higher
doses, among other negative health effects. A year later, her mother, also a
user, told me Kathy was in the hospital. "She had to have her gall bladder
out," she told me, "but then when they went in she had to have this much of
her intestine taken out [demonstrating the size with her hands] . . . from
methamphetamine eating her up."

Eve was a former methamphetamine user with brain and facial injury
from a drug-related accident. She was receiving no medical care when I first
met her, although she had been trying unsuccessfully to navigate the paperwork needed for Medicaid. Two years passed before she received a Medicaid
card that would allow her brain injury to be medically addressed, years after
it occurred. The next time I saw Eve, she described a long list of health concerns she had learned about in her recent hospital visit and began to cry. "My
blood pressure was like out of control. I was in the hospital for a week. The
doctor said that dialysis was next for me. Or a stroke. Or heart attack. So
what. So what. I'm tired. I'm tired."

Beyond lack of health insurance, the stigmatization of methamphetamine
compels users to avoid receiving medical attention. The data revealed that the

suburban environment, with its standard of middle-class values that are often violated in secret, influenced young methamphetamine users to fear exposing their failure to live up to these values. An example of what appeared to be a hypocritical value was the standard of not having sex before marriage, which research shows is typical among young suburban females. Bea was an example of how a middle-class young woman can take extreme measures to hide a marginalized status. Bea was a young methamphetamine user who at age sixteen became pregnant by an abusive boyfriend. Rather than tell her parents, she had a friend perform what she called a homemade abortion with a coat hanger. Although she bled for a week, with pain and blood in her urine, she said, "The [pregnancy] test came out negative next time I took it." She never received further medical attention for this. Although indirectly related to methamphetamine use, Bea's story indicated a limited access to confidential health services and risk-awareness education for young people in the suburbs.

Withdrawal

Withdrawal from methamphetamine includes both mental and physical symptoms. The lack of food and sleep, as well as the constant moving, eventually has an effect on the body. For example, Katy explained her withdrawal:

> Oh God, the first couple times that I ever did it, it was, it felt like my body was dying. Every part of my body ached. Like every muscle in my body ached. Just 'cause basically when you're on it, you're tense. Like you're tensing things you don't even realize you're tensing. My back was just knots all over my back. You'd have a headache. Sometimes, when I first started doing it, when I'd come off of it I'd get splotchy, like purple splotches sort of all up and down my arms.

Methamphetamine users recounted a wide range and diversity of withdrawal symptoms, some similar to withdrawal from opioids. Typically, women said they were extremely tired and had an irregular heart rhythm and a feeling of depression. Others described more severe physical symptoms. Madeline, a student, described a withdrawal that was so severe she was compelled to call her friends to bring her methamphetamine in an effort to stop the pain:

> I tried so hard to stop, and I didn't get out of my bed. My eyes were like swollen shut. Like when you're so hungry you just feel like you're going to throw up, and you just have to sit there because you're just like, okay, I was feeling like that but I was so hungry at the same time. So it's like you want to eat, but you feel like your stomach's about to explode. And you know when you're so tired that your eyes are just shutting? It was like I felt that but I couldn't go to sleep. And I was like really, really full. I was feeling like my stomach was going to explode. . . .

I basically felt like my stomach was out to here and my tongue was sticking out. And so I just laid there and then finally I was like, you know, I just called somebody, and I was like please bring me some [meth] and they brought me some and then I was fine. I did some and I was just like up and ready to go.

Withdrawal symptoms such as these make it difficult to stop using even when motivated to do so.

Beth, the seemingly perfect suburban soccer mom, described a process of withdrawal more physically appalling than most methamphetamine withdrawal stories I heard. After a series of binges that involved staying awake for fourteen days at a stretch, she decided to stop on her own:

I had sent my kids to live somewhere else with friends, and I said that's it, I'm done, I can't do this anymore. My youngest daughter was a baby and I stayed where Robby [estranged husband] was living. I went to bed for about four days, tried to get clean. Cold turkey, but it was so hard. Literally, I mean I wouldn't even lift my head off the pillow, couldn't lift my head off the pillow to smoke a cigarette. I was locked in my room. I didn't eat. I didn't drink. I don't think I went to the bathroom. Robby came over to the house because I wouldn't answer my phone. Somehow got in the house, ended up taking me to the emergency room. I had a 104-point something fever. I was dehydrated. Every orifice, my ears, my nose, my eyes, vaginal infection. I was in the hospital. I guess it was poisons. My scalp, I had like open sores.

The severity of the withdrawal appeared to be linked to an uncontrolled use pattern rather than duration. Beth engaged in bingeing behavior, whereas others, like Julia, learned to use in a more controlled manner. Unlike smokers, who tended to use repeatedly throughout the day, Julia injected methamphetamine and used only once a day. She described her relatively easy withdrawal:

Like dizziness. Like if you wake up and you don't have it for a little while, a couple days, like you get real dizzy, real tired. It's pain, a lot of time you'll hurt, like your body will ache really bad. You feel like fatigue, you know, you can't get out of bed. I mean I get up every day with or without it . . . if I don't have it, like, I'll start hurting, and I'll feel tired or weak or whatever, but I still stay up.

The universal symptom in withdrawal from methamphetamine is the overwhelming sense of fatigue and feeling of depression. Other symptoms appeared to be linked to the type of methamphetamine used, route of administration, and the number of days on methamphetamine without sleep.

Sleep Deprivation

After days of being awake on methamphetamine, some women became psychotic and began to hallucinate. Stella was part of a spiritually oriented young network who used drugs in the basement of a suburban home. She described what she saw after staying awake for days on methamphetamine:

> I stay up for three days and I can see energy, I can see demons and angels. . . . I do know a lot of people in my group of spiritual friends—that's why they do meth. Because, think about it—because Gandhi and Buddhist and stuff—they starve themselves. They stay up for days to get more closer—to see the energy—to know everything. All is one and one is all. So, you do meth that long, it's a way of cheating enlightenment. It's a fake, half-assed, stupid enlightenment that just, if you don't even know it, it just, it just freaks you out. Well, you have to be intelligent to be able to, um, do God's work. If you're trying to do God's work and you're trying to, you know, free people from their demons. And you can see the demons. You can see the demon on their back, and you know how to kill it. You have to be intelligent to be able to deal with that because the demon's going to jump on you. Demons jumped on me today.

Stella justified her insomnia-induced visions by relating them to spiritual experiences, and helping to rid her friends of unwanted demons.

Tammy, a former user from a middle-class neighborhood, described what occurred when she was sleep deprived for what seems like an incredible length of time:

> And I mean I've stayed up a total of sixteen days one time on some good stuff. . . . Whew. When you stay up for sixteen days you start seeing people's faces in windows. You start seeing people that, I mean me, I seen people that passed away twenty-something years ago that wasn't in my room, in the window, sitting up in trees. [Laughs.] It's scary.

When I first heard stories of meth users staying awake for a week or more, I was skeptical. But I heard these stories from so many users, it became evident they were somehow surviving the extended periods of wakefulness by taking short naps, which some called "power naps."

Sleep deprivation sometimes caused injuries resulting from lack of coordination or passing out from sheer exhaustion. Nancy, for example, was permanently disfigured and had little reason to hope she would regain her looks. She was involved in a one-car accident when she fell asleep at the wheel of her car. She had been bingeing on methamphetamine the week before when she had an emotional breakup with a partner, but she said she was not using the day she had her accident. A bag of methamphetamine and a good-bye note from her girlfriend were found in the car, so the police report called it a methamphetamine-related incident and attempted suicide. Nancy claims she was not trying to commit suicide, but because it said so in the report, she lost her insurance coverage:

> I hit a tree. When I crossed the road I hit a ditch. They said that the Sub-
> urban went six feet up in the air and when I came down I hit a tree. A
> tree that you can't see from the road and the officer said I tried to do it
> on purpose, but if I'm going to do it on purpose why would I go across
> the road, jump a ditch, and then find the tree instead of hitting a tele-
> phone pole right there. I was taken to the hospital . . . I died twice.
> I broke my neck. I shattered my heel. Broke my jaw in three places. . . .
> The officer that came out to the scene, I wasn't there when he got there,
> he came to the hospital and he wrote on his report that I tried to commit
> suicide. . . . I haven't been able to see any doctors because the insurance
> canceled. . . . I lost my insurance. I think they put me back together for
> my coffin, is what I think. I really do. I mean when I had the wreck my
> face broke the steering wheel of the truck.

Apparently, a clause in her insurance stated it did not reimburse for medical bills related to attempted suicide. Moreover, the medical staff treated her badly because she became known as the "meth addict" on the hospital ward. Nancy's face was patched together so she could be released. But with no reconstructive surgery, her face was unrecognizable from the beautiful face in the photo she showed me from a few years ago. She said she could not find a job to support herself with her face like this:

> I've tried to get a job ever since and I moved to [Suburban Town] with
> my daughter for about three months. She told me the Waffle House
> needed some help. Waffle House will hire anybody. It don't matter what
> they look like. There was three of them up there that needed help and
> wouldn't none of them have hired me. They kept shuffling me back and
> forth, back and forth. So another friend of mine was working at Waffle
> House in [another Suburban Town], and she said they're not like that
> here. Come on down here and we'll put you to work because we need
> help really bad. So I went down there. Moved down there for a couple
> weeks and her district area manager said that he couldn't hire anybody
> that looked like me—that I'd scare his customers off.

Nancy thinks she might have fallen asleep at the wheel because she had stayed awake on methamphetamine the week preceding the accident in order to work. Once she stopped using for a day, her body and brain refused to stay awake.

MENTAL HEALTH

The mental health issues recounted in the women's stories were difficult to disentangle from issues of childhood abuse, intergenerational poverty, long-term domestic violence, chronic unemployment stress, unhygienic social conditions, and homelessness. Almost all the women were either diagnosed with a mental health disorder or at some point in their lives had symptoms of depression or other emotional anguish they relieved with drug use. Since I was not qualified to diagnose symptoms of mental health disorders, I asked the women if they had been professionally diagnosed when they mentioned a mental health condition. Many reported a professional diagnosis for a range of disorders.

A commonly held assumption by both the women and outsiders is that the drug use causes mental health problems, but most of the women reported being diagnosed before they ever started using drugs. Some women preferred to self-medicate with methamphetamine rather than take the prescribed drug, while others simply could not afford a doctor or the cost of the prescription drug, and in the poor enclaves, methamphetamine was cheaper. Mental health issues mentioned by the women include attention deficit disorder (ADD) or attention deficit hyperactive disorder (ADHD), depression, bipolar disorder, and stress. Suicide attempts were also common.

ADD and ADHD

Emma was only a child when her mother thought the whole family needed counseling and Emma was diagnosed with depression. Her parents were middle-class but struggling to keep up their middle-class lifestyle. Emma had everything she wanted materially, but family life was strained. She was always overweight and her mother tried to keep her active in dancing, sports, running, and other after school activities. She was diagnosed with ADHD when she was a teenager, but since she already had a record of misusing prescription pills, no medication was prescribed. She said one reason she took methamphetamine was because it helped her to focus. This was a common reason for using methamphetamine and misusing prescription stimulants.

Twenty-two-year-old Grace was diagnosed with ADD and misused her prescription of Adderall. Although she also used methamphetamine, she said she preferred to use prescription drugs:

> I don't want some backwoods redneck making my drug. It sounds stupid that I want a pharmaceutical company feeding me drugs, but I don't know. And it was just a little too much for me. Whenever I abused drugs I like a very functional high. I like something that I can be high on in a way, but also no one else knows. I'm kind of secretive like that. And

that's something that I could never, never like master with meth. I just felt like I was in a constant state of panic.

Linda, also diagnosed with ADD as a child, reported using the two drugs for the same purpose:

One of the things I liked about it [Ritalin] was that it reminded me of speed, and I'd use it when I couldn't find any crystal meth. I would use Ritalin. Yeah. A lot of times it was just a matter of convenience too, it was just kind of around.

Unfortunately, many women were not diagnosed and appeared to self-medicate their symptoms without knowing the cause of those symptoms.

Depression

Depression loomed as an omnipresent theme in our interview data. Some who were diagnosed with depression reported that methamphetamine was better for their depression than the medication they were prescribed. For example, Dolly, a thirty-seven-year-old woman from a working-middle-class background, said she had been taking Xanax for stress related to her depression: "But then along came ice and no more depression, and no more pills. No more feeling sleepy and then feeling better tomorrow. You feel better now."

Quite a few of the women were affected by a traumatic childhood incident that still caused emotional pain. They said they used methamphetamine to forget. Mercedes, a Latina woman, described what she was trying to forget:

When I was eleven, I used to run away from my foster parents and I would go check on my mom because my dad was very violent. And several times my mom would be passed out drunk and my dad would come to while I was there and he'd [long pause] abuse me, both sexually and physically. And uh, when I was eleven I got pregnant by my dad and, uh [long pause] . . .

Did you have an abortion?

No, my mom pretty much beat the you-know-what out of me when I was about four and a half [months pregnant]. I was just really starting to show, um, to the point where I wouldn't go back home to my foster parents' house because I knew they would be able to tell and I was scared. I didn't know what to tell them.

Mercedes lost the baby, and twenty years later she was still having nightmares stemming from the emotional and physical abuse at the hands of her parents. She never received counseling for this incident. She told me the counselor she currently saw at a methadone clinic had rape counseling training, and she might talk to her. She hoped her new counselor would be able to put her nightmares to rest.

Like Mercedes, many of the women in the study said they felt depressed but were never diagnosed with depression. Others were not diagnosed until much later, after drug use had started. Mia said she had been depressed all her life. She was professionally diagnosed only last year at age fifty.

Bipolar Disorder

Julia was taken from her drug-addicted parents when she was young to live in DFCS group homes. While there, she was diagnosed as having a bipolar disorder. She described her experience during this time growing up:

> DFCS was like shoving pills down my throat and I didn't want them. I didn't believe I needed to go see a psychiatrist and go tell him everything that I had problems with. And I rebelled. . . I always said I didn't want to be like my mom and be strung out on drugs, because it was like they would say, "You're just like your mother," you know, and stuff like that. It was just harder for me. . . I don't know, I basically ran away from them [foster parents]. And that's what got me out of their custody.

At age fifteen, she was back living with her mother who was still an addict. Her mother gave her Lorcet, a narcotic pain pill, for her headaches. Her grandmother introduced her to methamphetamine at age sixteen. By age eighteen she was shooting methamphetamine with her boyfriend. At age twenty she was raped at a dealer's house.

When asked how methamphetamine affected her since she had a bipolar disorder she explained:

> Because I think when I'm high I don't think about, like, I don't see my depressed mode, and I don't start moaning, or thinking about past, or start thinking about stuff that makes me sad, or whatever. So I think it keeps my mind off of being so depressed. Because I used to be very, very depressed. I used to not come out of bed for days . . . I feel like I don't have to take medications. I don't get to where I'm wanting to hurt myself.

Hurting oneself, or self-harm, often involves self-*cutting*, which is associated with a range of diagnosable disorders, depression, anxiety, and stress, as well as with people who have experienced emotional, sexual or physical abuse. While many forms of self-harm are hard to identify, such as ingesting toxins intentionally to harm oneself, cutting is easily identifiable, especially when it is done on areas of the body that are visible, such as arms and legs. Some of the women had scars clearly in sight, such as Dee, who was introduced in chapter one.

Dee came from a middle-class suburban family and had lived in the same suburban town all her life until recently, when she either left home voluntarily or her mother asked her to leave; her story was unclear on this point. Her childhood, however, seemed idyllic. Her parents never divorced and she saw them argue only once in her life. She had no abuse or trauma in her childhood. Her father died suddenly of cancer when she was fourteen years old. She was very close to him and tried to put it out of her mind and move on with life, but she said she sometimes reflected on the fact that she had no father. Perhaps not coincidentally, she started drug use at age sixteen, and it quickly got out of control. She liked methamphetamine immediately. She had already used Adderall and said methamphetamine had the same effect only better. She left home at age eighteen and was living out of her car, sleeping in parking lots at night with other homeless people.

I noticed the cutting scars on Dee during our third interview, when it was hot outside and she was wearing shorts. The deep pinkish scars showed up clearly in contrast with her white thighs. She said the scars on her legs were from cutting she did when she was younger and still at home. She said she had been tempted to cut herself recently. I asked her why, and she replied with a smile, "You don't know how good it feels—it's a release."

Some of the women were cutters before they started using, like Dee, but others started cutting after their first use of methamphetamine. When I first saw some of the deep scars on the women's legs and arms, my stomach turned. There were so many women with these scars, I eventually became used to seeing them but still felt troubled. For these women, with their visible scars, the physical pain of self-harm relieved the mental and emotional pain whose scars I could not see.

SOCIAL HEALTH

I use the term *social health* here to refer to the infectious diseases that can spread across entire communities where drug-using networks live and work. I want to draw attention to the social implications of these infections, typically classified as public health concerns,. The infectious disease that receives the most attention is human immunodeficiency virus (HIV), which can lead to acquired immunodeficiency syndrome (AIDS). According to data collected by the Centers for Disease Control and Prevention (CDC), injection drug use has directly and indirectly accounted for more than one-third of AIDS cases in the United States (Centers for Disease Control and Prevention 2008). Among women, the increase in rates is alarming. In 2000, 57 percent of all AIDS cases among women were attributed to injection drug use or sex with partners who inject drugs, compared with 31 percent of cases among men. By 2008, the rate of HIV infection among female adults and adolescents attributed to injection drug use was double the rate for men. These recent statistics suggest that risk awareness and prevention education would be useful knowledge to disseminate among women who inject drugs and/or have sexual relations with men who inject.

Hepatitis C virus (HCV) is the most common blood-borne infection in the United States, and injection drug use is a primary risk factor for transmission of HCV. Recently called the "silent epidemic" because of the relative lack of attention it receives from the medical field, it is increasing among younger injectors (Tirrell 2011). Approximately 3.2 million people are chronically infected with HCV, which can lead to cirrhosis of the liver and liver cancer. The transmission of HCV is primarily through injection drug use routes, although sexual transmission is possible. Since 2002, the male to female ratio has declined and was nearly 1 in 2008 (Centers for Disease Control and Prevention 2008). This signifies that female risk behaviors for contracting HCV are increasing in comparison to men, indicating the need for more risk-awareness education and prevention efforts aimed toward women.

The primary route for the spread of infectious diseases among drug-using networks is through sharing syringes, cookers (where drugs are mixed with water), cotton filters (where drug mix is drawn through cotton to absorb its impurities), and other drug paraphernalia (crack pipes). Sexual activity is a risk behavior for HCV transmission if the woman has multiple partners or a partner who injects drugs. Most of the women in the study who injected said they shared injection paraphernalia with a partner. Women also reported they did not use condoms when they were in a monogamous relationship. For example, thirty-year-old Erin said, "I got them at home. But I'm in a relationship. I mean he doesn't cheat on me. We don't mess with anybody else." Unfortunately, relationships among many of the women were often short-lived.

Monogamous relationships were not the norm. Stella, who engaged in sex with about ten "ice-buddies" that year, used condoms only occasionally: "And usually when I start using a condom I say, 'Fuck this shit.' And take it off and keep going [laughs]." When Stella was asked if sex was better on methamphetamine, she indicated it was great for men primarily: "Most people, most men anyway, they do ice to be able to stay up and have sex all night. . . .Well, I liked for them to be able to do that. Yeah, it was better [laughs]."

Although Flo, a fifty-year-old former methamphetamine user, was currently monogamous, she was not monogamous while she was using methamphetamine. Informed while she was in jail that she had contracted HCV, she continued to have unprotected sex. Although it is rare for HCV to be spread by sexual contact, engaging in sex work with multiple partners is a risk behavior for HCV as well as HIV and other sexually transmitted diseases. During the last year that Flo used methamphetamine, she had at least ten sexual partners. I asked how many of these were steady partners (serial monogamous) and she replied, "None. These were people that had the dope. I'd go straight to the source. That way I didn't have to deal with the middle man." She did not use condoms that year.

Mia, the fifty-year-old woman who was an active injection methamphetamine user, had been diagnosed with HCV twice and treated with Interferon, although it was not clear if she completed this treatment. She was currently engaged in street sex work and drinking heavily:

> I haven't been checked for a while, but I would know if I had it. When I was twenty-one they said if you take one more drink you're going to die. And I'm fifty and I've been drinking ever since then so . . . but I do have damage. Every time they take any blood from me they'll say, "Well you're fine there's nothing wrong with you. I do see some liver damage but you're okay." But they can tell it from my blood and stuff.

As a result of insufficient guidelines and training among medical staff about how to effectively provide health care for HCV, many of the women diagnosed received no medical attention. The diagnosis and information women did receive was very confusing. Individuals newly infected with HCV typically were either asymptomatic or had a mild clinical illness. The majority of infected individuals might not be aware of their infection because they are not clinically ill. However, those infected serve as a source of transmission to others and are at risk for chronic liver disease or other HCV-related chronic diseases for decades after infection is detected.

CDC recommends HCV-positive individuals be evaluated periodically for possible development of chronic liver disease (Centers for Disease Control and Prevention 2008). Those who use or inject illegal drugs are advised to stop using and injecting drugs and complete substance abuse treatment with follow-up risk reduction and prevention. However, funding for medical care and treatment is typically not available. None of the women diagnosed with HCV infection received this type of medical attention. And as Mia's words show, most of the women took their HCV-positive status lightly after years of being ignored by the medical establishment. The medical establishment essentially discriminates against active substance users, making it almost impossible for them to obtain treatment for HCV.

Deb, a forty-six-year-old former methamphetamine user now on methadone, described how she tricked the system. Deb was diagnosed with HCV during one of the blood tests she had at a rehabilitation center years ago. Left medically unattended for years, Deb was taken to the emergency room by her sister when she became jaundiced and her liver swelled.

> Actually, I kept having to go to the emergency room because I don't have insurance. And I was so sick. Kept applying for disability; kept getting turned down . . . and I'm so sick. It started out . . . extremely tired. I'm talking about, you know, just worse than any, you know, I—I mean, just can't even get out of the bed tired. Um, not functioning tired. You know, getting up and going to the bathroom and coming back, that's how tired I was. My stomach was so swollen that it looked like I was

pregnant. My eyes had a yellowish tint to it. Um, my sister was like, something is bad—you got to go to the hospital. . . . So I went to the hospital and—you know, they didn't check for hepatitis C. I told them all the symptoms, and I told them I had hep C. They did not check. They did not do the blood work.

In and out of the emergency department, Deb eventually saw a doctor who recognized her symptoms of acute HCV:

I kept going to the ER. Kept going to the ER. And throwing up, you know. They'd give me fluids, you know. This really cool doctor—can't remember his name or I'd tell you. Just so that the world could know. I mean some—you don't find a lot of sympathy from emergency room doctors. Or any doctors—but I will say I have met several here, you know, that have tried to help me. Well, he did his residency or whatever out at the hospital. And he would, actually goes out and volunteers at the ER like maybe once a week or once every month or whatever. But he is the one that really went for everything with me. He didn't care about—I mean he ordered every test possible. He did everything within his power to help me . . . I had no Medicaid. No. No. Couldn't get it. Couldn't get it . . . felony. You can never get Medicaid unless you get Social Security. So he hooked me up with a doctor—helps with the hepatitis right. He said he had a program. The other doctor hooked me up with him through the hospital. And he had a program for the Interferon and all that and it was free. Well I called the doctor, you know, and they said yes. The nurse told me, "Yes we're doing a program, you know. Come in see if you qualify." Of course I have no income, you know, no—no—no nothing.

She was put on Interferon and Ribavirin treatment until one day the nurse told her that she was being dropped from the program:

Yeah. And she says, she's like, "Okay, what we'll do is . . . I'm going to show you how to do everything, and they're going to mail you your Interferon and your Rebetol every week, you'll get it. And you have to have a blood work done. Okay, you can—you know, so it will cost twenty-five dollars or whatever, you know, to come get your blood work done once a month." And so, anyway, you know, that worked out for about eight weeks. And then on the third visit, I didn't even make it to the back. The lady at the front said, "I'm sorry, but he's decided that he is not going to do this anymore for people who don't have, uh, insurance. But anyway, we're not doing it anymore. But we'll give you a number of somebody else that might be doing it. So you call him." Well, I called them and they said it was a three-month waiting list. So what

I did was I just went to the health department and got my blood work, and I did not tell the people that was sending me the medicine that the doctor stopped seeing me. They sent the blood work on. They never questioned me on that, and I wound up finishing it that way . . . I took, um—Interferon. I gave myself one shot a day. And I took eight hundred milligrams of the, um, Rebetol, which goes along with it. I did that whole treatment, you know, and that lasts close to a year.

The treatment Deb described is also extremely difficult to complete because of the severe nausea and flulike symptoms, as well as depression, it causes. Deb not only kept to her regime, but she also finished the medication program on her own without a doctor's oversight. This contradicts the popular opinion among local medical professionals who told me that drug users could not complete the Interferon program if they are still using drugs.

After several inquiries, I found no doctor in our area who would treat a current drug user for HCV, claiming regulations against this practice. Studies indicate that the more stringent treatment guidelines and commonly held practice of not treating current drug users for HCV is not evidence based (Sylvestre 2005). Instead, more individualized and targeted treatment for drug users should be standard practice, and medical treatment based on benefit assessments should be the same for drug users as for non-drug-using patients (Edlin and Carden 2006; Edlin et al. 2001). Recent research shows successful outcomes integrating HCV services for active drug users (Sylvestre and Zweben 2007).

The use of condoms reduces the spread of numerous sexually transmitted infections (STIs), yet for many women condom use was not their independent choice but rather one dependent on a male partner's preference. For women who wanted to keep their new boyfriend or needed the resources provided by a male sex partner, condom use was not practical in real-life situations. As discussed by the two women who participated in a focus group, it was a matter of priorities:

Do you always feel comfortable insisting?
Flo: Yes. Or no. And a lot of times and you're out there you didn't make your money. So, I guess I ain't going to get my money.
Mia: And my thing is the person that I would be with at the time would always have drugs, and I wanted the drugs more than I worried about catching anything.
Flo: Right. That's right. Yes. So you, yeah . . .
Mia: So you just don't even—that's not an issue.
Flo: It's just like, who's in control?
Mia: The drug [laughs].
Flo: Yes. And it is—bottom line. That's usually what happens.

Here we see one participant in the focus group changing her story that she always used a condom when another participant proposed a scenario based on the reality of what the male partner could offer in exchange.

Having access to sterile syringes and injection paraphernalia has been shown to drastically reduce the spread of HIV and HCV infection among drug users. Most of the women obtained sterile syringes from friends who used drugs, relatives who had diabetes, or from pharmacies. However, skill at buying syringes at a pharmacy varied. Twenty-two-year-old Julia explained:

> A lot of times, I mean I've seen some people bleach them out. Like they'll bleach each other's out. I mean I try not to do that because [laugh] there's too many diseases going on, you know, and this town is noted for hepatitis really bad. And most of the time you can get them from the store. I mean my mom gets them from like CVS and I've gotten them at the drugstores before. I mean if you know what to say, sometimes you can get them. Sometimes they'll turn you down, which I think is really ridiculous cause they shouldn't turn anybody down because, you know, they're going to go do something to get a needle. And whether it's from using somebody else's or whatever. If they want to get high then they'll do it.

Syringes were not the only drug paraphernalia needed by the suburban-injecting networks. Discussing the use of clean syringes and access during a focus group, Ada said, "I've seen somebody use lake water," to which Mia replied, "I've seen people use creek [water]. I've seen people use spit." The practice of using unsterile water is a risk factor not only for spreading infectious diseases but also for exposure to a host of bacteria-related health issues.

Recent public health reports show that young women are more likely to be infected with HIV and HCV than older women (Centers for Disease Control and Prevention 2010). According to the women's accounts, older women used their own syringes more than did the younger women who injected. Syringes were more difficult for younger female injectors, lacking the experience of the older women, to obtain. Twenty-five-year-old Lea described her experiences buying syringes:

> Because it's so hard to find clean ones, and everybody's scared to go into the pharmacy and ask for them, so when I got the balls to do it, I would make sure, cause nobody else would go get their own, and it took so much courage to do that cause I was high and there'd be all these fucking people around, and the pharmacy tech keeps looking at me. . . . I'm not even fucking kidding, because I always got turned down at CVS. The only time I was ever able to get some was when I went to Walmart, and it was when I covered up all my tattoos and when I actually didn't look like I was shot out. Because if I was shot out, they would ask me

questions, I am not kidding; I think that is so wrong to me because they can refuse you, it's not gonna stop you from doing drugs. They *make* you share needles with somebody. It does not make any sense to me. You have to ask the right way . . .You have to ask for the right gauge and you have to ask for the—it's a certain size and I had to look it up online every time because I'd forgotten the numbers. But if you don't say it right they won't give it to you because they'll think you're an addict or a junkie. And if you make them think you're a diabetic they'll give it to you. And I had to cover up my tattoos when I went. And everybody always paid me to do it because everybody was so scared to do it. But I'd go and get it every time. I'd get a box of a hundred and make a lot of money off that. Because nobody would go themselves and so they'd— they'll pay five dollars for a rig. And I'd give them out clean.

For Ada, the twenty-one-year-old woman who had been told while she was in jail that she had contracted HCV, learning how to get her own syringe was a lesson that came too late. She already knew that she contracted HCV from sharing syringes with a group of injectors:

Any person that has injected, I don't care how many times they say they only use clean needles, there has been a time or two that they've been careless and not. Because people that use needles, they're going to get their fix however, whatever limits they got to go to, I don't care what they say. And I think if the community, instead of having to have ID or something to get clean needles, I think it should be community service to give them out. It would cut hepatitis and AIDS in half.

Syringe exchange programs (SEPs) are increasing around the world but are still illegal in some states in the United States. Moreover, state regulations vary on whether pharmacy staff can sell syringes without a proper prescription. In the state where the women lived, SEPs were illegal. Although one SEP operated undisturbed by law enforcement in the city, only one of the suburban women knew of this program, and she did not know where it was located. Until I had talked to Ada about harm reduction, she was not aware that SEPs existed. Even after being informed of the program, the women mentioned that lack of transportation to the city or other barriers would prevent them from obtaining this free service.

SUMMARY OF GENDERED HEALTH RISKS

The patterns of health issues related to methamphetamine use found among our sample of women included physical, mental, and social health problems. Methamphetamine use also was found to result in exposure to violence and injury. This syndemic pattern could be linked to the lack of health care services in suburban communities. The study findings show that female methamphetamine users living in the suburbs not only experienced multiple barriers to health care services, but they also lacked continual care or injury prevention awareness. ERs, one of the main health providers used by the poor in urban areas, refused uninsured drug users who presented in the suburban ERs, or they dismissed them within a few hours when they were medically stabilized without addressing their chronic diseases. Primary providers and emergency health care staff in the suburbs seemed to lack sufficient knowledge to provide proper service for drug users, and some openly discriminated against them. Health care and social services often were overburdened, underfunded, and intimidating to drug-using women, especially those who lived in the outer suburbs or exurbs.

Lack of services or access to services leaves women and their children vulnerable to the risk of injuries and more severe health conditions that can lead to disability and death. Some of these women received health care attention only while incarcerated. These findings support the call for public health interventions that take into account the social reality of drug-using females and the everyday gendered violence they encounter due to their increased exposure to injury and disease (Bourgois, Prince, and Moss 2004).

None of the women diagnosed with HCV were receiving any health care oversight at the time of the interviews. Typically, drug users are not treated until they cease all drug use, primarily due to the belief that they will not complete the treatment, although this view has been challenged (Sylvestre and Zweben 2007). The one woman who managed to receive treatment was dropped from what appears to have been a clinical study. Yet she completed the treatment on her own.

The women's aggregated stories on health, illnesses, and health care issues show an enormous gap in health care for the most vulnerable and marginalized. Moreover, the discrimination against drug users by health care providers appears to be unfounded. All of the women wanted to be treated for their health problems related to drug use, and most were willing to stop drug use if their pain and suffering could be addressed medically.

The lacking services included access to syringes and other paraphernalia that have been shown to greatly reduce the spread of infectious diseases. Harm-reduction strategies were not an option in the suburbs, and SEPs were illegal in this state. This political situation resulted in a rapid spread of HCV among one injecting community made up primarily of suburban youth who were aware of harm-reduction messages but did not know how to obtain clean syringes.

An aspect of harm reduction in methamphetamine use that is rarely addressed in the literature is the threshold level for the negative effects of illegal drugs. The "quit or go to jail" message by law enforcement becomes a "quit or die" message from the health care and treatment community. Yet we cannot ignore that the women's stories reveal varying effects from similar amounts, routes of administration, and lengths of time of methamphetamine use, indicating that for many women, drug use continued for years despite health concerns. The literature shows that amphetamine-type medications do have beneficial effects for some people, most notably for children with attention deficit disorder (Weisheit and White 2009). We know that each individual has her own threshold level for tolerance, and some substances that are dangerous for one individual are not for another. Selenium, a trace mineral, is present in the gun bluing ingredient used in the production of cold cook methamphetamine. Although selenium is toxic when used in high doses, only one woman revealed negative health effects from ingesting this drug. Likewise, some women were able to use methamphetamine for many years at high doses and appeared physically and mentally healthier than women who used for only a short period of time. Individual tolerance and threshold levels should be considered in any assessment of substance use and health needs.

Another aspect of health that needs to be examined under a political economy lens is that chronic physical pain increasingly is addressed in our society through the use of pain pills. Likewise, deep emotional pain that is more difficult to identify and treat is also addressed by a wide array of prescription pills. Those who can afford these expensive treatments and medications do so legitimately. Those who cannot afford them obtain drugs illicitly, as did many of the women in the study who self-medicated physical pain and emotional suffering with illegal drugs. They used prescription pills concurrently with methamphetamine, sequentially, or in a switching pattern from methamphetamine to prescription pill abuse. When they had access to legally obtained prescription pills they typically reduced their methamphetamine use. Who is allowed access to these pills, why, and how pills are made available are political and economic issues affected by social stratification.

CHAPTER 6

Gendered Risks

VIOLENCE AND CRIME

SKY

Sky is a thirty-eight-year-old white woman who was raised in the suburban enclaves of poverty. She was born in one of the larger suburban towns surrounding the city and lived in this same area at the time of the interview. Both her mother and her father were methamphetamine addicts, and her grandmother raised her. When her grandmother died, she was sent to live with her mother and stepfather. Her stepfather proceeded to rape her regularly when she was only eleven:

Did you tell anyone?
Well, he used to threaten me because, right before this happened my grandmother died. The one that helped raise me. And my grandfather just didn't feel as though he could take care of me by his self. So he sent me to live with my mom and my stepdad. And he—my stepdad used to threaten me if I tell anybody, then he'll kill—he'll do something to my mom and I'll lose my mom. I'd just lost my grandma so I was scared to tell anybody. But after two years it got to the point where any time I wanted to do anything or go anywhere or anything, I had to have sex with him to do it. And one of my mom's best friends had came and got me and my stepsister to help her do some yard work. She was going to pay us; it was during the summer. And I told her I really don't want to do anything I just want to go sit outside on the swing. And when she came outside I was crying. So I broke down and told her what happened. And then my mom didn't believe me so she made me go live with my dad. . . . I ran away at thirteen. I was gone for seven and a half months to [another state]. I started stripping in a club and snorting cocaine . . . me and the girl that ran away with me, we went to [Big City] and we ran into these two men that said that they were going to New Orleans, and they could help us get a job. And we were what—thirteen? So get a job, yeah, let's go! So we went with them. And the job ended up being

stripping in a club. They didn't even have a—they didn't even have a stage. We just stood on top of the pool table.

How'd you get away from that?

He had two locks on the door. One lock had a key to it, and if you didn't have the key you couldn't get out. Well he left the door open one day— we were cleaning up for him in that room and he had the door open. And I guess, not thinking, he went to the bathroom and when he did I told my friend I'm leaving. If you want to go let's go. And she didn't go with me, so I left. And I ran into some people, this guy name Robert, and he asked me what was wrong because I was sitting in a baseball field in the dugout and I was crying. And he said, "What's wrong?" I said I want to go home. I miss my family. So they called my family, and my family came and got me. My stepdad and my grandfather came and picked me up. Then I ran away again. I ran away until I was old enough to get a job and be on my own.

Years later, her father and stepmother introduced her to methamphetamine. By then Sky was a single mother trying to make ends meet. She complained how tired she was when her father offered her methamphetamine:

I seen him do it, and I was like, "Dad, what is that?" And he told me. And I asked him, well what's the point of it, and he said, "It gives me energy." And at the time I was working two jobs trying to take care of my kids, so I was like, "I don't know if I can do that though—shoot it." And my stepmom was like, "you don't have to shoot it. You can smoke it. You can snort it." So that's how I started snorting.

Why did you continue to use methamphetamine?

I guess the addiction. When I get up in the morning I want a line or eat a little. I can get up and clean my house and go outside and function and just [long pause] it doesn't make me feel better. It just kind of drowns out all the issues that I have [becoming upset and crying].

Sky had a lot of issues to drown. By age thirty, she not only worked at two jobs but also engaged in sex work and sold drugs on the side. By age thirty-eight, she had so many felonies related to drug distribution that not even the public ex-offender employment office could help her find work. She explained to me that all she can do to survive is sex work, "I'm not going to lie. I do drugs, you know what I'm saying. I can't find a legal job, so if I can't sell drugs then I do whatever you know is necessary to keep myself going." She estimated she had one hundred sex partners in the last year.

Sky lived in one of the trailer parks surrounding a suburban town. The trailer park where I picked her up for the first interview had seen better days. The next time I picked Sky up she was staying in the nicer trailer park nearby where the trailers were better maintained, and some sported handkerchief-size yards with flowers. Sky told me why she moved there:

> This is what I'm going through, my grandfather just passed in December. He had this mobile home for twenty-three years. He owned the mobile home. But the mobile home park says I have to fill out the application, and they have to run my [criminal] background. And my background is very extensive, and that's what I'm struggling with right now. See if I take this application to this lady, is she really gonna run a background? Because my grandfather's been there so long.

Sky informed me that she had a new boyfriend who was living with her. He did not have a criminal record, and she was hoping that maybe a background check could be done on him instead. Obviously stressed about where she will live, Sky questioned why she might not be able to live here in her grandfather's mobile home when presumably illegal Hispanics were living in the trailer park:

> I'm not racist in no kinda way. My best friend is mixed. My boyfriend is black. I have many Hispanic friends, but you have all this Hispanic people that are out here, and the majority of them is not legal. . . . It's a very nice mobile home park. He's [grandfather] been there for twenty-three years. And we have all these Hispanic people out here and probably I'm gonna say 75 percent of them aren't legal. I'm a U.S. citizen but y'all wanna run my background check and tell me if I can stay based upon my criminal—not if I'm legal to be in the country or not. Y'all just wanna worry about if I got a criminal record?

We moved on to a conversation about employment, when Sky brought up her problem with a criminal background check again:

> Me, cause I'm still waiting on [Suburban City Works] [an employment service] to call me back about that felony criminal background thing. They still haven't called me. I called them eleven times.

Sky recounted the story of how she was able to get into one of the few nonprofit treatment programs for women while she was in jail, with the help of a well-paid lawyer:

> I was incarcerated when I was approved to go to this program. I was in there for possession of cocaine, trafficking, manufacturing, sales and distribution, and all that extra good stuff. I had like ten different charges, and the stuff that I was caught with, it wasn't mine, but it was mine. 'Cause some of it I had already purchased, she just didn't end up giving something that I purchased yet. When the police busted in and busted

her, they came to bust her, but with me being there, I got in trouble too. So my ex-husband, he paid twenty-five thousand dollars to an attorney. They got it to where I could, instead of going to prison for twenty-five years, I got into residential rehab, and I was on probation for ten years.

Sky was an active user when I interviewed her. A few months after her graduation from the residential treatment home, she relapsed. Her story revealed years of sexual abuse, followed by drug use, dealing, sex work, and low-wage jobs that did not allow her to rise above poverty. She was without a job and potentially without a place to live if she was not allowed to stay in the trailer park due to her criminal record. Staunchly pro-American, as most of the women interviewed were, Sky questioned why foreigners, perhaps even illegal immigrants, appeared to be more accepted in her community than she. Did she choose to engage in activities that resulted in her present situation? Or was she constrained by her structural forces? Sky's predicament can be explained from various perspectives, but here I employ interaction ritual chains theory to analyze Sky's drug-seeking behavior.

INTERACTION RITUAL CHAINS THEORY

This chapter is about the violence that occurred in the lives of the women before and after initial methamphetamine use, and the crime associated with their drug use, typically involving time in jail or prison. Interaction ritual (IR) chains theory offers an in-depth look at the processes that are going on in the women's lives and why they do what they do. IR chains theory is used here to focus attention primarily on changing situations and the people interacting in these situations. The center of the focus in IR chains theory is not on the individual but instead on the situation. In this sense it is a "theory of situations" that explains the process by which individuals do not *choose* but are instead swept along by shared emotions when in a group of two or more.

Developed by Randall Collins (2004), IR chains theory provides a useful tool in the concept of emotional energy seeking, which explains the motivational processes for all interactional behavior. IR chains theory draws from social capital theory, which Collins views as the shared trust and ground rules embedded in cultural and economic structures. The essential aspect of IR chains theory is emotional energy (which Collins calls EE), and social capital is important in this theory in the way it affects the EE payoff. Collins writes, "IR chains is a model of motivation that pulls and pushes individuals from situation to situation, steered by the market-like patterns of how each participant's stock of social resources—their EE and their membership symbols (or cultural capital) accumulated in previous IRs—meshes with those of each person they encounter" (xiv).

A successful IR situation can result in a strong social bond that gives a feeling of pride and joy. An ambiguous IR situation may leave the individual with a feeling of concern or confusion. An unsuccessful IR situation that results in a broken bond can generate a feeling of shame or anger.

The solidarity, meaning, and purpose provided by group membership—even a group of two as in the case of husband and wife—explains how seeking emotional energy bonds people in an IR situation. For example, as a child, Sky experienced a lack of trust in her closest network—the adults in her life. Her parents turned her care over to a grandmother, and her grandmother died while Sky was just beginning to contemplate life as a sentient preadolescent. She was then confronted with the bewildering situation of her stepfather violating what Collins (2004) called the shared morality (values and norms) of mainstream society she was taught by her grandmother, and her mother's seeming indifference to the violation. IR chains theory posits that without trust, EE is low and the IR chain is weak. Running away from her unsatisfying IR situations, Sky looked for a situation and a network where she could find high emotional energy—in layperson terms, *where she could belong*. Unfortunately, like many young women who seek belonging, she found it among men who used her for their own purposes.

An IR chains lens helps us to understand the process of embracing two contrasting standards of morality: that of the mainstream society where each of the women started and that of the drug-using network where each woman participated at the time of her drug use. Most women straddled these values, like Maggie, the supermom and dealer introduced in an earlier chapter who occupied both conventional and unconventional roles with contradictory values and norms.

A theoretically informed IR analytical lens reveals how women jump the gap between the conventional and unconventional roles that encompass the phases of a drug career. IR chains theory explains why and how the women move between these phases motivated by EE seeking. The women's stories are used to illustrate this process in real life. In some cases, the women lose a role that acts as a turning point into uncontrolled use; in other cases the loss of a role impels a turning point into seeking treatment for their problematic drug use. In both cases, IR theory highlights their EE–seeking behavior, which can be found in drug-using situations as well as conventional situations.

A successful IR provided the women with more confidence in themselves through the ritual. For example, almost every woman began to buy and sell methamphetamine to help supply her own use or to earn money, but the women also gained confidence by being part of a successful IR. Additionally, they gained trust and respect from other members in their deviant network, such as drug dealers, and continued the ritual that provided them with emotional energy.

The interacting influences of violence and crime, and the effects of violence and crime on the women's lives, are the focus in this chapter. Violence is organized by the main themes of molestation and rape, domestic violence, and other violence in the drug environment. The broad theme of crime includes sex work, dealing and manufacturing, and incarceration.

VIOLENCE

Sexual Abuse: Molestation and Rape

The term "sexual abuse and molestation" here refers to any abuse that was sexual in nature perpetrated on the women whether or not it fit a legal definition of rape. Typically, this occurred when they were children or adolescents. In order to further protect anonymity and because of the detailed violence depicted in some stories, in this section the women are not identified by pseudonym; instead, the perpetrator is identified by his or her relationship to the woman (boyfriend, father, partner, and so on).

Molested by father and stepmother as a child:

Oh yeah. She would put dildos up me. I mean how graphic do you want me to get?

Did you ever see a doctor?

No. They don't take you to doctors when they re abusing you. . . . *They* got mental problems because I've never sexually abused a child in my life. So they can't use that as an excuse. That was my stepfather's excuse. "Well I was sexually abused by my mother and father." Well excuse me. I was sexually abused too, but I don't go out here and sexually abuse children. So don't use that as an excuse because it happened to me.

When this woman was given prescription opioids for an injury, she said they made her forget her emotional pain as well. She continued to seek drugs from that point and became a methamphetamine user who injected drugs daily, supported by sex work.

Molested by mother's boyfriend, who became her stepfather, from age nine to eleven:

Oh well, I had a rough childhood and some of the things that's in my childhood I wanted to forget about, because I was molested by my stepfather. My biological father divorced my mother and then before she was even divorced she had already hooked up with this guy . . . and my momma was a real bad alcoholic at the time. And so she got with this guy and I was molested from the time I was nine years old until the time I was fourteen when I had to leave home. I left home at fourteen years old.

Did you tell your mother you were molested?
Yes, and she didn't believe me.

Molested by father since puberty:

> I don't know, my dad, I mean . . . my dad used to be a partier. And then
> he quit, and they started going to church because my mama and him had
> split up at one point in time but they got back together, and they started
> going to church and stuff. And then he got hurt at work and he was at
> home. My mama worked nights so I would come home from school,
> she'd leave to go to work, I'd take care of my—when it first started, it
> was just my little sister—I'd come home and take care of her and I'd
> cook dinner. I guess I took over the role of wife. I guess, and, I really
> don't know. But he started, I was thirteen [long pause] Oh its, this is
> hard (crying) . . . Um, when it went on for, until I was sixteen before I
> ever said anything. And I finally told one of my teachers at school because
> I started thinking my little sister's growing up, and he didn't start with
> me until I was thirteen, but she's still a baby and what's going to happen
> when I'm not there to protect her? And I ended up telling my teacher
> and then I told my mom and—I don't—I really don't know what hap-
> pened. I know she talked to him and he admitted to doing it. He admit-
> ted to doing it. I mean, I never, I didn't tell on him until he finally—he
> had sex with me. He come, got in the shower with me, and had sex with
> me. . . . But then after she [mother] found out, I mean to begin with,
> she act like she was going to really do something about it. And then the
> next thing I know, *I* gotta leave the house. Or somebody has to leave
> the house. And she goes, "Well which one should it be?" So I was sent
> off. Yeah, oh yeah. My daddy definitely come first. He definitely come
> first. Whatever my daddy want my daddy got.

Molested by uncle at nine years old:

> I can remember I was—he was giving—I took a bath and he came in
> with the towel and like when he was drying me off he was fondling me
> and then he took me in the bedroom and he was laying on the bed and
> he had his penis out. And he made me suck it and made me play with it.
> He never, you know, penetrated me but he did all the other stuff. And
> told me that if I ever told that, you know, I think he told me I would die
> or my mama would die. Something would happen that scared me that I
> didn't tell for a long time. And it went on for a while until finally I told.
> And apparently he was a pedophile and he had been molesting other chil-
> dren. And he ended up in prison but not because of what he done to me.
> It was—he was molesting other children too.

Molested by father at age fourteen:

> I came out of the bathroom and he was in the kitchen with his—in his hand, and said come over here and touch it. And I still cringe right now. I'm embarrassed right now. . . . I still get real emotional about it [crying]. Even though nothing happened—*it* still happened. It's kinda like, okay. I guess it wouldn't have been such a big deal if it had been somebody else, but when it's your dad. And you see your mom struggling to work. And you see that your mom is good and she's a Christian lady. And you don't understand why your dad is, like—it's like, almost a betrayal to your mother too. It's like what in the hell are you doing? Why you doing this? Oh, I was so angry. I internalized it. I mean I was just like, I hated my dad. I couldn't stand to be around him. I'm sorry [emotional] . . . Now here's the real kicker. I was a virgin until I was twenty-six years old.

Raped by drug dealer:

> [My boyfriend] went to jail, and I was working with these girls that I thought were my friends. We knew this guy who was a drug dealer, but he lived with his mom that was dying. She's an older lady, and he told me I could live in her house while he [boyfriend] was in jail. I could stay there and just pay money, go to work every day—and the guy like, he mixed it up together [a drug cocktail], and I didn't know what it was. And he did it, and like the cocaine like hit me at first and I was like coughing and choking—thought I was going to die. Like I kept blacking out, and then the Ecstasy hit me so I like passed out. And that's when I got raped, or whatever. And I'd wake up and be all disoriented and not know where I was.

Raped by a gang:

> I went to a party and I got intoxicated and it was—I basically went home with the wrong guys, and one of them was actually a drug dealer, and the other one was just his best friend and they had a third friend. And the third friend actually kind of protected me, but when he got up and went to work the next morning I got up to use the bathroom and that's when the other two guys, the drug dealer and his friend, pulled out their guns and basically had their way with me. And, um, I didn't know where I was in the city. Turned out to be in [Suburban Town]. And I found that out because I ran out of their apartments. I was trying to find a pay phone or a phone to call the police and I saw the water tower. And I called the police. And the police told me I smelled like alcohol and was probably still intoxicated, and told me I probably deserved it. I probably got just too drunk and, you know, went home

with the wrong guys. Which is probably what happened. But I had a black eye. I had bruises on me because I tried to fight them off.

The normalization of a child-adult sexual relation is not something easily explained by any theory after one listens to the stories told by grown women who were molested and raped and were still suffering. Their accounts of what occurred, in some cases when they were children, acknowledged the imbalance of power relations inherent in the life-altering experiences, which in mainstream norms should be *mutually* shared pleasure. Obviously, the women did not receive any positive emotional energy from these IR situations, and it affected their relationships and behaviors for many years.

Just as we cannot measure the extent of harm and damage to a child who is molested, so we cannot assign ranks to the act of rape. Tragically, although rape is always violent even if the woman is unconscious, rape is often treated and discussed as two kinds: simple rape, which does not involve physical violence, and aggravated rape, which involves physical violence. Since these distinctions are made by police officers, social workers, health professionals, lawyers, juries, and judges, even the victims themselves learn to accept them. The rapist who commits simple rape is typically never charged, or if charged, never convicted (Goode 2011). Knowing this is the likely outcome, many women never even report it. Some women in this study internalized society's trivialization of sexual abuse.

Domestic Violence

Domestic violence started early in life for most of these women. Beth, a former user with high-bridging social capital, described a typical middle-class childhood as the daughter of a police officer, until she told what happened behind closed doors:

> We were middle-class. I always went on vacations in the summer, every summer to [Beach Town]. The house was nice. The cars were nice. We had to keep up, I guess status, you know. What people thought is the way that—nobody knew how, I guess, how bad it was inside the house. To the point when the ambulance showed up. . . . They [police] were protecting him. My dad never went to jail. . . . I have tried to commit suicide twice.

Her father remained violent throughout her childhood, and while Beth remembers the beating her mother and sister received, she does not remember her own. Like many of the women who recounted a troubling childhood, Beth married early:

> My husband was a heroin addict. He was abusive. He was very violent . . .
> He would disappear for days. Bring women home. I would come in with

the baby, into the apartment, and there would be other women there, and he'd be all shot out and—it took me a long time to get up the guts to leave him.

So how did you get away then?

We moved to [another state], and he had gotten abusive one night. We had just moved into a duplex and I had gotten a good job. I was working for the hospital, and he beat the crap out of me one night. Put my head through a closet door. And the next day my daughter who was only about maybe two, three, came out and she pulled—I had put like a towel rack or something over the door—bathrobe—so nobody could see the hole, and my daughter came out and moved the bathrobe to the side and said, "Daddy's not nice," or she didn't like Daddy or something like that. And I said well that was it, and I put him [husband] on a plane. He thought he was going home to visit his mother and I mean I had worked it out with the travel agent and everything. My boss paid for the plane ticket and I put him on a plane to his mother and then that was it.

In IR chain terminology, Beth found high EE in her work situation, which gave her the motivation to leave a failed IR chain. Her colleagues at work saw the bruises on Beth's body, and eventually she gained enough trust in them to tell them the truth.

In contrast, Ely was like many of the women who said they would never tell:

When did he start beating you?

That was probably within probably the first month we were married.

And did you ever report him to the police or anything?

Of course not . . . it's not an option. No. It's just not an option. I guess it's cultural. You don't call the police.

You don't call the police when you get beat up?

Nope. You keep your dirty laundry to yourself. [Laughs.] You know, my life ain't *Jerry Springer* [a tell-all television show].

The police are trying to protect you though, aren't they?

No, you don't see it as protection because they want to come in there and just basically say, "Look don't you have a mother, a father?" And then when you say no I don't, [they say], "You don't have anybody that can help you?" Well no, because I'm not allowed to leave my house or check my mailbox. So I come from a physically abusive father right into a marriage, never had dated or nothing. You see what I'm saying? So that was all I knew.

We see that even if the emotional energy payoff is low, women like Ely did not have the social capital to find more positive EE relationships. Yet even those with higher social capital fell victim to abuse.

Dee said she came from a nice suburban neighborhood, with loving parents, and described her home as "a pretty happy family." Yet she felt alienated at school and associated with older age groups. After her father died suddenly, she became emotionally attached to a "crazy boyfriend." Dee, at the age of nineteen, was in a negative EE situation:

It was very abusive relationship. Well, one time he locked me in his bath—it was like the public bathroom at the pool in the neighborhood we were in. He locked me in there and he beat me senseless. . . . I finally like got the strength to get up. And I was like, I was in my bathing suit bottoms, just a tee shirt, and I didn't even have my shoes. He had my purse. He had everything of mine. My keys. And so I started walking home. Like I actually—he was chasing me in the neighborhood. I was trying to get out of the neighborhood. I was screaming. So many cars were coming by and no, not one person would stop to help me . . . and I was stuck walking home in the pitch—and it was dark. It was nighttime.

So how did you get away from him?

Well, my friend who sold me meth actually. Because she—I'm a really bubbly person. I love talking with people. I love making friends. But I also get run over and treated like a dog because I just—I take it. And she gave me—you know she, she told me listen, I care about you. I don't want you to do this. You know, just like everybody else did but she just—for some reason there was just some sense of her being there that helped me just stop talking to him. Like I broke up with him one night and I just, I never went back to him. Ever. And it just like—she helped me out with that a whole lot. Just because like I felt like I had no one because he had, you know, run off all my friends. All my family. All my everything! I didn't have anything. And then when I started hanging out with her again it was like I have somebody that cares about me, and that will stick by me.

The IR chain model explains Dee's attraction to a man who gave her a sense of belonging, especially after she lost her father, the most important man in her life. Dee had few social and emotional resources at this time, and she was responding to whatever gave her the most emotional energy for the least cost. It was not until her friend, with whom she already shared the culture of methamphetamine use, showed genuine interest in her situation that she had the strength to leave an abusive situation. Even though her mother and others had tried unsuccessfully to encourage her to leave this man, it was only through a friend with mutual focus—you can trust me because we use methamphetamine together—that proved successful.

Some of the women who suffered domestic violence at the hands of husbands or partners when they were relatively young and inexperienced, like Dee, had few other alternatives. Others learned to defend themselves or leave, although alternative options for women from poor communities were few. Ely, mentioned earlier, was young when she suffered years of domestic violence. Unlike Beth, she did not have the bridging capital to engage in an IR chain with friends who could help her. After many years, she gained the courage to leave, spurred by an emotional situation:

I'll tell you how the [prescription] pill thing started—with my mouth. See he broke my jaw. My husband . . . but see, I was so young and dumb, and I thought abuse was a part of my marriage. You know what I'm saying? And I had to seek help because of the blackout. I had blackout headaches. He hit me one punch right there and shattered my jaw. . . . What's so sad is I lived right there in my home town and I would have to hide. I'd go months and months at a time without my family knowing where I was. Disappear. Because I knew my brother would kill him. Bottom line. I knew my brother would kill this man. So I would hide. The jawbone thing—it's kinda hard to hide with your mouth wired together.

But what did the hospital do when they wired your mouth together?
I didn't say he did it. I lied. I told them that me and a team of girls was playing ball and, uh, a ball hit me.

How many times did you have to go to the hospital because of your husband?
Oh dear God, repeatedly. Repeatedly. Repeatedly. From black eyes to bald spots in my hair being pulled out.

Ely left her husband with the help of a psychiatrist who was treating her for her blackout episodes. After the divorce she became addicted to pain pills, and then to methamphetamine when she moved to a new suburban town with her second husband. Here she encountered a different type of violence—that inherent in the drug world.

Violence in the Drug Environment

The environment of drug dealing is known to be violent, but typically we do not envision a quiet suburban neighborhood as the setting for drug-related killings. Beyond domestic violence, the suburban women recounted scenes of violence related to dealing, sex work, and homelessness. For example, Tammy described how her boyfriend, a dealer, was murdered:

So the guy that I was dating at the time . . . he ended up getting killed over dope so . . . he got shot. Yeah, it was my boyfriend. He got robbed and they shot him at one of our friends' house. I was gone to look for a job that day. And I came home and mama had told me that he shot—they thought he shot himself. And a friend of ours had shot himself in the foot a few days before so I just thought it was something like that, but it wasn't. They shot him right between the eyes so—he knew him though. The guy that killed him ended up getting killed a year later in the exact same way.

Over meth?

Yeah.

Many of the trailer parks were settings of violence. Joy had lived in the same trailer park for years in her own trailer thanks to her steady income of disability checks. During a focus group with another woman who used to live in this suburban enclave of poverty, Joy discussed how her association with violence helped her obtain Medicaid, which was very hard for most women in the study to obtain. Another woman in the focus group, Ava, piped in that the violence in the area where Joy lives was contagious:

JOY: I'm disabled. I got my first check thirty days after I applied and I didn't have an attorney. I went and applied for myself. I had four nervous break-downs. I've been institutionalized against my will for years, 'cause I'm homicidal. I've shot people, and stabbed people, and cut people . . . more than three people at one time.

AVA: Where you guys are living . . . I was there for three weeks and I put a knife to what's-his-faces neck, because he was doing crazy stuff to me, and I was losing it. It's really easy to lose it in such an area, especially when you're shot out.

This exchange between a forty-four-year-old and a nineteen-year-old shows how violence was a part of the drug-using world and became a part of the women's lives. Ava entered this world, and although she was raised with middle-class norms that rejected violence as a response, she quickly learned to defend herself. Dee, another nineteen-year-old from a middle-class subur-ban neighborhood, was living in her car for weeks until a man with a trailer offered her a room. She sounded excited when she told me on the phone that she finally had a place to stay. I warned her about men offering shelter, but she said, "No, he's cool." Within a few days she had to run from the trailer while he chased her with a hammer.

Being homeless was a risk situation that many of the women in the study experienced. In the year preceding our meeting, Ida was not allowed in the homeless shelter because of her drug use, so she slept in the woods nearby. She explained how she got a large scar across her forehead:

There was no drugs involved in this incident. There was no connec-tion—I didn't even know this person. It was an attack. It wasn't like any-thing dealing with drugs. I didn't know him. He didn't know me. It was just like he came out of the woods, he looked like Satan, and started slashing . . . but I was in a drug area, in the area where they sell drugs in the hotel where I got cut—up the hill. And he thought well, gee, there goes a—let me go cut her up. Nobody's going to miss her. I've even had police officers tell me that: "How many man-hours, how many tax dollars do you think we're going to spend on you. I can guarantee you right now," they would look at me and say, "I can guarantee you right now you have a crack pipe on you. Or you have some kind of—something illegal on you right now. How many man-hours do you think we're going to spend looking in the woods for your butt? If you're stinking in the woods, you're stinking in the woods. We'll find you one day." Now if Ms. So-and-So from wherever, you know, dies—Ms. Proper Lady, the judge's wife—it's going to be front-page news.

Ida had already lost her home and children and was unemployed. She somehow managed to earn enough money to stay in a cheap motel overrun with bedbugs at the time I interviewed her, but she disappeared when the motel was shut down. Sadly, the police prediction was correct—nobody seemed to care whether she lived or died. Her story, recounted, on these pages might be the only record of her last days.

CRIME

Sex Work

Sex work is a crime in the state where the women I interviewed lived, and some women were arrested, charged, and sentenced for this activity. The law reads, "A person commits the offense of prostitution when he or she performs or offers or consents to perform a sexual act, including but not limited to sexual intercourse or sodomy, for money or other items of value." While most of the women in the study exchanged sex for drugs, they did not always consider this prostitution, and none said they were arrested for a sex for drugs exchange.

Mia was arrested the first time she went on the street as a sex worker at age twenty. After a short period as an exotic dancer, giving her boyfriend all her money, she struck out on her own:

> Then I left him and just kind of went on my own. Walking the streets. Living in motels. . . . When I wasn't working in the clubs I'd be walking the street. I got arrested for prostitution at that time. I got arrested for prostitution in [Big City]. The police officer was undercover, . . . I didn't stay on the street very long because I wasn't good at it. You know, I'm used to being raised in—not in the city. So here I'm thrown into the city trying to be a tough girl. And strung out and mostly was looking just for the sugar daddy that I found to take care of me. But, um . . . no pimps. Nothing like that. . . . Oh, the police. Um, once I realized he was a

police officer, he was not nice at all. Very hostile. I mean it didn't even last but a minute as far as I got in the car and I, we verbally discussed what was going to happen, and he said, "Okay you're arrested." . . . And at this point I was twenty-one, and my sugar daddy, um, he was like a twice-a-week thing. But he didn't want to keep renting motels, so he set me up in a little apartment by the airport. And I got sick and had to go to the hospital with the hepatitis. All during this twenty-one. Still dancing . . . but yeah didn't have to really walk the streets much because I had this older man. Married man that, you know, took care of me, but I mean for four years he was really good to me.

While Mia eventually left the city street and acquired conventional work roles during her adult life, she had come back to streetwalking thirty years later, when I met her in the suburbs.

In contrast, Joy, at forty-four, had supported herself through sex work all her life. Like many women in the study, she started prostitution to pay the rent: "I was working. But I lost my job, and—I came to [Suburban Town] and I turned my first trick, and I told you, I got four hundred dollars remember? To pay the rent for the month. . . . It's damn financial because I don't enjoy it. I don't have sex for pleasure. If you don't give me no money, you ain't getting it." One of the more unusual stories was Ely's account of being what appears to be a madam managing female sex workers. Ely was selling methamphetamine and crack at the time from a motel room, where she prepared what she called "crack whores" for the professional men:

Lawyers. You wouldn't believe. That whole motel—I had the whole motel. Because on Fridays the lawyers would get—they would pay me a hundred dollars to clean up a whore. A crack whore.

What do you mean clean her up?

Give me the money. Go buy a new outfit or whatever they wanted her to wear. Bathe her. Clean her up for action. They'd rent the front rooms and there would be five, six men and one girl. They paid me a hundred dollars just for the girl. Was always white girls. Beautiful white girls. I was a crack seller. I sold the crack. See what I'm saying?

The girls were using crack too?

Oh God yes. They didn't get a damn dime. They got to smoke crack and do whatever them men wanted them to do. . . . Freaks is what I call them. I mean, you know, what I'm saying? . . . No, I would never do that. I would never—there's a lot of them out here now [for] twenty dollars. For what? I'm from the old school. I don't, you know—I believe in get out here and find you some kind of hustle. Find you something—you know, you don't—to me it's selling your soul to the devil.

Dealing and Manufacturing

Every woman who engaged in dealing drugs eventually did so for money. As discussed previously, many of the women sold drugs to support their families. Some women sold drugs instead of having to engage in sex work. For example, Linda was financially stretched and wanted to stay in her middle-class community. She had the social connections to make good money by selling marijuana, cocaine, and methamphetamine. She describes how she started and how her business grew:

> Right after the wreck, I was single at the time. I think I was waiting on the divorce, and had the wreck and I couldn't work. I was holding out for a settlement with the lawyers and all. I had to support my kids. I started selling drugs. And at that time I wasn't smoking it. . . . I had a friend that was a bartender, we bartended right after high school, and uh, I took some by to her, to try, we had grown up together, and she said, "I'll give you the hookup, okay?" I knew who to get it from. That man came to me. He said, "I know you've been hurt. I know you're struggling to raise your kids. If you can get rid of it, here's what I'll do. I'll front you this. I'll front you pot." I can make a killing off of [marijuana], I hate the stuff [laughs]. Well, he gave it to me a real good deal. Pot, meth, and coke. Then I had somebody that I sold it to who was a manager at a grocery store. One of them owns a string of restaurants. One of them owned a very exclusive nightclub down in [coastal town]. And another owned a business, and that's where I went and met him. He owned a furniture store. And he also owned a car body shop. . . . This man that I was buying it from is, uh, he's higher up in a church right here in this town . . . he did it for a business venture. He was a very intelligent man.

Linda's story illustrates how her mutual trust and sharing with a few social networks provided her the opportunity to have a trusting relationship with a high-level dealer in her church who fronted her the drugs that she sold to middle- and upper-class clients. Her casual remark that she did not like the *stuff* [marijuana] shows that she was not dealing for drugs but for support. When she started to sell methamphetamine, she began to use it herself for energy and to stay awake. In a few years she went from being a controlled occasional user to a problem addict.

For some women, the emotional energy gained from this type of work was evident in their description of their dealing days. Lea, a single mother and living at home, is an example of this. Her quest for a better-paying job ended up in the city at a club where she met her next boyfriend, a cocaine dealer much older than she was. Still precocious, at age twenty she started to help him deal cocaine from the city to the suburbs—employment that brought her into a world she had never imagined from her suburban home:

> I'd never seen an atmosphere like this. It was the kind you see on TV. And I got really caught up in it. I made lots, and lots, and lots of money . . . and we'd go out to every VIP club in the city and spend so much money. And he was, like, he was a different kind of dealer. Because like he was— he sold to the corporate America. The people that were his age, that they're thirty and forty. And I was still young, but I was like, you know, I was the girlfriend. So nobody really said anything. And all these people would come that had really—like movie directors in the city and like people that were like insurance company executives, and people that were so rich and would come there so often and get eight-balls of cocaine.

Collins (2004) incorporates Bourdieu's (1986) version of social capital in IR chains theory by showing how IR markets are highly stratified, and those without the symbolic knowledge to understand the attraction of elite IR markets are excluded. Lea, much like Sky, came from a position of powerlessness and with access only to IR markets at the lowest level of the power hierarchy. Being included in part of elite IR markets is certainly very appealing to these young women, who are essentially being used to run drugs while exposing themselves to risks of violence and incarceration. But the emotional energy they received in this interaction is apparent, even years later as they recounted their stories. Collins bridges the agency and structure theoretical divide. Viewed through the lens of IR chains, the drug-dealing behavior of these women is explained as a social process instead of an individual action by a person with agency, or as a structural force acting on a powerless individual caught in a cog of the machine.

Although the women did not say they manufactured methamphetamine themselves, many saw it being produced. The state bureau of investigation where the research took placed estimates that each person who produces methamphetamine will teach ten others to produce it. Recipes for methamphetamine production abound on the Internet and are available to almost anyone who seeks them. Known as *Uncle Fester's Meth Cookbook*, the "Secrets of Methamphetamine Manufacture," written by a chemist, is a popular underground book of recipes for manufacturing methamphetamine and other drugs. While many women described different methods of manufacturing, none recounted the process with as much detail and zeal as Zoe, the mother of five who started using methamphetamine while married to her third husband.

Zoe had only used crank a few times with her husband before she discovered he was producing it. He left her and started living in a house he inherited located in the woods. She visited him at his house in an attempt to regain his love and discovered he was manufacturing methamphetamine.

Needing the extra income, she began to deliver his methamphetamine to clients. As she explained the minutia of how he made it, I asked her if she knew the dangers of being in a house while methamphetamine was produced. She replied, "That's what I don't understand. I guess because my feelings for him are—I don't know. I don't know why. I feel crazy sometimes."

Zoe was very good at the business and soon became an accomplished dealer with more connections. She took it quite seriously and appeared to gain EE from the excitement and relationships involved in this activity. She had few other options for financial advancement. Desiring to have the best product, she sought out the highest level of traffickers without fear for her personal safety. She described a few scenes:

> For a long time I didn't find a good hookup, I would find somebody to buy it from and I'd get an ounce and it'd have . . . maybe an eight-ball and a half of good in it, and the rest would be cut. And I would go up in the middle of 'em and demand my money back. I would raise hell with 'em, you know . . . there was some God-awful places I went into. I'd have one guy with me and even if he didn't even go—I'd go in by myself—I don't know how, but I never got hurt. And sometimes I'd get my money back or get dope, and sometimes I wouldn't. I lost a lot of money. But I finally found this guy who had these Mexican friends— used to be his neighbors but they're not anymore, and he hooks me up with them, and they come with five-gallon buckets full or meth with lid—they put their foot on it and mash the lid down on it shut. Full of pure meth, crystal meth.

The image of this mild-mannered, petite, suburban woman, who looked more like the stereotypical image of a librarian than a meth dealer, demanding good methamphetamine from her Mexican hookups seemed bizarre. But the minute details of how the methamphetamine looked, how it was made with different ingredients, and how she distributed it provided evidence that she was not making this up.

It was only a matter of time before Zoe was caught. One of the clients to whom she had just sold methamphetamine was stopped by the police just after leaving Zoe's house. He ratted her out. She did not feel betrayed. She said she would have done the same thing rather than go to jail, and later she did. In her view:

> Yeah, they were out somewhere and got pulled over and they [police] found dope on 'em. And the police said, "Well, if you'll help us do this, then we'll drop your charge." So they helped 'em get somebody who's bigger, you know. Somebody who's selling more or somebody they want. They were already in trouble, they just didn't want to be—go back to jail again.

What about "you better not be a rat or you're gonna get killed on the side of the road."

That's just too—this is too small for that, but when it gets on up into the . . . like the Mexicans . . . I told on someone to get out of trouble once too, and that's what it was. The police pulled me over on the way home from work. I had bought a twenty sack from my friend at lunch that day, and they found it and I was facing prison you know. And [the cop] said "if you'll help us get [friend] then you won't go to prison" and I said okay, you know? They already had the cuffs on me and I said I'll do anything, and I told on my best friend.

Here we see that Zoe, a white woman with white and Mexican dealers, readily disclosed her suppliers at a low level in order to avoid prison. Her bonding relationship with her social network of dealers and users appeared very weak.

In contrast Ely, the white woman from the suburbs, spent nine months in jail without revealing her supplier, an African American man from the city whom she trusted. After her second divorce, Ely worked extra shifts at a diner to support her family and ended up selling crack from the kitchen:

Because when I come to this state, I lost my husband, my car, my home, my everything. I lost everything I had. I went to work there. I opened it and shut it. You know what I'm saying. Every—every two weeks we got paid, every two weeks. I might bring home six hundred and something dollars. And I couldn't make it. My rent was three something. And I got involved with a black person, a cook there. And he told me, that, I'll show you how to make you some money. And it was cocaine. You could take, you could take a, you could take a little bitty bag of powder cocaine like that and you could do this [cook it] and make it like this [into crack]. You see what I'm saying. And I—oh dear God. I was selling it out of the restaurant. By the grace of God.

The police eventually caught Ely. Her story reveals that she was not only a woman who can be trusted but, unlike Zoe, she had a strong relational bond with her dealer that crossed racial barriers. She went to jail rather than reveal her dealer to the police. I asked her how long she stayed in jail:

Nine months. I had a year probation and it was a twenty-six-thousand-dollar [fine]. But the day I went to court after nine months I went to court. The man that I went down for—and I never told on him, that's who they wanted. They didn't want me. They wanted that bigger person . . . I got one hundred dollars a week on my books. And—and the day I went to court, his wife stood up, a black lady, and paid twenty-six thousand dollars cash for my everything. No. I wouldn't tell on nobody.

No. No. That's no. No . . . But that was the deal we'd made from day one. Anything ever go down . . . because he had four little kids, you know what I'm saying. It's called protection.

Ely had embraced the morality of the shared culture of drug dealers—which included, at least in the old school network, a sense of honor in not being a snitch. She did not tell on him, and he took care of her as agreed.

Manufacturing methamphetamine takes on local traditions, so a recipe in one area may not be used in another (Weisheit and White 2009). As mentioned previously, during the first year of the study, I heard reports of a local production method in which methamphetamine was grown on strings in a fish tank; the resulting product was called cold cook meth. Zoe, who learned the methamphetamine recipe from watching her husband, provided one of the most detailed accounts of this method:

> That's crystal meth. That's how they grow—they grow that meth. I sold that kind of meth. I know how they make it. I've seen a guy throw away six ounces of meth that he grew because it was black and he didn't know how—the method of cleaning it—and he threw every bit of it away cause he thought it was poison and it would kill someone, so he threw it away. And he didn't know to clean it with lighter fluid or nail polish remover. They just get an empty fish tank and they dig a hole or a good place where its gonna be still and dark. And they take coal that you get from the rail road and they chunk it up into little—crush it up and spread it out on the bottom of the thing, and then they take like sheet metal or sheet aluminum—aluminum I think, and they chunk it up into little pieces somehow and sprinkle it all in there with the coal. And then they take a string and like, a thin piece of paneling or something and lay it over it and make little holes all over—all in there and run the pieces of string down through there, and then . . . they take the gun blue and the anhydrous gas, and they run it through some kind of tube that goes into that. They put it through a thing and it starts—the fumes from it starts crystallizing on the strings, and it just grows for twenty—you have to leave it for twenty-eight days and you chunk off the bottom part of it and the top part 'cause the others is too poisonous to use it, and the users use the part that they don't throw away.

Stella, a twenty-four-year-old from another suburban town, described the cold cook meth recipe made by her boyfriend:

> I can actually call right now and get all the ingredients . . . you can get it from the surplus store—he's got the hookup. And he takes yarn and he

gets it to where the yarn, it's just about touches, all these liquid melts mixed together at the bottom. The yarn can't touch it or the dope will be bad and it'll be yellow and ugly and won't work. So the strings just go right above it like a centimeter to an inch away from the liquid. And eventually it all evaporates and on the strings you have big, huge crystals, just drop it off the string. You pull the strings out and you break all the crystals off the strings, and that's real ice.

These women were from different social settings, different networks, and different dealers, but with similar recipes for cold cook growing methamphetamine. Whether or not it was methamphetamine, the women said they smoked it, snorted it, and injected it to get high. Some sold it for money, and if caught with cold cook meth, they went to jail.

INCARCERATION

Incarceration and a criminal record typically resulted in the women breaking bonds to mainstream society while building bridges to unconventional networks. Every woman who was classified as part of the suburban poor had been in incarcerated, often multiple times. Charges and conviction included drug possession, distribution, prostitution, resisting an officer, and parole violation. Joy, who had been in and out of jail and prison many times, was charged with using excessive force when she was attacked by a drug dealer and a john (sex work client): "Let me see. . . . Oh, I cut this guy up with a box cutter. And then the next time I shot this man in the side of the head with a shotgun." Joy became very familiar with the legal process and had set aside money for these situations: "I bonded myself out. [I stayed in] long enough to get my paperwork done." A few women reported being put in jail when they called the police on their abusing husbands, and their husbands convinced the police and judge that it was he who was being attacked.

At least four women who participated in my study were put in jail during the course of the study. Two were sent back for probation violation. One was out in a few weeks and completed her third interview and focus group. The other woman, Uma, contacted me from jail before she could complete her third interview.

When I first met Uma, she had only been out of jail for forty days. She lived at Buddy's house, the older man mentioned in chapter 4 who hired women for his cleaning business. He drove her to the library to meet me for the interview. She said he was not her boyfriend, but I learned he took care of her financially. Uma was born into a poor suburban family and put into foster care when her mother died. After two abusive relationships, she became a single mother. Introduced to methamphetamine and cocaine late in life, she quickly became addicted. She began engaging in street prostitution and was arrested for stealing from a client:

> Well, because you got a lot of illegal immigrants and they're scared to put the money in the bank and you know this one time, you know. I got the wallet and I got the two thousand dollars, and he didn't get nothing [sex]. And then that gets into my criminal record. That's why I got a robbery charge because—that's what originally got me put on probation. I sure did . . . We all went to jail. He went to jail for soliciting prostitution.

Uma was in jail or prison at least seven times after this incident—for drug possession and probation violation. Two days before we were to meet for another interview she was already back in jail charged with check fraud. Ironically, the man she stole from was Buddy. He appeared to really care for her and he contacted me to ask if I could help her get into treatment. I had a few long discussions with him, and he seriously believed that Uma deserved treatment more than prison.

I visited Uma in the detention center, and she was desperate to find a treatment place to stay. During the visit, I called a local treatment facility for women, and someone at the treatment home conducted an intake interview with Uma over the phone. She said the intake coordinator would get back to me regarding her case. A week later, when I heard nothing, I called the treatment facility again. There was no record of either the interview or the staff person I had talked to from jail. Contrary to previous reports I had heard, the staff person now told me they would not take anyone from the detention center.

Because of her existing criminal record, Uma was given a three-year sentence. Buddy called to let me know that Uma wanted me to find her an educational program in which she could participate while in prison so that she could have a better chance of finding employment when she got out. I told him I would look, but educational programs for prisoners, despite the overwhelming evidence of their success in reducing recidivism, were not supported in our state.

I knew too well that the chances for all the women in the study to find employment with a living wage after a felony charge were slim. Women could not obtain any resources from the government if they had a felony record. For example, Ely, who kept her promise to not rat on her supplier, was now challenged by the barriers she faced due to her criminal record: "I'm not on anything [drugs] now. I've never, you know, I've never drawn welfare. I've never done anything like that. And I can't get food stamps because I have a drug charge. I have a drug charge. And this can be on—for the rest of my life."

Summary of Gendered Violence and Crime

The majority of the women in this study were abused physically, emotionally, and/or sexually by family members, boyfriends, or partners. Often this occurred in silence and was addressed years later by drug use. The women's life trajectories indicate that they participated in drug roles such as dealing and running primarily out of economic need. This in turn drew them away from mainstream roles. Once caught by law enforcement, they often lost any remaining mainstream roles. Children were removed from their homes when their mothers tested positive for drugs or were sent to jail or treatment. Once released, the women were stigmatized by a criminal history, and if they received a felony conviction they were barred from receiving any of the government resources they desperately needed to return to mainstream work roles. This resulted in a drain on their extended family's resources, and when this was depleted, the only means of income was through continued criminal activities. While the women's lives seemed charged with emotional upheaval as a result of their own choices, their choices were constrained and influenced by structural inequalities and policies that condemn drug users without regard to their reasons for using. The women did what they needed to do in order to survive. In IR chains theory terms they did what they needed to do to gain EE.

The IR chains theory explains how their behavior was motivated by EE seeking and constrained by social resources. While the women were incarcerated, their bonds with conventional situations were broken. During incarceration they learned to gain EE from unconventional situations and were constrained to interact only with other prisoners. When released, their EE seeking was limited.

What made their stories even more tragic was that the social agencies and nonprofit organizations whose job it was to address these issues, to reeducate, retrain, and help prisoners reenter society typically failed them. Often the staff in these agencies was openly hostile or passively indifferent.

CHAPTER 7

The Revolving Door

TREATMENT, RECOVERY, AND RELAPSE

BEV

Referred to our study by a sponsor in twelve-step, Bev was in former-user status when I first met her. At age forty she was living with her mother, who had helped to raise her child. Bev had more mainstream social capital than many of the women I interviewed. She came to the interview dressed in a crisp white blazer with her hair stylishly cut. She might have been dressed to go to church or work. I learned she had performed semiprofessional work all her life, often while using methamphetamine. The long sleeves she wore to the interview covered track marks from years of injection. The conservative-looking middle-class woman sitting before me recounted her years of running drugs between the city and wealthy clients in the suburbs. Her high bridging social capital provided the resources she needed in both her conventional and unconventional roles.

Bev had spent the last ten years in and out of treatment or jail. Other than her drug-dealing work, she had been employed in offices of local businesses and professionals. Her acumen and good business sense made her valuable in both roles, and she was eager to have a job in the conventional world. She explained why she was currently unemployed:

> If you have a drug felony, nobody will hire you. You can't get any kind of help . . . you can't go back to school . . . food stamps. You can't do anything. And it's like they just want you to go back to selling drugs. . . . I mean if you can rape somebody, you can kill somebody, you can still get food stamps. You can do anything you want to do. But you do some drugs and they don't give you a second chance. It's making you want to go out and do it more. I mean, it does. It makes you want to relapse because you can't get a job, you can't do this. I mean, I can't work at the Dollar Store . . . I can't work at a bar. If you have a drug felony you cannot get a serving license. And I've never had an alcohol problem in my

life. I think I've maybe been, even what you would consider drunk, maybe three times in my life and I'm forty.

Bev expressed what most women with a felony charge on their record told me—that it was almost impossible to be legally employed. Some of the women eventually took a service job off the books, as Bev did when friends of her mother offered her work cleaning houses. For her last offense, she served one year in prison and still had five more years on probation. She took methamphetamine on her first day out. "It makes me numb," she said. Given her bleak prospects as a felon, I could understand her feelings.

During her time in treatment programs and twelve-step fellowships, Bev learned that she was *codependent* on men. Although she was legally married, her estranged husband lived in another state; Bev currently was seeing a man she called her boyfriend.

Bev reached her rock-bottom period a few years ago. Estranged from her family, she was covered with track marks, bruises, and sores from months of bingeing and a general lack of personal hygiene. Bev described the place where she picked up her methamphetamine during that time as Deliverance. She stayed there when she was homeless, and another time when she ran away from a treatment program. "You ever [see] the movie *Deliverance?*" she asked. "That's what they [dealers] were . . . honey, they live in a shack—or a trailer . . . it's down a gravel road." Deliverance, I learned, was near the library where we met in the suburbs, not in a remote rural location.

Bev's husband was in jail, and she was about to be evicted from her home, when one of her neighbors called her parents to let them know their daughter had come to their house asking for food. Bev described what she remembered when she answered the door that day:

I had been up for five or six days and I had bruises, and I had, you know, been shooting. And now my mother had never seen me like that. And [clears her throat] she showed up at my house. And when she showed— I wouldn't have opened the door if I'd known it was her. But when she opened the door I couldn't even see straight that day. I'll never forget it because I couldn't see straight. . . . My dad came the next day, I mean, my stepdad. When he came the next day he looked at me and he said, "You know, your mama came home crying. She thinks you're going to die. You know, you look rough." And I was like, "Oh I'm fine," you know, because I'd had a little bit of sleep that night. He was like, "You're not fine." My mother had seen the needle marks all over my arms, and, you know, she was like she tripped out. And I was so embarrassed. And my son's birthday was going to be two days later, so that's when I quit. I went to my mom's house and spent the night.

Bev had been in a few treatment programs prior to this time. After one arrest, Bev was bonded to a treatment center awaiting her court trial. "That's a joke," she retorted, "It was a transition center. . . . They're just made for money purposes." After her second arrest, her mother convinced her to go to a church-sponsored treatment program for women called the Angel Street Ministry (pseudonym). It was run by an elderly woman who also coordinated an adoption service. I had heard of this service from a few other women we interviewed who described it as a "baby mill." Bev, however, was not pregnant and did not have a small child to put up for adoption. She said she was basically free labor for the woman's businesses. Bev's assessment of the program was insightful, but nobody believed her. She ran away.

"I went straight to Deliverance," she said. Her mother picked her up later at a nearby gas station and drove her to a hospital. Bev explained how she was able to get to a stabilization unit:

> They were not going to take me. That's where, um, [County Hospital] sent me. They were not going to take me because I was a meth user. And there is no detox for meth. So you have to tell them—you know, I was to the point where I didn't, I didn't even think I was going to cut myself or anything like that, but I didn't care if I woke up.
>
> *Did you have to say you're committing suicide?*
>
> That's right. That's right. You are so correct . . . right, I didn't care. I mean I didn't care if I woke up. But then, when I got out of the [detox unit] I started using again.
>
> *They don't take you to treatment afterwards?*
>
> No. No. They give you some, you know, some advice to go get counseling and things like that, but no, they don't . . . they gave me meds. I got diagnosed—well they sent me to the health department for my follow-up. And that's when I was diagnosed with my bipolar. And they prescribed me meds, but then, you know, when you don't have a job and you don't have any money, um, because see I lost my job when I went to detox. Well, I didn't want to go back. I was embarrassed.

She was convinced by her mother to return to Angel Street Ministry. Bev described the program and the woman who ran the house with an iron rod:

> But to me, it wasn't no rehab. I mean because when you're coming off meth or any drug, you're going to have bad days, good days, and you're going to rest. You want to sleep some—you don't want anybody to bother you some days. But she don't believe in that. She believes in putting you [to work] that first day and you're up at 6:30 and . . . there is no resting if you lose, you know, if you're upset or anything like that, she'll tell you dry it up. There's no crying. There's no . . . you know, you don't show

no emotion. You can't show any emotions. . . . They don't have no counseling. I mean, if she does any kind of counseling, *she'll* do it for the people. . . . She's in her seventies and she tells you that she knows things. I mean, like she knows spiritlike things [that] come to her . . . and then there's no lock on the bedroom. So they can, you know, you can just walk in. You had no privacy. And there's no going to your room during the day and laying on your bed and reading. There's no TV. She wants you— if you read, you're reading Christian. I mean it's very, it's like—I said it was a cult convent . . . I was on Zoloft and Trazodone. Because I had gone to the [detox unit] and then they had told me that I was bipolar. Well I was supposed to get on this bipolar medicine but I hadn't got on it yet because I couldn't afford it. Um, but she took me off of my Zoloft and my Trazodone as soon as I got there. She told me I didn't need it no more. God would help me. . . . She tries to get you to, um, get insurance through her nephew—health insurance and life insurance policies for myself. That way I'm respecting my parents in case I die, they can bury me.

Bev worked in the thrift shop connected to the ministry from 6:30 a.m. to closing and then waited to be driven back to the home, arriving about nine at night. She said they cashed about five hundred dollars a day, but she never saw any of it. She worked six days a week with one day off so she could do her laundry. Bev left Angel Street Ministry for the second time and stayed with her mother again, working temporary jobs provided by her mother's church friends.

Bev still communicated with some of her former colleagues to whom she used to sell methamphetamine. She said she knew they still used and had told one woman to call me for an interview, but the woman refused, saying she did not want anyone to know. Typically, I hear from middle-class and upper-class people only when they are in their recovering phases—like Bev. But we lost Bev by the third interview. The twelve-step sponsor who originally suggested Bev call us said she had not seen her for a long time.

Bev tried both formal and informal treatment. Among the choices of treatment options available to suburban users were residential, outpatient, counseling, and the twelve-step program. But as Bev and others revealed, there was no specific treatment for methamphetamine users.

Many of the women in this study reported routes to cessation of methamphetamine other than treatment. Stopping use of methamphetamine or other drugs without any help or a formal treatment plan is often called "cold turkey," a phrase borrowed from the heroin addiction literature. Most cessation by cold turkey was linked to another reason to stop, such as having a new social role, incarceration, acute illness, or reaching the metaphorical rock bottom. Although cold turkey is typically not a strategy suggested by most treatment programs, many of the women in the study who learned that they were pregnant did stop cold turkey, which highlights the initial influence of the mother role. Some started using again later after they gave birth, but others were drug-free for many years while their children were young. There is no stereotyping a drug-using mother, since every situation is different. Yet, relapse, is a well-documented fact, even among the most caring of mothers.

Every woman in this study relapsed; most relapsed multiple times. Collectively, the women attempted every type of cessation strategy several times. After a relapse, most of the women internalized their addiction status. Twelve-step was the strategy most often used for attempting recovery, which explained the widespread acceptance of the recovering addict status as a life-long situation.

Addiction has been called a "troublesome concept" without a standard definition or diagnosis (Akers 1991; Bailey 2005). For example, the widely used *DSM-IV* (*Diagnostic and Statistical Manual of Mental Disorders*, fourth edition) uses the term "dependence" rather "addiction." Few women could define what addiction meant or what being an addict meant. Yet, recovery was predicated upon the respondents accepting that they were addicted and somehow culpable for their status (Granfield 2004; Weinberg 2000).

THE SOCIAL CONSTRUCTION OF
ADDICTION AND RECOVERY

When sociologist Craig Reinarman read his paper "The Achievement of Addiction: Discursive Construction of Phenomenological Reality" at a conference in 2001, one member of the audience responded that whether addiction is a myth or not, the suffering of the addicts is real. The audience was reacting to a divisive academic discussion over how the disease of addiction was invented, promulgated, and internalized by discursive practices. In other words, it was a socially constructed concept. In the published paper, Reinarman wrote, "Understanding how the dominance of addiction discourse was accomplished in these ways does not imply that the lived experience of what is called addiction is therefore any less acute or compelling. But it does invite attention to the contradictory uses of disease discourse: a humane warrant for necessary health services and legitimation of repressive drug policies" (2005, 307). This debate on addiction discourse is mentioned here to explore how the concept of addiction might help or hinder the women in this study who wanted to stop using methamphetamine. My focus is on the lives of women who were immersed in a society that advocates the addiction model. Therefore, understanding how the women perceive addiction is crucial for this analysis.

People who use drugs rely on the concept of addiction to understand and explain problematic features of their drug use. The difficulty with the concept is the vagueness of its meaning and the interchangeable usage "substance addiction," "substance dependence," and "substance abuse." Moreover, the use of the terms "addiction" and "abuse" tends to homogenize what is a very heterogeneous group of drug users who have diverse using patterns that change over time. Less derogatory terms used in academic literature are "problematic use" and "problematic users," which I prefer, but these were not the terms used by the women in the study. As an ethnographer, I did not want to impose my academic terms onto their lives.

Addiction is a disease model—more specifically a brain disease (Leshner 1997; Leshner and Koob 1999). In contrast to a punitive response to drug use, the disease model implies that the user is not completely at fault since it is the addiction that does not allow the user to stop using. This raises the complication of integrating the concept of a disease causing loss of control with the therapeutic model espoused by virtually all treatment programs that require the addicted individual to control his or her use. In other words, "participants in drug abuse treatment discourse must somehow reconcile the view that they can be socially empowered to overcome their drug problems with the view that those problems are, indeed, caused by a disease over which they have little or no personal control" (Weinberg 2000, 618).

Moreover, the criminalized aspect of illegal drugs creates a challenge for those seeking aid in cessation, as they cannot pursue all the overt means of recovery available to someone abusing legal drugs, such as alcohol or tobacco, for fear of exposing their illegal behavior. Twelve-step programs do provide anonymity, and this may explain some of their appeal and success as treatments. Additionally, as informal organizations run by self-defined recovering addicts, they require no form of payment. The recovery meetings themselves are an alternative to drug use and provide an interaction ritual (IR) chains situation for emotional energy (EE)–seeking behavior. The social network also provides the recovery-minded individual support when beset by cravings. However, as previous research shows, twelve-step groups are not conducive for all those who seek help for their substance-use problems (Peele, Bufe, and Brodsky 2000).

In this chapter I discuss recovery and relapse in the lives of the women, focusing on the phase called relapsing addict junkie. As explained in appendix B, the respondents referred to themselves and others as addicts or junkies, and this was not a term I chose to use to define them. Typically, these are the terms they heard used by others. Likewise, the women in this study used the term "recovery" in the same way that treatment professionals tend to use it, defined as the abstinence from all drugs except tobacco and caffeine.

In this study, recovery, treatment, and relapse appeared to be a revolving door with no clear beginning and end. If we accept the popular addiction perception that former users are always in a recovering state, the revolving door is not problematic. Moreover, the literature tends to discuss relapse with no time-limiting boundaries. When is a person free from fear of relapsing? The answer appears to be never. If this is so, then when can a treatment model be judged successful? The criteria for success range from retention in a program to graduation from a program to no relapse within six months or one year or longer (Barrick and Connors 2002). A widely used treatment protocol manual differentiates between short and longer periods between a relapse: "Classical relapse prevention approaches make a distinction between "slips" and relapses, with slips defined as mild episodes of use that are viewed as learning experiences" (Substance Abuse and Mental Health Services Administration 1999). The recovery literature conceptualizes recovery as a career of its own, involving many periods of abstinence and relapse (Hoffmann 2003).

In this chapter I present vignettes of the women's lives depicting the entire cycle of multiple recoveries and relapses within their social, biographical, and historical context. The analysis of the data show that while treatment (including twelve-step programs) emphasized the self-control aspects of recovery, it was the social-control aspects that instigated a turning point in the women's lives toward achieving recovery. The most consistent finding was the universal acceptance of a cycle of treatment, recovery, and relapse by professionals, semiprofessionals, friends, family, volunteer workers and virtually everyone concerned about the women's addiction status. There were a few exceptions, and these were among women who sought and found their own way out of problematic use.

The following tales of recovery and relapse include those with formal treatment, informal treatment, and self-recovery, or what is often called natural recovery. Multiple routes existed in each woman's career, and often one process was a catalyst for another, so the effect of one or the other is difficult to identify. Because of the overlap of different routes to recovery at different times or at the same time, particularly the use of a twelve-step program while involved in formal treatment, one quote may represent more than one route or strategy. I do not intend to compare these processes for efficacy but instead to highlight the common aspects found across all processes that led to effective recovery from problematic use of methamphetamine.

FORMAL TREATMENT

Formal treatment included legally prescribed medications to help with detoxification and other diagnosed medical problems, professional psychological counseling, and social support, although this support was often provided by twelve-step groups as part of the treatment program or as aftercare recovery maintenance. Formal treatment can range from expensive private residential rehabilitation to nonprofit or government-supported treatment. Nonprofit treatment is usually not entirely free of cost but often offers a sliding fee that allows the poor to pay a reduced rate or be sponsored by donations.

Free government-supported treatment is rare. The nonprofit and public treatment residential programs were the most sought after by the women in this study, and typically the least accessible. Women with money or private insurance easily gained access to a treatment center of their choice, but only for the time period allowed by their insurance—usually two to four weeks. Women with Medicaid had access to some treatment, again time-limited. Women without financial means needed to gain access to treatment programs through the emergency room, detoxification facility, or jail. Rarely was a woman accepted into a nonprofit or public funded treatment program without being connected through the treatment hierarchy, composed of nonprofit and public social service staff, medical staff, and individuals working in law enforcement or legal representation. A reference from one of these insiders usually was better than a cold call from a user looking for treatment.

Having social capital among nonprofit professionals emerged as a factor that helped some of the women. Directors and staff at the homeless shelters, domestic violence shelters, and residential treatment homes knew each other and referred women to each other's programs. A referral from one of the directors ensured a bed. Not having this social capital was a great disadvantage. Recall Ida, the woman introduced in a previous chapter who was homeless and could not gain access to treatment. Had she been referred to any of a number of treatment programs by the homeless shelter director, she would have had a place to stay and a cessation of her drug use—even if only for a short time. Yet in what appeared incongruous cruelty, the very reason she needed treatment was the reason she could not get a bed in the homeless shelter. She had a nighttime job in a twenty-four-hour restaurant, so she was not allowed to stay in the homeless shelter. With this low-paying work, she could only afford a motel infested with methamphetamine users, and soon she was using methamphetamine, without a job, and without a place to stay. Her attempts at entering treatment were met with one exclusion criterion after another, as she explained:

> Treatment centers would say that I don't fit a certain category, that I wasn't messed up enough, or I was too strong for this, or I needed to have this, or that, whatever, to enter into their organization. Either I didn't have insurance, or I didn't have what I needed to have at that time to enter into these programs. And the shelters as well. They have shelters for women and children, but no shelters for single women. I mean it's kinda like, wow, you got all these shelters for men. You have these shelters for women and children, but you have no shelters for women. You know, and at my age, my children are not with me. And if I'm having a hard time, or struggling with drugs I need a place, I need an option to say well look, I'm out here; I do need treatment. I've been using drugs. I want to

do something with my life. And you've got all this history on me where I have done good things in my life, and I have been stable. But I've got to have a base of operations to do that in order to comply with their rules and regulations or whatever what have you. But, I'm a good candidate for probation or some kind of structural program, because I can comply.

Almost every woman who attempted to find a place in a treatment facility in the suburbs, especially during the last two years of the study, ran into the same barriers as Ida. Based on the women's stories, gaining entrance to treatment was not as difficult in previous years. The Great Recession appeared to activate social circumstances (unemployment, divorce, loss of health insurance) that resulted in a greater need for drug treatment. The women were given a range of reasons why they could not enter the program. Beyond the program not having a bed (the typical response), women were told they had not used enough, were not ready, or did not live in the right county.

Tammy had been in a few treatment programs before and recently moved back to the suburban county to be near her children. She told me she tried the treatment homes that were on the resource list we gave her. "I've heard about them, but I heard it's so hard to get into there. 'Cause see, I'm from [Suburban Town], but I haven't been a resident here in four years. So they told me that I got to wait a year to make me resident eligible or whatever before I can actually get in there."

Others opted for the outpatient program rather than wait for a bed. Aby attended an outpatient program that required she stay at the residential treatment home during the day and return to her sister's home at night. A few weeks earlier she had tried to be admitted to the emergency room:

I went up to the hospital, and told them, I'm HIV. I use needles, can you get me some kind of rehab? And they said that President Obama had passed something and they don't really do detox. They wouldn't admit me. I thought they'd at least take me to [nearby city hospital], and they wouldn't do nothing. They let me go back out the doors that night. I had a bag packed thinking they're gonna take me to rehab. I sat at the dope dealer's house thinking they're gonna take me to rehab. I had the dope dealer take me up there, and they sent me back packing. I had to have my dope dealer pick me up that night. And I stayed up there [at dope dealer's house] for two more weeks. I was just miserable, and I had heard of a couple people that I had done dope with that had left the [treatment program]. And it took two weeks from the day, I called them [treatment program] and they took me in. I started going and they wanted to put me in-house, and but at the time they had no room for in-house, and 'cause I was voluntary, I was passing all my drug screens and stuff, so they didn't make me go. . . . Yeah, but I mean I've heard of people being rejected you know. I've ran into a couple of people since I've been clean. One girl was trying to get her kids back, and they didn't have no room and she was wanting to go into [the treatment program], and she had to go back out on the streets cause sometimes they're full.

Aby's travel to the outpatient program involved a sixty-mile round-trip each day from her sister's home to the treatment facility. She stopped attending the day program when she obtained steady employment. Although Aby had been in and out of many treatment programs, based on her current sobriety it appeared this program was helpful in her recovery. She also was diagnosed with bipolar disorder while at the facility and was prescribed antidepressants.

Other women emphasized the lack of transitional services available when they left drug treatment. One of the older women said she went through a treatment program and then started going to twelve-step meetings. She was drug-free for eight months but started again because, she said, "My husband went back to sellin' drugs—cutting up enough for me to see it. Of course I'm gonna want it—I'm an addict." The recovering addict status she learned to embrace while in treatment appeared to have the unintended consequence of facilitating her relapse, and she justified it as just a slip in her recovery.

Most women identified a lack of work-training or life-skills opportunities while in drug treatment that would prepare them to deal with their needs once they left the program. Many women who used methamphetamine for emotional or psychological issues were given no substitute to take the place of the self-medication they had previously used. For those who used both methamphetamine and heroin, methadone maintenance treatment was viewed as a nice escape from the daily chaos created by drug use. Some women who primarily used methamphetamine reported using heroin or pain pills in order to qualify for methadone.

Ironically, it was easier to get access to treatment through the criminal justice system, an unintended consequence of overpopulating the jails with drug users. Most often the respondents who received formal treatment while in a criminal justice program did so through the drug court treatment model. The drug court is a voluntary alternative to incarceration that incorporates drug treatment with close judicial supervision. Typically, drug court treatment programs include mandatory counseling, twelve-step group meetings, attendance at regular court sessions, random drug testing, and, in some cases, life-skills training (Boeri, Lamonica, and Harbry 2011). Some drug courts emphasize employment and education as integral parts of the treatment program (Deschenes, Ireland, and Kleinepeter 2009). Most studies find drug court participants have substantially lower recidivism rates than comparison samples (May 2008).

The drug court treatment program was the most complete model we found in terms of training, counseling, social control, and motivation to stay drug-free in order to avoid jail. Because of the multifaceted nature of the program, it is difficult to identify one single factor or even a group of factors to credit for its apparent success. The women, however, generally pointed out one aspect they felt was most important, which was different for each woman. For example, Dolly, a thirty-seven-year-old housewife who voluntarily turned over her children to her sister after years of using methamphetamine, reported that her sobriety was learned in the drug court: "They took me off intensive [treatment] last week and I've got a new probation officer, and I've done all my community service, and I've done everything I was supposed to do. All my programs, and all my treatment, and all my evaluations, and therapy and everything. And it's all helped, you know. But honestly the biggest thing is depending on God." Dolly, fresh out of drug court, mentioned the required regular visits before the judge, the coordinator drawing up a plan for her, and the counselor's interest in her life as factors she liked about the drug court program. Others highlighted different turning points in their lives that landed them in court, which acted as a catalyst for effective recovery.

Audrey, at only nineteen, already had been through an expensive private treatment program and attended aftercare twelve-step fellowship before she was arrested for drug use and chose to participate in the drug treatment program instead of going to jail. She said the drug court rules helped to keep her from relapse:

> Honestly, right now it's the fact that I'm in drug court. It's the fact that I get random drug screens. I haven't been tested this week, but like last week I got tested three times. So it's like very random. But going back to speed—like I graduate drug court in March. I'm finally going to be done with this. But I have no intention on ever using meth again. I mean I can't tell you the future, like I can't really, I'm not a psychic, but I saw what it did to me. . . . Yeah, and when I got my first job, it was July that summer, and I had to wear long sleeves to work because I still had track marks on my arm. Like, I mean, it sucked.

Audrey's description illustrates a convergence of factors that made the drug court program more successful for her than the private treatment program or twelve-step groups she attended. Her attraction to drugs waned to the point of feeling disgusted at her former self.

Drug court also provided (or enforced) a sense of purpose and structure. Madeleine recounted how, previously, her whole day was filled with getting and using drugs: "I didn't do anything but sit around and smoke speed. I didn't have a job. I didn't go to class. I only hung out with people that did speed. I was either going to get speed, like setting up the deal to go get it, or selling it, or doing it. I didn't go out anywhere. I didn't work." A traumatic event was the turning point for Madeleine before she went to drug court. While waiting for her court date, she was kidnapped by her abusing boyfriend. After being returned safely to her mother's home, she stayed inside the house until she appeared before the judge and asked to enter the drug court program.

Drug court, like methadone maintenance, provided the women with enough time to develop positive IR chains outside their drug using networks. While drug court appeared to be one of the best chances for recovery for women who could not afford treatment, not all the suburban counties had drug courts, and some had very narrow admissions policies.

Lack of time to develop positive emotional energy (EE) in a non-drug-using interaction ritual (IR) was a primary reason for relapse (Collins 2004). Most treatment programs were not long enough. The consequence was increased problematic use that led to serious health and social issues. For example, Ada, a twenty-one-year-old woman, voluntarily admitted herself to treatment a few years ago but could not stay because of a lack of insurance. She had signed herself into treatment when she started injecting methamphetamine and wanted to stop, knowing the risks involved with injection. "They only kept me for seven days cause I didn't have insurance," she said. "Yeah, I was hoping to stay six months to a year but they only kept me seven days and then sent me home." Ada returned to injecting methamphetamine with her network of injectors. Within a year she was in jail for trafficking, where she learned of her recent HCV status. Because of exclusionary criteria for participation in drug court in her county, she was unable to enroll in the treatment plan. With a sense of hopelessness arising from her HCV diagnosis and lack of health care, she started using again soon after her release from jail.

In recent years, a few of the women were released from jail or prison straight into a residential treatment program. Unless they had participated in a drug court program, they were required to find a place in a treatment program on their own. For example, when Zoe was incarcerated the second time, instead of prison she was allowed to go to residential treatment, but she had to find a treatment facility that would accept her. Zoe was as zealous in her attempt to get a bed in a treatment program as she had been in trying to get good methamphetamine.

> I was on the phone every day. I had money that I had hid, you know, while I was selling the drugs and I had—I was able to call a lot. Stay on the phone all the time. In jail it costs a lot of money to make one phone call for fifteen minutes. There was like six-hundred dollar, seven-hundred dollar phone bills while I was in there; I stayed on the phone so much. I had all of my sisters on the phones; I had everybody I could think of calling them every day bugging the heck out of them.

After spending fifty-one days in jail, she got a bed in a residential treatment center in the city, where she spent six months. She liked being there and thought the staff was great. "And a lot of 'em I love to this day. I'll always love 'em." She attended twelve-step meetings almost daily after leaving. Six months later, she relapsed. Her probation officer told her to find another rehab facility. She related how hard that is to do without money. Her savings from dealing had been depleted by court costs and probation fees, so she contacted all the programs with a sliding scale payment plan:

> I've called all them places on there [the resource list] and all of them says you have to pay, and the ones that don't, they've got long waiting lists or else your child has to be on Medicaid, or food stamps, and my daughter's not on either one. Not because she couldn't be, because she [mother-in-law who has custody] is too damn lazy to go up there and sign her up for it.

Many treatment programs, especially those using twelve-step models, tell parents and family members not to "enable" their addicted loved one. Typically this is translated into withdrawing financial support but expressing your love as a process called "tough love." The process as enacted in real life is fully described in a book written by one famous father, George McGovern, a former United States representative and senator who was the 1972 Democratic presidential nominee. His daughter Terry was diagnosed with addiction to drugs and alcohol, and the family spent years paying for her to go to the best treatment programs and helping her start a new life afterward. Terry always relapsed, and finally, encouraged by treatment professionals, the family agreed to practice tough love and stopped supporting her. A few months later she was found frozen to death on the side of a street. The senator wrote a book about Terry's story in which he mournfully describes the guilt he felt for following the tough love approach (McGovern 1997). Yet tough love appears to have worked for some women with addiction problems, such as Isabella.

Isabella was the former methamphetamine user who lived in a gated, guarded community where her mother bought a house for her so she could attend school without having to work. Instead of going to school regularly or working, she sold drugs from her house. She described what happened when her mother withdrew support:

Well, my mother of course suspected that something fishy was going on, but then she really found out that I was using, and she took my car, and she sold the house. And I was kind of living from place to place. Friends' houses, motels. And I was really tired of that.
So your mother took away the money and everything?
Mm-hmm. [yes]
And then what happened?

I called my mom and told her to come get me and take me to rehab on her birthday.

Isabella's mother sent her to a private residential rehabilitation center where she became immersed in the twelve-step philosophy. After leaving the rehab center, she attended twelve-step meetings while she lived with her mother, stopped using all drugs, and returned to college to obtain a degree in substance abuse counseling. She plans to start a new career as a drug counselor helping others.

Isabella's social capital likely had more to do with her recovery than did tough love alone. Ada's mother could not afford to pay for a treatment program that her daughter wanted, and now her mother cried every time she talked to me about Ada's lack of health care for HCV. Likewise, if Bev's mother had practiced tough love, her daughter might have been found dead at Deliverance.

INFORMAL TREATMENT: THE TWELVE-STEP MODEL

The twelve-step program started with Alcoholics Anonymous (AA) and is now used for every type of addiction. It was the primary model used outside structured outpatient or residential programs—here referred to as informal treatment. In addition to requiring abstinence from all substances except tobacco and caffeine, twelve-step programs strongly encourage regular group meetings, daily at the beginning and at least weekly for most individuals in recovery, which is a lifelong prospect. The program's use of a buddy system (the buddy is typically called a sponsor) provides individual help for someone who is contemplating relapse. The recovery tools employed in twelve-step participation involve social support, reliance on a higher power, and socially enforced cessation. Because the meetings are free, they are incorporated into virtually all treatment programs. Since they are anonymous, they draw people from all social classes.

Participation in twelve-step groups allows a new identity to be enacted for those who desire to overcome their addicted selves. The "myth of addiction," according to Gibson, Acquah, and Robinson (2004), protects a central value within mainstream Western society—the value of individual autonomy and self-control (601). To be an addict requires individuals to believe that they have some sort of pathological inability to properly manage themselves (Hammersley and Reid 2002). Drug users, in forming a new social bond that requires describing themselves as recovering addicts, are not simply cultivating a structure of support to overcome the physical pains of withdrawal but also to develop a new identity. The twelve-step terminology that describes this group interaction highlights the emotional aspects, such as calling the meeting a *fellowship*.

Beth is an example of a long-term user who depended on twelve-step for her current sobriety. This seemingly perfect suburban mother used methamphetamine for years and became economically trapped by the money that dealing provided for her family. Unfortunately, she lost her family because of it and was in jail and treatment a few times before she managed to stay drug-free and regain custody of her children. Beth complained that methamphetamine was everywhere in her community. When asked what she would do if it were offered to her now, she replied: "Go to a meeting. . .My big thing now is I don't have to be on top of everything. I don't have to be supermom. I guess it's like where, you know, for whatever reason things just aren't going right. Robby and I could be fighting, the kids could piss me off, or things aren't going well. I thought about it, I will get up, call somebody, and go to a meeting."

The dynamics and efficacy of each twelve-step group will vary even within the same group from time to time. This aspect of twelve-step groups is apparent from the varied responses of the women—all of whom knew of twelve-step by experience or reputation. Some women did not find a particular twelve-step setting that contributed to their recovery. In contrast to the coerced sobriety required by incarceration or maintained by urinalysis tests, twelve-step uses social control to enforce a self-proclaimed sobriety, which results in various stages of recovery among its members. A few respondents reported some displeasure with this arrangement. Other respondents also claimed that users pose as recovery-minded individuals, but a recovering user usually will know a hidden user. This was aptly described by Lucy, an avid twelve-step participant: "There are a lot of people that are in your twelve-step programs that are still current users. And being a user, you can look across the room and, you can't hide it, you know. You can't hide it. You can talk all the good talk and walk all the good walk, and I can sit here with you and la, la, la—angels and sunshine. But when you are a user there's something that's going to flow out of you as a drug addict. It is something that you cannot hide." Lucy's words give evidence of her migration from a drug addict to a recovering addict who recognizes a user faking recovery. Most respondents, however, accepted that while multiple failed attempts at recovery were typical, twelve-steppers needed to hit rock bottom—the essential stepping-stone to effectual recovery.

Even among current participating members, the social construction of the eternal recovering addict who needs group help as well as help from a higher power was not embraced wholeheartedly. Rachel, for example, described the aspects of twelve-step she did not like:

Whether I'm going to meetings, whether I am talking to my sponsor, whether I'm working the steps, whether I'm praying, whether I'm reading my books, whether I'm like doing all the crap AA recommends me to do, which I'm getting tired of AA recently. 'Cause I feel like I can't think for myself. I can't think for myself anymore. I've like noticed that recently, that I can't think for myself. Like everything I think is something AA told me to think. You ever been to an AA meeting? They sit around, they tell you everything. Over and over and over and over again. Like, I can't think for myself. When I have to make a decision I want to call my sponsor or someone else for everything. I never make my own decisions. And that's part of AA, not making your own decisions, and I don't want that.

But you've been clean for a year.

Seventeen months. I mean it works. It keeps me clean . . . but I can't think for myself. And that's why I'm still clean.

Rachel's critique draws attention to the group-think aspect (letting the group think for you) of twelve-step, a key to the program's success, but one that makes the requirement to choose to be drug-free questionable. If one cannot think for oneself, where is the choice or agency?

A number of accounts by women who attributed their current success at being drug-free to their participation in a twelve-step fellowship were presented in previous chapters. However, many others had participated in twelve-step programs in the past and relapsed. We discussed twelve-step during a focus group with two women who had differing views on the program:

Flo: I was mandated by the court to go to NA [Narcotics Anonymous], and the twelve-steps for me, personally, I didn't like it. I didn't like it because it was something that they were like drilling in my head. You know, you have to live, eat, and breathe every step. And the fourth step was really hard to do. And I couldn't expose myself to somebody that had just the same problem I had. I didn't see the reason behind it. I really didn't. And I got put down a lot. And they eventually kicked me out because I didn't want to, you know, if I made a face or something . . . and the lady that ran the place said, "Oh, I know you feeling like this." No I'm not. I just don't—I don't know what I was thinking but, you know, I wasn't feeling what she was telling me I was. And they were just trying to get in my head too much. I didn't like that. I really, really didn't like that. They didn't want to hear what you have to say about what you were feeling. You know, I just came out of doing all that crap. You know, it was hard. But I didn't like—the twelve-step program didn't work for me. It really didn't. What worked for me was God really. I started going to church. I started going to church and I let Him get in my head and in my heart but yeah . . . and that worked for me personally. Just me personally.

Mia: I've been in and out of twelve-step programs for years. I started doing twelve-step programs twenty years ago. The longest I ever made it was three months. To me it's like, you're going to live drunk and on drugs and you're miserable, or you're going to live clean and sober. And because you have to fight it so hard and you think about it every day, it's miserable to me. I don't know which is worse. I've been trying to find the fine line my whole life and there is none. There is none. And I've come to be aware that there is no fine line. You either drink or you don't, or you either do drugs or you don't. But AA and NA doesn't fix it. I have to fix it in myself. Going to NA and AA and reliving all the old stories and trying to get all what's shoved down in my gut out does not work for me either. If I wanted to pull all that out I'll pull it out. And I don't want to have to pull it out in front of somebody that really don't want to—number one don't want to hear it anyway.

Flo: And they don't care.

Mia: Yeah and they going to sit there and act like they care. Don't act like you care!

Flo: And then they'll talk about you after group.

The women appeared to have some relatively harsh words to say regarding their experiences with twelve-step groups. Of course, not all groups are the same, and some of what goes on in a particular twelve-step fellowship cannot be censored or controlled. But their words were echoed by many other women in the study.

I knew these two women had expressed a desire to attend group fellowships, so I asked what they did like about twelve-step:

Flo: If it was a group with just women . . .

Mia: Yeah, those are good.

Flo: If it was a woman's group where it's not head programming it would—I would've went. I would've went. You could talk about things to improve yourself, not live in your past. Like, you know, coming here [focus group] is like, you know, what did you do to get—or how did you come about this? That's a whole lot different than, you know, you reliving it all the time that you're going to that group so.

What if we had a women's group that just met to talk like what we're doing now?

Flo: Like having a set—a rap session. This is fine. This—I love coming to y'all. I really do.

Mia: It's not a programming your head. If it's like, okay, you know, what did you do? When did you do it? I'm like whoa, ok, I screwed up. Please forgive me. And then it's messing with my head, because if I use, you know, why am I going to come here?

Flo: If I use I should be able to come here. And let's get it—try to get it right. Why did you use?

Well we don't have to talk about your use. We can talk about your other life.

Flo: Other life. That's what I like about this group.

Mia: Some of the people when they started getting started on that, you know—it's like oh wow! And then it's a revolving—it's a vicious revolving door. It really is, but I'd love to go to a women's group.

To set this conversation in context, both women had had recent transitions in their lives. Flo had just met a new boyfriend at a twelve-step group, and although they no longer attended the twelve-step fellowship, they were deeply immersed in church functions and both were drug-free. Since some twelve-step groups discourage relationships among members, this new relationship may have been why she stopped attending. Mia had recently had her heart broken by a fellow homeless addict who led her into weeks of uncontrolled drug use after she had been in a treatment program, attending twelve-step meetings, and drug-free for over six months. On the day of the focus group interview, she was staying in a halfway home for women in the city and doing relatively well, although her words indicated she was still experiencing stress from her recent relapse, as evidenced by her comment on the vicious revolving door.

Mia's poignant statement "I've been looking for that fine line my whole life" was in response to a question on whether a former addict can ever take another drink. She knew according to the twelve-step philosophy this was impossible. While it might have been impossible for her, other women did find some moderation in drug and alcohol use, one of the strategies used in a natural recovery process.

NATURAL RECOVERY/SOCIAL RECOVERY

The confluence of several changing relationships was a pattern we found among all women who achieved sobriety or controlled use of methamphetamine, whether or not they used any form of treatment. Many women in the study showed that they learned to control their use by first achieving social recovery—recovering their social life—without participating in any kind of treatment or supportive twelve-step group. Some eventually became abstinent from all drugs and alcohol; others continued to use alcohol or other drugs in a very controlled and occasional manner without relapsing.

Routes to recovery that were not treatment or twelve-step included social support, goal-focus, avoidance, spiritual experiences, and using a substitute drug. Social support encompassed support from family, friends, counselors, health care providers, social workers, or even strangers. "Goal-focus" refers to specific actions taken to replace the methamphetamine-user role in the respondent's life with a goal in mind other than abstinence, such as graduation from college or learning a new hobby. "Avoidance" refers to avoiding the people and places that tempt one to use a drug or otherwise cause craving, often described as "triggers." Spiritual help includes any type of otherworldly influence mentioned as instrumental for recovery. Finally, women mentioned the use of substitute drugs when referring to a legal or illegal drug used to substitute for the problematic drug. While some of these routes may be used in treatment programs that allow a substitute prescription drug, and others are used in twelve-step, here they were employed by the women outside of a formal or informal treatment structure.

Stopping drug use on one's own is rarely discussed in the literature, with some notable exceptions. The process is often referred to as "natural recovery" (Biernacki 1986; Cloud and Granfield 2001; Waldorf 1973), or "self-change" (Sobell 2007); I use the term "social recovery" to highlight the social nature of these strategies (Boeri, Lamonica, and Harbry 2011). Social interaction was present in all the routes to recovery used.

Social Support

While for most women social support came from associating with an established social group, such as a church or club, other women needed only the support of one person to help them stop problematic use. For example, Madeline, the twenty-two-year-old who was kidnapped by her boyfriend at gunpoint, indicated the need for constant support from her mother: "And so I called my mom and I was like, 'Will you please come get me?' And she said, 'Only if you're completely done with those people and everything.' And so I moved back home and I stayed with her like twenty-four hours a day. That's basically when I stopped."

Goal-Focus

Three popular goals mentioned by our respondents included keeping or acquiring gainful employment, completing higher education, and participating in volunteer work. For example, a few of the younger women indicated that the social environment of school provided positive social capital they did not want to lose. Audrey, who had started methamphetamine use at age fifteen and had been incarcerated a few times, developed a new focus on achieving a college education: "I have no intention of ever using meth again. . . .I'm going to school full time, I've got a boyfriend, and I work part-time." Like many others, Audrey described various new social roles, all of which were incongruent with the role of a drug user.

Avoidance

The avoidance strategy in natural recovery occurs when a conscious decision is made to avoid the settings and people associated with former methamphetamine use, without being coerced to do so by incarceration, probation, or residential treatment requirements. Some women claimed that even thinking of associating with any of their former network would be problematic. Many of the women indicated that they had to avoid all contact with other users in their social network in order to remain in recovery or in control. This was not always possible when the women lived in a drug-using community with no resources enabling them to leave. Some women illustrated amazing resolve to be able to associate with drug users selectively and not allow the association to interfere with their own drug-using status. Sophia said, "I kind of just stopped hanging out with that whole crowd for a long time. I only hang out with one of the girls that I used to do it with, but I don't do it with her now." Her recovery strategy indicates that in contrast to the strict avoidance of drug users required by treatment and twelve-step group participation, a range of avoidance levels based on personal decisions was also successful.

Spiritual Experiences

Since a higher power is part of the twelve-step process, it was impossible to distinguish the influence of twelve-step from the spiritual experiences mentioned by the women, who had participated in twelve-step programs at some point in their drug career. Here I highlight those who focused on the spiritual experience not merely as a belief or a step to recovery but rather as something that was life-changing. Lucy, who spent one year in a private rehabilitation center and attended twelve-step for a short period afterward, said her spiritual life was the most important factor in keeping her away from using methamphetamine:

> You have to work on your personal self. And now today, sitting before you, I am a true believer. There is nothing on this earth made by man that is something stronger made by God, and that is your mind. Nothing in this earth, nothing in this world is stronger than what God made, and that's your mind.
> *So you're a true believer in what?*
> Your mind over matter. Over any matter. Drug matter, social matter, depression. Mind over matter.

Although many former twelve-steppers gave credit to the twelve-step program for their recovery, Lucy instead gave credit to her God-given mind. And while others replaced drug-using networks with twelve-step fellowships, Lucy replaced her drug use and drug-using network with religion and church.

For some women, a spiritual experience resulted in a temporary cessation without treatment. When her mother died, Ida said her cessation of all drugs was due to a spiritual experience. The daughter role was very important to Ida. She loved her mother, and contrary to expected outcomes, the death of her mother made her stop drugs for years: "Surprisingly, you would've thought that, you know, my prior drug use—and my whole family too, I'm sure they thought I was the one that was going to crack and go off the deep end and probably kill myself with drugs. But surprisingly, I went cold turkey. Just didn't want anything to do with drugs. Felt like I had wasted all these years, the moments that I could've had with my mother, I wasted them. And I guess I just wanted—in respect to her death, to stay clean." Here we see an unexpected turning point that comes at one of the greatest emotional times in the life course—the loss of a beloved parent. Instead of using more drugs to console herself, Ida stopped using out of respect for her mother. This lasted for about two years, but even today, Ida speaks of her faith in God to help her overcome her addiction: "And I would depend on him [God]. And there would be a while that I would be okay. And I would depend on the Lord for my strength. And I still do." Most of the women in the study considered two years a long time to be drug-free.

Substitute Drug

The most controversial strategy discussed by the women was the use of one drug to stop or slow down the use of methamphetamine, which is a substitution strategy. Most often the women mentioned using alcohol, marijuana, or prescription pills on their route out of problematic methamphetamine use. For example, when I asked Chloe how she stopped methamphetamine, she replied, "Sometimes I want to smoke weed but just because I feel like, you know, I feel like a bitch sometimes so I think weed can, like, I think it can mellow me down."

Other women mentioned using legally prescribed medications that are typically employed as a medically prescribed substitutes in formal treatment, for example, buprenorphine. Even though buprenorphine is used for withdrawal from opioids or heroin, many of the women were polydrug users and had enough pain pill use to qualify for this substitute medication. Some of the women, however, switched to pain pills to stop methamphetamine. Generally, methadone maintenance was successful for stopping methamphetamine use when the women concurrently used another drug (heroin, opioid pills) that qualified them for a methadone program. For example, Mercedes was a long-term methamphetamine and heroin user, but eventually the withdrawal effects of heroin forced Mercedes to abandon methamphetamine: "I got so strung out on heroin that I didn't have any time anymore for speed." As a heroin addict, Mercedes was eligible for a methadone program, and since the program randomly tested for other drug use, she could not receive her daily methadone if she used any other drug. Mercedes recounted how she stopped using methamphetamine as well as heroin:

I just want to get my life together. I've spent more of my life on drugs than I have not on drugs. And between that and—mainly my daughter.

She's at an age where—she's sixteen and I want to be a role model for her . . . and that was a big motivating factor for me to get my life together. . . . Basically I try to fill up the void, the time that I used to use with getting high, um, with positive things that are going to, uh, enhance my life, and cause me to grow and not, um, go backward so to speak. . . . I go to a charity health clinic downtown. Instead of buying each other Christmas presents this year like the [methadone treatment] staff normally does, cause I'm on the Patient Advisory Board, this year I got them to donate something, some money, to the Health Clinic.

We see a convergence of motivations in Mercedes' account of her recovery. She is on methadone, which is critical to fulfilling her need for medication and alleviating her need to self-medicate with methamphetamine. She is tired of the drug addict life and desires to be a good role model for her teenage daughter. She feels a bond with the methadone clinic staff, and she keeps her life full of social activities that provide a bridge to new social capital, such as her role as a board member of a local nonprofit clinic.

Mercedes appears to have been given enough time, thanks to the methadone, to learn to appreciate the other social activities in life that drugs took the place of before. When her life was impoverished—during the time she lost her daughter to foster care, was incarcerated, and raped—even a low temporary interaction ritual (IR) chain situation was appealing. With the help of methadone, she had time to develop positive emotional energy from new IR chains, as shown by the excitement Mercedes had in her voice when she narrated her story. Her time in the methadone program also provided her a mainstream role that offered more bridging social capital.

Many women told us that when they tried to get into subsidized treatment, or they relapsed, they were told, "You are not ready yet." What Mercedes' and Lucy's stories show is that the women need time to migrate to a new role (Hughes 2007) and to gain emotional energy from their new IR situation (Collins 2004). For example, Mercedes' migration to her role as a nonprofit board member gave her a successful IR chain, but it took time for her to find this situation and for others to accept and trust her as well. Lucy's migration was through twelve-step to a church fellowship that took over a year to find. For many women who need time to learn to control their drug use or cope with their problems without drugs, unless they can afford to pay for the time needed in treatment, they typically will not get it.

Unfortunately, new users spend years in problematic drug use, experiencing much suffering, losing social roles, and participating in damaging relationships as they make their way to the rock bottom. Dee, a young woman from a middle-class background who had substantial social capital, was currently following this destructive path. At only nineteen, she had already acquired an attraction to the ritual of injecting methamphetamine and had broken most of her social bonds to mainstream roles. Confronted by her boyfriend and mother in a failed intervention, she responded with the treatment and recovery discourse that she was not ready to abstain from all drugs:

> So he was in rehab. I was at home. He started to get very controlling kind of, like worried that I was going to go run off and do drugs, or do just like stupid things. And I told him—like I dealt with it for a good month or two, and I'm like listen, I'm not going to do everything you think I'm going to do. I want to do drugs. I want to do meth again. I'm not going to just like stop because you want me to. Like I have to stop because I want to, and I don't want to. . . . It's like, I know that if you go to treatment you have to be 100 percent. And like, I want to fix my life, but I'm not ready to stop using drugs. . . . I feel like he was just in rehab just because it was a place to stay. It was food to eat. He told me straight up that he wanted to do it [use meth] the minute he got out. The minute he was released. And so I'm not going to be wasting my time in a place that is not going to do me or anybody else any good, you know, if I'm just sitting there just waiting to get out.

Of course there is no real evidence that the addict has to be ready to stop or want to stop for recovery to be successful, but like many beliefs, it works because people believe in it. As Lucy observed, "It's mind over matter." The Thomas theorem, "If people define situations as real, they are real in their consequences," explains this concept.

Instead of suggesting Dee stop using, I encouraged her to get her GED so she could go to college as she had said she wanted to. I was surprised when she called a few weeks later to let me know she had taken a practice GED exam and passed.

SUMMARY OF GENDERED TREATMENT, RECOVERY, AND RELAPSE

In this chapter I looked at all recovery strategies used by the women, categorized as formal treatment, informal treatment, and natural or social recovery. While some of the same social recovery strategies were used in formal treatment and twelve-step programs, treatment is often inaccessible for those most in need. Furthermore, by all accounts in this study, more types of programs, targeted services, and longer periods of time are needed for a successful treatment outcome. The advantages of twelve-step include its anonymity, accessibility, and cost-free participation. However, participation in twelve-step can limit one's social network considerably, and the status of being a recovering addict implies that even a glass of beer is taboo. Although this might be true for some, it was not true for all. The advantages of natural recovery are the opportunity to learn moderation and not being forced to leave one's entire social network, which are both prohibited or highly discouraged in formal and informal treatment.

In most of their stories of recovery, the women focused on their own agency, or ability to make a choice, because that is the recovery discourse of the majority of traditional treatment professionals and experts. Choice includes the decision to surrender one's agency to a higher power, as Lucy claimed, or to a sponsor, as Beth did. However, viewed with an understanding of the power dynamics involved in this discourse, the assumed choice of the women to surrender to the addict perspective involved an almost total relinquishing of individual choice. Granted, they do choose to surrender; however their choice is highly constrained by their social circumstances, available social options, and professional opinions.

By including successful strategies used by the women in this study beyond treatment and twelve-step, the number of attempts at sobriety might be reduced and therefore relieve the public burden of institutionalized treatment centers and the overpopulation of incarcerated drug users. It also takes the focus off the individual. Instead of blaming the individual for being weak in the face of a constant barrage of drug use in community and social networks, why not provide opportunities for social inclusion in conventional roles? Currently, recovery and relapse is accepted as a revolving door that could last a lifetime. I suggest a focus on social recovery instead of abstinence as the first goal.

"Social recovery" refers to acquiring the skills, resources, and networks needed that enhance people's ability to live in society without resorting to problematic alcohol or drug use (Boshears, Boeri, and Harbry 2011). Social recovery might be a more beneficial conceptualization of recovery for those who seek recovery but fail to achieve the complete abstinence from all substances required by abstinence-only recovery models.

While more treatment is needed, it also must be better, longer, and cost-free. The economic and political environment of the contemporary United States continues to invest in punitive solutions that are not working for many, as this study shows. It seems unlikely that government will invest in other options in the near future. However, as the recession continues, the jails and prisons are over capacity and are being forced to release prisoners whose only crime is drug possession. The hordes of men and women incarcerated due to laws constructed to punish drug users and rid communities of low-level dealers will be released to a chaotic array of underfunded after-prison programs and poorly funded social services. As shown in this book, health issues identified while in jail or prison frequently do not receive adequate medical attention after the prisoner is released. Unless harm-reduction initiatives are funded, effective reentry programs are implemented, and health care is made available, the imminent massive release of inmates will result in infectious diseases spreading throughout communities unrestrained, and the formerly incarcerated will engage in the only gainful employment they can find, whether legal or not.

The women's lives recounted in this book give ample evidence that incarceration merely exacerbates the problems that instigated drug use. To adequately begin to address the impending criminal justice upheaval and resulting public health implications, the attention we gave to criminalizing the lives of drug users must be transferred to providing medical attention and social recovery where it is most needed. To do this we must first acknowledge the barriers to these services in contemporary social and economic context.

CHAPTER 8

Policy Implications

KAT: IN SEARCH OF SHELTER

Kat was one of the more resourceful women I interviewed, but she was also one of the most disadvantaged in terms of having no material possessions and little social capital. She had not always been in this situation. A hard worker, Kat took a service job right out of high school and held it for a short time until she found an office position. "I worked there until I got married when I was twenty-one," she said, "And then when I was twenty-two, the company relocated to [Big City], so I quit. I didn't work for a few years after I got married."

The city was about thirty miles away, but Kat, like many of the women in the poor suburban communities, did not have a car and did not often venture there. The first time I met Kat she had a home and a job. She had recently left an abusive husband, taking her teenage son with her. At forty-four, she looked worn out from a difficult life and damaged by domestic violence. But her will was strong, and she appeared to be able to handle emotional issues, judging from her calm recounting of her story.

The next time I saw her, she was homeless. Kat was a proud woman, and she told me she was ashamed of her current situation. Her son was living with friends temporarily. She did not want to tell me where she was living now, but she asked me to drop her off in a deserted trailer park seemingly inhabited only by dogs, cats, and rats. Based on her recent history, I suspected that she was squatting in an empty house near where she used to live. As I mentioned, she was resourceful.

I recounted my third meeting with Kat in chapter 2, describing how I spent twenty-four hours looking for a motel manager who would take her and her son without an ID. I personally paid for her extended-stay room for a week. Although I asked her not to allow other women to stay with her, since the manager might charge more, when I came by I saw another woman living with her and her son in the one room. Kat did not lie. She told me her friend had nowhere to go and that they help each other out. She also told me that the manager would not mind. He had already propositioned them both to exchange sex for an extended stay in the room. They refused and had to be out at the end of the week.

My two assistants and I made calls all week to find Kat a place to live temporarily. When we started, I had no doubt that with our combined contacts for service providers, professional credentials, and technological resources (we had a phone and a computer), we would find something in a week. We were surprised when we had nowhere to send Kat by the day before she had to leave the motel. Most of the places we called did not return our calls, even though we each left a phone number on the voice mail recordings. When we did get a real person instead of voice mail, we were told that they did not have room or that Kat did not fit their criteria for acceptance. The three of us called more than twenty services, including domestic violence shelters, family shelters, women's homes, temporary housing, emergency services, and churches.

We documented all our calls for the study. The evidence we collected that week supported what the women had told us: "They never call back." If a person answered the phone, it was typically a low-level staffer or volunteer who did not have real answers but merely read a long list of exclusion criteria. The reasons that excluded Kat included no photo ID, she had to pass a criminal background check, and her son, now fifteen, was too old. I also was worried about the drug testing that every shelter performed at intake, since I knew Kat smoked marijuana and might have taken a few prescription pills recently that were not prescribed to her. She had been suffering from terrible tooth pain for weeks, and I had driven her to a dental service that claimed to provide free and reduced services for the poor. In fact, the service had a base fee, that I offered to pay, but Kat said no, she would get over it. I suspected she had someone with pain pills to help her "get over it."

The day before Kat had to leave the motel, I gathered my team in my office to begin a phone-calling marathon, starting with a particular well-funded nonprofit whose Web site guaranteed help for the homeless. Every time we reached a real person on the line, we were told to call another number. The number we were given was either not working or went straight to voice mail. After hours of calling, I returned to the first person with whom I had spoken. I learned she was a volunteer who did not have answers to my questions, since they were not on her list of responses. I asked to speak to a supervisor, suggesting that my next call would be to report them. I was put on hold and cut off three times while waiting but called back repeatedly. Finally, a self-identified director came to the phone to tell me the nonprofit was out of money and was not taking any names for their waiting list until next year. I suggested they update their Web site to reflect this change.

Knowing that a personal connection would help obtain a bed in a shelter, I called friends and colleagues to see if they knew anyone who worked in nonprofit homeless shelters. A colleague who organized conferences and workshops on homelessness forwarded my request to a person she described as a "mover and a shaker" in the area. This person sent me a list of homeless shelters in the city. I emailed back explaining that the homeless woman lived in the suburbs and did not have transportation to the city. I asked if she had any contacts in the suburbs for shelters and if she knew where homeless people could obtain a photo ID. Keeping an ID was one of the major difficulties faced by the homeless, and I thought a community leader known as an advocate for the homeless would surely have information about how to obtain one. She sent a name and phone number for a homeless shelter, another number for the ID, and directed me to the resource list we were already using. I tried the numbers, with disappointing results, and sent the following letter in reply to the "mover and shaker" for the homeless:

> Dear Madame:
> Just so you know, the first number you sent is disconnected. We already tried the resource list numbers you sent, since these are the same contacts found on the *Homelessness Resource List* widely used by people who serve the homeless in this area, as you must know. Moreover, the people we talked with at the final number you sent for obtaining an ID told us they do not help obtain an ID. I appreciate your referrals, but I just wanted to point out that the referral system is not working for us. It also does not work well for the homeless it was meant to help.

I did not blame this person or my colleague for not being aware of the faulty resource lists they distributed, which I am sure they thought were helpful. I used to give these same resource numbers out to others, and I never would have known how ineffective they were since no one came back to tell me they did not work. Until we incorporated a mechanism to document the usefulness of this list into a longitudinal study, we did not know that virtually every name and number on the list was closed to the most vulnerable and needy for one reason or another. We did not know because, contrary to popular opinion, the poor do not complain; they typically suffer in silence.

On the very last day, when Kat and her son had to leave the motel, I spoke with a personal friend who I knew donated money to a women's shelter. She told me to call the director and mention her name. The director told me to call the shelter and tell the staff they should give Kat a bed. I thought we had found something. When I called the shelter staff contact, a person I had already talked to a few days prior, she said that because Kat's son was too old, they were not allowed to take him.

"What do you expect her to do?" I asked in frustration. "Leave her son on the street while she comes to your shelter?"

"I suggest she call DFCS," the woman answered without a trace of shame in her voice. She knew what DFCS meant—foster care. I knew Kat would not do that.

At the very last hour, after Kat had already left the motel, I found a shelter for women and children to which I was referred by a friend. I had spent more then twelve hours on the phone. It was already evening. This shelter told me she could not come that night because intake only occurred in the morning hours. She could come tomorrow with certain stipulations:

1. She had to pass a drug and alcohol test.
2. She may never leave her son alone for a minute in the house.
3. Her son must wait outside for her when he came back from school until she arrived.
4. She must find at least part-time or temporary work within a week.
5. She had to have a full-time job within a month to stay there.

I told Kat about the shelter, located in another suburban town; she was not as familiar with it but knew where it was. Kat agreed to the rules. She stayed in the trailer park with a friend that night, ready to go to the women's shelter in the morning. The next day I got a call from her. She said she had gotten a ride to the shelter and saw it was surrounded by crack dealers on every corner. She could not expose her son to that environment, especially given the rule that he had to wait outside for her. She was very sorry and thanked me for my help. My assistant visited the shelter and confirmed Kat's observation of crack dealers. Kat continued to stay with friends in the trailer park until another man took her in.

In choosing the title for this section, I was reminded of the similarities and differences between the inner-city environment for marginalized males and the suburban environment for marginalized women. In the mid-1990s, Philippe Bourgois wrote a groundbreaking ethnographic study of urban social marginalization in East Harlem in which the male street-level crack dealers were "searching for respect." Women who used methamphetamine were the marginalized population in my suburban study. Instead of searching for respect, Kat, a proud and resourceful woman when I first met her, swallowed her pride when she was reduced to searching for shelter for herself and her son. The image of her turning her face while sitting in the backseat of my car so I would not see the tears swelling in her eyes portrayed the symbolic violence of a merciless society on a humiliated suburban mother. Much like the East Harlem protagonists, Kat "internalized her rage and desperation"; as was true for her urban counterparts. Bourgois wrote of his study protagonists that "the painful and prolonged self-destruction of Primo, Caesar, Candy, and her children is cruel and unnecessary" (2003, 327). "Kat" could have been substituted for "Candy" and the meaning of the sentence not changed.

Bourgois posited that "the inner city represents the United States' greatest domestic failing, hanging like a Damocles sword over the larger society" (ibid., 326). I posit that the sword of Damocles came dangerously close to falling during the Great Recession that began in 2008, and it is the blighted suburbs that will represent our greatest failure to motherhood.

After six months of hearing the women tell us they never found any help from services on the resource list, we decided to call every resource number on the list and identify which were useful and if they were not useful, why not. Since we were working directly with the women in our field, we knew their concerns. For example, the suburban poor expressed a deep mistrust of DFCS, and the stories they told seemed to corroborate their belief that if they reported their homelessness or issues with drug use to any government agency, their children would be removed by DFCS, and they would have no support in trying to regain custody. The case of Dot, introduced in a previous chapter, illustrated how difficult it was for her to merely understand what was required by DFCS let alone try to achieve it without help.

Women who had been in foster care as children told us numerous stories of how they had been abused or mistreated. Parents who had children in foster care were visibly devastated and often cried as they recounted their concerns. Nan, whose children were divided between foster care homes and a camp facility, said her son liked the camp and was involved in activities, but her daughter was having trouble and had already run away a few times to try to come home. Each time she was picked up and sent back to foster care. The last time she ran away she did not come home, and she was now missing. The women had all heard horror stories about DFCS and foster care, and their worst fear was having DFCS get involved.

We coded the resource list based on our findings. Our legend included the following codes:

R = referral service only

RO = referred out to a nonhelpful resource

WL = waiting list

$ = need money

T = need transportation

NI = need insurance (Medicaid)

L = legal risk (DFCS-related)

ID = need ID

M = men only

W = women only

NK = no kids

NOB = no older boys

NWN = nonworking number

NH = not helpful

VO = voice mail only

GR = geographic restriction (located in the city)

LM = left message

LM/NR = left message that was not returned

We eliminated the resources we found not useful at all for the women in our study, which were all those coded with RO, $, M, NWN, NH, and LM/NR. The remaining resource contact numbers were provided to the women with the various exclusion criteria inserted and fully explained, so they could decide if the resource was worth calling. At the end of the two-year study, we were left with a much reduced resource list—about one-eighth of the original list. First to come off our list was the Angel Street Ministry, the home for troubled young pregnant women.

ANGEL STREET MINISTRY

Angel Street Ministry was discussed briefly in chapter 7 by Bev, the woman diagnosed with bipolar disorder and whose story included multiple relapses. However, I first heard of the Angel Street Ministry (pseudonym) from Emma, a woman from the youth culture. She described the home she went to when she thought she was pregnant:

> She was supposedly this very Christian lady and she believed in the Bible and how precious Jesus Christ was, but did not lead the life of Jesus at all whatsoever. It was just one big scam. I found out the reason why she wanted me to come to her place was because she thought I was pregnant and that's how she lured her prey in. You know, she gets women who are battered, who are on drugs, who have no place to go, who have been kicked out of their home because they're on crack and they're pregnant. They don't know where they're going to go, much less what they're going to do with the baby that they're carrying. So she takes them in, she gets their hair done, their nails done. She makes them get up at six o'clock in the morning to clean chickens and mow the lawn by hand, and do Bible study at six a.m. every day.
>
> So all the battered women that come in, all the children that they bring in—that's how all the money comes in from the state. So you're only allowed to stay there if you're either pregnant or have children, you know, that you needed harboring; you needed help. You know what I'm saying? So she would get these mothers who were battered

and love them, who were on drugs most of the time, and she would collect money from the government. She would collect money from all these churches, all these donations. . . . My friend was one of the ones that, you know, was pretty much conned into giving her baby up for adoption because this lady brainwashed her into thinking she could do no good for herself to the point where she did give this baby up for adoption.

Thank God I wasn't pregnant. Once she found out I wasn't pregnant she tried to get me to do things that I didn't want to do . . . doing things for her and her organization that I didn't want to do, like intakes. Like I had to help con ladies into wanting to stay there, you know. I had to tell them this place was awesome. I'd be responsible for doing their first administrative paper work when they first would come in there, and tell them how awesome this place was and how she had changed my life. And it was a bunch of crock.

After a few more young women mentioned this place, I decided to investigate it. Already influenced by stories of the women I interviewed, I thought I would be too subjective to conduct research on the woman who ran the home. I sent a research assistant with a colleague from my department to inquire about the services and program. They were honest about our research study, since we were collecting information for the resource list and the Angel Street Ministry was on the list. Following are some of the notes from their report:

We were greeted at the door by the [owner/director], Cathy [pseudonym]. She stated that the ministry started in 1973. She said there are roughly twenty-five to thirty people in the up-to-eighteen-month program. When asked where she gets the participants, Cathy said, "The police department brings them," and from schools and hospitals. When asked if they work with the courts, Cathy responded, "Yes, and when they're court ordered they're easier to work with, they gotta get real or go back to jail." Cathy continued to say that their ministry provides an "opportunity to start over and live a good life." She said there had been instances where she had to call to get them "picked back up, because they were not going to get with the program." Cathy said the judge may sentence them, or a parent of a young woman may suggest the place to her, or the "PO [probation officer] makes the choice and then suggests it to the judge."

Cathy said participants are not allowed to smoke and are subjected to random drug testing. If they need detox they are sent to the local hospital detox unit. When asked what type of services they had, Cathy responded that they assess for anxiety or depression, and provide one-on-one parenting skills, Celebrate Recovery [a drug recovery program], and life skills. When pressed about police bringing women in, Cathy said that "officers may find them wandering on the corner, maybe with a sign 'will work for food,'" and will take them to Angel Street. Cathy said the officer will "run a background check on them," as a requirement for admittance.

When asked about the mothers' care of their babies, Cathy said, "If you're gonna stay here, you have to take care of your baby, if you can't, we'll have to find care whether at [a nearby Christian home for children], or 'adopt the child,' or find a family member." When asked at what point she decides or suggests the girls adopt out or turn over custody of their children, Cathy responded, "It's an individual thing, each person is different. We have good volunteers and mentors come in and work with them." Cathy gave a few examples of babies and small children who were adopted recently by prominent members of the community.

Cathy mentioned the girls must get a job and go to work. Asked if the girls stay there totally free, Cathy said, "No, they pay fifty dollars a week. They have a banker on board who works with them to help them get checking accounts at the local bank." Some of the donors were businessmen and church leaders in the community. Megachurch pastors, local politicians, and other local and prominent names were mentioned as being on the board of directors.

The drug recovery program at Angel Street Ministry appeared to be a recent innovation, since the young women we interviewed told us there was no drug treatment program or even twelve-step fellowship when they were there—just Bible lessons. None of the women we interviewed who had lived there mentioned being brought by the police or seeing police officers come to the home, although I did not ask about this specifically in the interview. We could not confirm with the local police department if officers actually "dropped off" young girls at the Angel Street Ministry.

The fact that so many prominent community leaders were on the board brought respectability to the ministry. Moreover, having a clean, safe place to stay was preferable to being on the street or exploited by men, especially for women who were homeless and pregnant. However, the lack of autonomy and the consistently negative reports we heard from the women who had stayed there were problematic. Angel Street Ministry had been involved in controversy in the past. My colleague found an old newspaper article that mentioned the Angel Street Ministry in connection with a church pastor accused of molesting little girls. Apparently he was a strong supporter of Cathy and her ministry. He and his wife "took in" some of the children from the ministry. He was arrested on charges of child abuse. We crossed the home off our resource list, but it was still on the list distributed by nonprofit organizations (NPOs) in the area.

IDENTIFICATION CARDS AND HOMELESSNESS

Not having government-issued identification—photo ID—emerged as one of the most frequent barriers to receiving any aid from government social services or nonprofits. For example, the largest NPO for the homeless and needy in the area, a conglomeration of services under one director and supported by donations from local churches as well as government grants, had ID restrictions for using the shelter and most other services. Only one daily hot meal was allowed without an ID, and homeless people formed a long line at noon to receive that hot meal. In the evening the line started hours before the door opened for the shelter, and anyone without an ID was turned away. The facility also had a clothes closet (the clothes equivalent of a free food pantry) staffed by volunteers, typically young people working off court-mandated community service hours. A brand-new warehouse distributed food for the needy families. All these services except the one hot meal at noon required a valid government-issued photo ID. Unfortunately, a photo ID was one of the hardest possessions for the homeless to keep, largely because of theft. A conversation during a focus group revealed the difficulty women had obtaining an ID once it was lost or stolen:

You still don't have an ID?
I haven't even had a chance to—I just got my birth certificate. Oh my god,
   I had been shooting for a birth certificate for three months, actually
   longer than that, cause my boss started shooting for it when I was in
   prison, I finally got one a little over a week ago. I was born in [another
   state]. First when you order out-of-state it's forty-five dollars. It cost
   more to have it shipped than it does for the actual birth certificate. Birth
   certificate wasn't but eighteen dollars itself.
What kind of documentation did you need to get your birth certificate?
An Act of Congress [laughter], and my mother, and a old prison ID. They
   didn't even want to accept that. My state is not having an old prison
   ID. Now if it had been the new one that I lost, it would have been a
   different story. It's a release ID
You need two documents to get your ID, so the prison ID would be one?
No, the state is not hearing no prison release ID. They're not hearing it. They
   want this, this, and this, and that's that. I got my [last] birth certificate
   just in time for my boss 'cause he had it in his safe. Four days ago somebody broke into the office and stole the safe . . . so matter of fact I got

the birth certificate and three days later the safe was stolen. So, I still don't have an ID. It was more aggravating 'cause they give you a runaround. They want you to have two forms of ID. Okay, I don't have an ID. They don't want to accept the ID that I have, you know. I have a social security card. If it wouldn't have been for the prison I wouldn't have got a social security card, 'cause to get a social security card, you gotta have a birth certificate, and to get a birth certificate you got to have a social security card.

So what has not having an ID blocked you from doing?

Jobs, house. Not having a birth certificate and a social security card can stop you from having an ID, and the ID can stop you from having jobs and everything else. The birth certificate and the social security card is your . . . if you don't have those two together, you don't have nothing.

How many times during that three-month process did you feel like using drugs?

Several times, because I got so frustrated because they were sending me around in circles to where I go from point A to point B, and not having a car . . . you know, I was going back and forth, and I never could go to point C.

Unfortunately, this was not a scene from a 1920s Kafkaesque society. This was the reality of the poor attempting to navigate bureaucracy in the twenty-first-century United States. And without an ID, these women did not have access to many of the services ostentatiously for the poor in the suburbs.

SYRINGES AND COMMUNICABLE DISEASES

The difficulty of obtaining clean syringes has been discussed in previous chapters. I was surprised, however, at the primary need for access expressed during a focus group with suburban youth:

What is most needed in terms of services for drug users in the area you live?

LEA: Drug users? I used to get really mad that like it was so hard to get some clean rigs [syringes] because I'm not even fucking kidding, I always got turned down at CVS [a pharmacy chain].

MAY: I remember when I was a kid, well not too young, probably ten or twelve years old, I remember hearing it on TV and stuff—this is when I was still in [another sate]. They had to give them away, the clinics and stuff, to IV users. They used to just give them syringes.

In the city they do that.

LEA: Well, see I never had a problem in [Big City]. I've gotten [them] one time in [Big City] at the CVS with no problem. They hand it to you in a brown paper bag. But in the suburbs . . . like at the CVS, I remember having some friends that would go before I started trying myself, and they would ask them for their diabetic cards, and I don't even know if they have those for real.

What if you never got your needles? What did you do?

LEA: We would run into them one way or another, but I would like getting them myself because then—this is the fucked up part about it, I would not give them away for free to my friends, I would charge them.

But did you ever use a dirty needle or a used needle?

LEA: Yes, I shared with my boyfriend all the time because we did not have a clean needle, we would—

MAY: Bleach it out?

LEA: Yeah, push the plunger with bleach, but I wouldn't do that with him because we shared shit all the time.

Did you share with other people besides him?

LEA: No I never did, but I know that, this shit used to piss me off really bad when we would be in a group somewhere. We'd be at somebody's house, and I only like to shoot up with him. I don't like to shoot up with other people out when I'm walking around doing shit, but he did. And if he could not find a needle, he would get one of his home boys' needles and rinse it out with bleach, and I don't trust that.

This discussion illustrated the need for a syringe exchange program (SEP) in suburban areas, especially for the young people who were less aware of where and how to obtain syringes, more reliant on their peer group, and rarely in the city where a SEP existed for injecting drug users. One of the reasons the SEP was allowed in the city was because they had shown local law enforcement and public health workers they could effectively dispose of dirty needles, which are a public health danger.

Safe syringe disposal was the topic of another focus group discussion with women who lived in a suburban enclave of poverty. I asked how they think syringes are disposed of in their community:

AVA: Needles would be pouring out of my septic tank. That girl that you had talked to previously and her boyfriend, flushing needles down my septic—I can get kicked out for that. My landlord come around and see we've got syringes pouring out of my septic tank.

JOY: Tell them to bend the needle, you put the cap back on, put it in like a Pepsi or Coke can and crush the can.

AVA: If anything bury the damn thing in the yard.

JOY: No, don't bury it in the yard cause some child might step on it barefooted or something.

Infectious diseases, hepatitis C (HCV), were a primary concern among the suburban injecting networks. I tried to find out what one reticent young woman was doing now that she knew she had contracted HCV:

Do you ever go to a support group?
Mm–mm [no].
Would you like to go to a support group?
Yeah.
Are you getting any care yet?
No.
So how long has it been now that you've had this?
About three years.
And how many times have you seen a doctor?
None. I don't have the money to go.
Why aren't you on Medicaid?
Because I can't—I applied for it and I can't get it. I don't know. Um, they didn't really give me a reason.
When you went to the hospital, the emergency room, and told them you have hepatitis C, what did they tell you?
To go get social security [SSI]. And I went and tried to do that and I got denied.

Ethical standards dictate that medical treatment based on benefit assessments should be the same for drug users as they are for non–drug-using patients. For example, the Centers for Disease Control and Prevention (2006) recommends that injection drug users (IDUs), a high-risk population, should be tested for HCV and HIV annually, vaccinated for hepatitis B (HBV) and hepatitis A virus (HAV), and referred for substance abuse treatment. The reality of the situation is that the majority of drug users who are uninsured do not have access to testing, vaccinations, or treatment unless they are incarcerated. After incarceration, medical and substance abuse treatment is typically terminated. This results in an unknown number of IDUs who do not know their infectious disease status or who know their status but do not have access to appropriate treatment. Public health practitioners and social workers often address this lack of knowledge by offering risk prevention education and focused interventions; however, these are not evenly distributed nationwide, and states vary in legislative endorsement and funding for such public health initiatives.

Infectious diseases such as HIV and HCV were not the only communicable health concerns among the poor. Ida, the homeless woman who stayed in a cheap motel, was scratching everywhere on her body by the end of her interview due to an undiagnosed disease or parasite. She was bleeding in some areas. A fungus had blackened her gnarled fingernails, and I wondered if it would get into her bloodstream as she scratched open sores. She cried intermittently throughout the interview. She had already been refused a bed at the homeless shelter, which would have given her access to more services through the continuum-of-care process. I gave her some resources to call for counseling, shelter, food, and treatment. I already knew that these resources would be nearly impossible to access, but if anyone needed them, Ida did. I never heard from Ida again, and I had no contact number except for the motel, which was permanently closed a few weeks later.

These vignettes illustrate merely a few of the many incidents that occurred during my ethnographic study among women living in the suburbs who were marginalized by the confluence of poverty and drug use. Based on the literature and my previous research, I anticipated these issues would be present, but I had no idea of the extent and depth of the difficulties and hardships the women faced in their daily lives just to survive. What this study shows beyond a shadow of doubt is that our social system, including social services and NPOs whose sole existence is to help poor people like Kat, Dee, Ida, and others, is broken. Some are sham services; some are scams. Others may be overburdened and underfunded, but service providers often appeared unsympathetic, or at best misguided. When even the homeless directors look the other way, we know we are in trouble. I am not the first to speak out about this issue (Allard and Roth 2010; Eliason 2006; Felland, Laeur, and Cunningham 2009). However, the recession of 2008 exacerbated the problem, and by 2011 the much anticipated "hope and change" in political power had not yet altered the structural issues that were the root of the problem—a lack of consistent health care for the poor and the criminalization of people who take drugs to self-medicate but do no harm to others. Several grassroots and government-supported programs do provide feasible, tested solutions.

Policy Implications

The issues revealed in this book on the reality of the daily lives of suburban women who use methamphetamine add to what others have exposed in the current "institutional quagmire of state-mandated social agencies" (Bourgois 2003, 243). This quagmire is made no less murky by the siphoning of funds by ineffective NPOs. In this section, I explore how policy change and new initiatives might provide the opportunity to stem the increasing problems associated with a criminalized drug user population. I use reflexive insight drawn from my own personal and professional experiences with agencies, bureaucracies, and social services, supported by the women's life experiences. Rejecting the crime-control model driving policy today, I join the call for harm reduction, decriminalization, and a focus on social recovery for problem drug use—a more humane policy and more pervasive social justice.

Drug policy in the United States is poised for change. Policy change has already occurred in many countries, as the focus on criminalization of drug users produced unintended consequences, such as the rapid spread of HIV and intergenerational poverty in families. Such change is usually slow, and the rising tide of pleas from the public for a shift favoring treatment over incarceration is yet to be broadly heard and honored. My voice and the voices of the women in this book add to the mounting demand from diverse corners of the political spectrum for ending the war on drugs, which is a war on our communities and the families living within them. Ending the war on drugs will not address all problems identified in this book, but it will be a giant step toward effective and more humane policy. Others have voiced the theoretical support for why policy change is needed (Bourgois 1999, 2003; Reinarman and Levine 2001; Singer 2006; Sterk 1999). In an effort to offer concrete and feasible solutions, I propose six other workable initiatives that underscore an already well-formulated blueprint for implementing drug policy change: harm reduction; social recovery; treatment on demand; housing-first models; restorative and transformative justice; and female-initiated programs.

Harm Reduction

"Harm reduction" refers to the practical strategies aimed at reducing the harm caused by drug use. There are no directives in terms of a global movement (see www.ihra.net) on how to practice harm reduction, but common principles include the acceptance that drug use is a complex issue with a wide range of behaviors, not all of which are problematic. Harm reduction emphasizes quality of life for the individual and the community. With a strong adherence to human rights tenets, harm-reduction strategies strive to achieve a nonjudgmental delivery of services to those who need them. Acknowledging the power differentials inherent in race, class, gender, age, and economic realities, a harm-reduction approach is sensitive to individual vulnerabilities. While respecting the rights of drug users, the approach does not minimize the real harms associated with drug-use behaviors.

Harm reduction, in many people's minds, has become synonymous with SEPs, although the services of harm-reduction programs usually are much broader. The SEPs receive more attention since the goal is reduction of infectious diseases that can spread throughout the community. Harm-reduction programs tend to receive more government aid in other countries than in the United States, although different states in the United States vary in their support and presence of harm-reduction services available in underserved communities. While the core of the program is the SEP, a harm-reduction center also provides education and risk-reduction programs as well as prevention, diagnoses, and access to treatment of substance use,

HIV/AIDS, STIs, hepatitis, and other communicable diseases. As shown in the stories told by the women in this study, there is a need for access to clean syringes in the suburbs, as well as safe disposal of used syringes. Moreover, suburban youths need risk-reduction education and testing for infectious diseases.

The barrier to these services for the suburban poor is lack of transportation. Mobile units have been the most successful response to such barriers (O'Connor et al. 1998). Until more centers can be implemented in communities across the nation, the use of mobile medical units operating from established harm-reduction centers and sent to surrounding suburban and rural areas is a feasible solution. It is also evidence-based and cost-effective. Mobile harm-reduction units have been shown to be successful in reducing the spread of infectious diseases and preventing deaths around the world, but they have been slow to be incorporated for harm-reduction purposes in the United States (Mbopi-Kéou et al. 2007).

The social significance of a harm-reduction approach to drug-use problems is thoroughly appreciated by most academics and professionals in the medical field. Based on their review of studies, the authors of the Global Commission on Drug Policy Report (2011) concluded: "Countries that implemented harm reduction and public health strategies early have experienced consistently low rates of HIV transmission among people who inject drugs. Similarly, countries that responded to increasing HIV prevalence among drug users by introducing harm-reduction programs have been successful in containing and reversing the further spread of HIV. On the other hand, many countries that have relied on repression and deterrence as a response to increasing rates of drug-related HIV transmission are experiencing the highest rates of HIV among drug using populations" (6). Beyond public health concerns, harm-reduction strategies ensure the social inclusion and participation of the most marginalized citizens by providing access to services that improve their quality of life. Without focused funding, the provision of harm-reduction services will remain virtually stagnant, yet only two years after the ban on federal funding for harm reduction was lifted, Congress reinstated it in 2011.

Social Recovery

"Social capital" refers to "the social norms and networks that enhance people's ability to collaborate on common endeavors" (Putnam 2000, 35). The concept is used to explain the unequal distribution of social resources available to individuals within their communities and across social networks that act as a barrier to obtaining desired goals (Bourdieu 1984; Coleman 1990; Portes 1998). Sociologists Richard Granfield and William Cloud (2001), noting a direct correlation between social capital and recovery, coined the term "recovery capital," defined as the combined physical resources, skills, knowledge, and social capital available to a recovering person. While recovery capital is used to predict cessation of drug use and sustained recovery, it focuses again on the individual abuser and less on the social aspects of use (Laudet 2008).

I use the term "social recovery" to direct attention to the social environment and *problematic* drug use that impacts and is impacted by the user's social environment (Boeri, Lamonica, and Harbry 2011). "Social recovery" refers to acquiring the skills, resources, and networks needed to enhance one's ability to live in society without problematic alcohol or drug use. The key is to focus recovery on the social aspects first. The stories of the women indicate that, for many, efforts directed on their social lives resulted in less problematic drug use and eventual cessation. For example, Mercedes, who was impregnated by her father, a runaway foster care child, raped by gangs, a drug injector and drug dealer, and without a high school education, by any statistical prediction should have been found dead in an alley. Instead, supported by the social safety net thrown by a caring methadone director, she had the time to enroll in a technical school and by age thirty-five be fully employed, living with her daughter, and drug free. The methadone counselor helped her social recovery, and she was able to resist using drugs by having access to the only legal substitute drugs available to her—methadone. A second example is Flo, who also experienced terrible abuse as a child at the hands of a violent father, was involved in gangs and crime, an ex-felon drug addict who might have remained in and out of prison for most of her life. Instead, while she lived at the house of Buddy, who allowed women to stay in his home while they worked for his business, she was given respite from living on the street and her social environment changed. She became involved in a church where she felt she belonged, advocated for the homeless, became engaged to a dedicated fellow church member, and was drug free by her last interview.

In contrast to recovery conceptualized as a total cessation of all drug use, conceptualizing recovery in terms of social recovery facilitates the use of targeted and personalized strategies to reduce problematic use. The stories of the women show that abstinence typically follows a reduction of use when accompanied by improved social context; however, social recovery is conceptually the cessation of problematic use that may or may not result in total abstinence from all substances. As shown, some of the women did not seek total abstinence but instead desired controlled use, or that "fine line" spoken of by Mia. If people wavering between drug use and sobriety were given access to more tools for social recovery, it could relieve the public burden of institutionalized treatment centers. It would also take the focus off the individual and helps to put the emphasis back on the social structure that constrains and facilitates recovery from problematic drug use. Social recovery draws on social capital theory. Incorporating social theory into public health issues is an acknowledgment that the two are inseparable (Potvin et al. 2005). A refocusing on the social practices that constitute the lived experience of drug users and reveal the pervasive aspects of social influences on their drug-use trajectory is needed. While I emphasize the social aspects of drug use in this book, I do not repudiate the scientifically supported biological mechanisms that may lead to dependence, and the need for medical treatment in those cases where a medical disease or psychiatric disorder can be identified. However, I suggest that if we start with the social aspects, we can more easily identify individuals whose problems are not social but instead psychological or biological (a status often called addiction). The influences on drug use can be conceptualized as concentric circles, as shown in figure 8.1, representing layers of genetic, biochemical, psychological, and social causes (Boeri and Tyndall 2012).

The inner circle in figure 8.1 represents those genetic influences that may predispose drug users to become dependent on a drug. The layer surrounding the inner circle represents physiological and chemical causes of drug addiction. These changes that have been found to occur in the brains of long-term drug users can influence continued dysfunctional drug behavior (Dole 1980). The next layer in the concentric circle represents psychological factors, such as early childhood trauma and mental disorders, that have been shown to influence the initiation into and continued use of both licit and illicit drugs (Miller 1995). The outer ring in figure 8.1 represents social influences. The illustration acknowledges the influence of all the factors; however, I suggest that starting at the outer ring on the social aspects allows us to focus more medical attention on those influences from the inner rings.

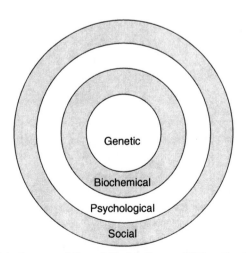

Genetic

Biochemical

Psychological

Social

8.1. Integrated Causal Model. Source: Miriam Boeri.

The problems stemming from social issues can be better addressed through social initiatives rather than medical ones. For example, Ada, at only twenty-one, offered social insights based on her experience as a child growing up in a suburban enclave of poverty:

> Young people just need more things in schools and stuff that they can do to get them away from the drug crowds. Like people don't need to be, like in high schools, cliques, and stuff. And less of a money issue, like sports and things should be cheaper. Things should be like, you know, the government should pay it. The government should pay for more things in the schools rather than the kids have to pay it themselves. Because it all starts with a lot of poor kids doing drugs in schools. That's the main group of kids that start doing drugs, are the poor ones and the ones that don't fit in.

Danielle, a woman who typically controlled her use, identified a suburban town she moved to briefly where almost everyone used methamphetamine, and others confirmed her assessment. Danielle proposed that there was nothing to do there, which is why users in this town could not control their use:

> I moved to [Suburban Town] and that seems to be all anybody ever does. I never met people like I have in that place anywhere in my entire life, and I've lived in like three or four different states. . . . It's just horrible. I've never seen anything like it. And people say [methamphetamine] is everywhere. And yeah, it might be everywhere but it's not as concentrated as it is in [Suburban Town]. It's just, there's nothing for them to do there. There's no YMCA. There's nothing to break the cycle. I mean all they do is steal and do drugs. That's all there is for anybody to do up there. I mean the cycle really needs to be broken. . . . It needs like a YMCA, like baseball teams or something extracurricular, but like structure. They need structure. They need, they need to be shown that there's other things to do because they really don't know.

Here, Danielle expresses the need for a social response to a raging methamphetamine problem in one small suburban town whose young people had nothing to do. This town was identified by many other respondents in our study as the capital of methamphetamine users. The majority of those we interviewed from this town were unemployed and lived in enclaves of poverty. The youths were most affected by the suburban poor social environment, and as Danielle pointed out, they had nothing to do. With no public transportation, they relied on older adults with cars to take them to any social event. The main social events they participated in appeared to be using methamphetamine and pain pills.

Social activities can fill the void that drug use often fills. For example, Tiffany, the Latina woman introduced earlier, was helped by her boyfriend to stop using methamphetamine. He replaced drug use in her life with social activities that kept her interest and eventually became ritualized:

> He's just a completely positive character. He would just calm me down a lot of times. I don't know. And he had like more of a life. Instead of like waking up every day like "how am I going to get high today," his was, "let's go do this, let's go do that," you know. It was more of like activity was a way of, you know, trying not to think about it. Like he was taking me everywhere. We'd go to the beach. We'd go to the lake.

While social recovery helps us to focus on the primary influences of drug use in contemporary society, we cannot disregard the fact that some drug users have problems that extend beyond the social. Some require structured treatment other than social recovery. The two do not need to be mutually exclusive solutions to a social problem. Nor does treatment need to focus on one aspect (mental health issues) at the expense of the other (social isolation). Instead of emphasizing consumption of drugs and other individual behaviors referred to as a choice or agency—as if the stigmatized, downtrodden, ex-felons have much agency left to call on—we can first focus on the social environment to identify what could be done to ameliorate their recovery in this area. Social recovery extends recovery capital to include the areas of life that the women are most affected by in their quest for reintegration into mainstream social life. If we first focus on social recovery, the number of people needing treatment will be reduced, and professional treatment providers can focus their efforts on the targeted few.

Treatment on Demand

The disease model of substance addiction appears to be one effective means of replacing punitive approaches to drug abuse with therapeutic approaches, although it remains highly controversial (Reinarman 2005; Weinberg 2000). Nevertheless, the argument that addiction includes a disease component has prompted the recent trend in the criminal justice system to establish drug treatment courts, which allow those who are incarcerated with drug offenses access to specialized courts that mandate treatment instead of time behind bars (Hora, Schma, and Rosenthal 1999). As discussed previously, these treatment plans typically last for two years and have shown variable but primarily positive results. Moreover, because drug courts are operated locally, with diverse eligibility criteria, disciplinary structure, and treatment protocol, it is difficult to establish valid outcomes across drug court programs, and success is typically measured by reduction in recidivism rates, not by reduction in drug use (King and Pasquarella 2009). Drug courts are, however, the primary response to the swelling of the prison population by prisoners with drug-related crime. According to FBI reports, 83 percent of drug arrests are for possession of illegal drugs alone, and a drug offense is the most serious offense for over 50 percent of prisoners in federal prison (Justice Policy Institute 2009; West, Sabol, and Greenman 2010). From 1972 to 2007, the number of people incarcerated in the United States for drug offenses increased fivefold. For many participants, drug court is the best treatment attention they will ever receive; if they are suffering from a health problem, however, they should be treated by the medical system and not the criminal justice system.

Decriminalization of drugs is necessary to make it possible both to differentiate between those whose only crime is drug use and those whose criminal behaviors include drug use and to address the root issue more effectively. The increasing criminalization of drug users destroys their lives for years. According to the Office of National Drug Control Policy Web site, five million of the nearly seven million American adults under the supervision of the criminal justice system are supervised through probation or parole, and about two-thirds are substance users (Office of National Drug Control Policy 2012). The "reentry myth busters" provided on this federal agency Web site do not adequately portray the reality of reentry for the women I interviewed in this study. For example, the statement that "an arrest or conviction will NOT automatically bar individuals from employment" is deceiving. It might not be automatic but unemployment it is generally long-standing for ex-offenders, particularly those who have a drug offense. A felony conviction is usually a barrier to housing, employment, social services, and federal aid for education. As shown in the women's stories, strict regulation through probation and parole often result in permanent unemployment and increased recidivism. If humanitarian concerns do not provide the impetus to address this ongoing social injustice, the economic consequence of millions of unemployed and homeless ex-felons should scare the public and politicians into realizing the logic of decriminalization.

Housing First

Women who use methamphetamine, as shown in this study, tend to have what is called a dual diagnosis, which means they have a mental health problem and a substance abuse problem diagnosed as addiction. The effect of society's reaction to their drug use, which may be self-medication, results in increased use and suffering. Moreover, the health and social services created to help the poor instead hinder their access to needed care (Boeri, Tyndall, and Woodall 2011).

A new social control framework identified by postmodernist scholars explains the seeming inconsistency between goals and actions by contemporary social service bureaucracies (Beckett and Herbert 2008; Cohen 1985). According to this school of thought, those in power control through surveillance and repression. A postmodern view of society's social control mechanism reveals endless social workers, police officers, government bureaucrats, and even medical staff working to control, coerce, or repress populations into submission. Few involved are aware of the interconnectedness of these control systems, which when working on behalf of the state appear to be working for the good of society. The subjects of this control are the same people—social deviants, as defined and identified by the state.

The cross-institutional arrangement of control includes not only the traditional agents of control such as law enforcement, courts, and penal systems but also our assumed social safety nets of welfare agencies, child protection services, mental health services, and those whose stated purpose is to provide for the homeless and sick—although rather than provide for they serve the purpose of controlling. Katherine Beckett and Steve Herbert (2008) credit the theoretical origin of the new social control not only to Foucauldian thought but also to the political economy account of increased segregation that enforces the exclusion of the most vulnerable. This includes the banishment of the drug users and homeless from public urban spaces, the proliferation of gated communities in the suburbs and peripheries of cities, and the implementation of ordinances that support increased police surveillance on the poor. The mechanism used to control the vulnerable poor, who might unite in protest if not socially controlled, is through the formal institutions that were created to help them (safety, health care, social services) but instead act as "instruments of surveillance" and punitive bureaucracies (Wacquant 1998, 25). The expansion of these social control regulations includes greater control over probationers and parolees as well.

As shown in the stories told by the women and confirmed by my own attempts to access shelter, health care, and food for them, the increasing forms of surveillance and social control mechanisms over the poor create barriers to accessing these services, yet those directing these services often remain indifferent. For example, the directors of NPOs could not adequately explain to me the need for a government-issued photo ID, and issuing a temporary photo ID would not be considered. When the director of the one homeless shelter in the suburbs agreed with me that a temporary photo ID for the homeless he served might be a short-term solution, he said he did not have the staff to implement such a process. When I offered to provide photo ID equipment and an intern to facilitate the process, the director protested, "They [the homeless] will just lose it anyway within a few days."

The social control of the poor through restrictions to services was omnipresent among providers of social services and health care in the suburbs, but the affordable housing shortages caused by the recession and the concurrent increasing need for housing ensured that shelters of all types became even more restrictive. Recognizing the growing need to house the homeless with mental health issues and chemical dependencies, Sam Tsemberis, a psychiatrist and advocate for the dual-diagnosed, developed a housing program focused on providing housing first without restrictions or exclusionary criteria, such as the need to be drug and alcohol free, in order to be housed (1999). The model came to be known as *housing first*. Combining housing with supportive treatment when people desired it, his experimental model for housing the homeless with dual diagnosis had significantly better outcomes than those served by the dominant continuum-of-care model practiced by virtually all standard programs (Tsemberis 1999; Tsemberis and Stefancic 2007). For example, after a two-year experimental study in a suburban location, results showed that the housing-first participants were placed in permanent housing at higher rates than the traditional treatment-as-usual group, who had received the standard array of services and processes (Tsemberis and Stefancic 2007). Not surprisingly, the services providing the standard array were not pleased with this finding.

The controversial model eliminated the two most problematic requirements for what agencies called "housing readiness," which requires treatment compliance and sobriety, by giving immediate and autonomous housing to people who lived on the streets regardless of substance abuse status (Tsemberis 1999). Continued success in transitioning the homeless with dual diagnosis to permanent housing, as well as reducing mental health problems, injuries, and deaths, have gained this contemporary innovation for the homeless worldwide attention. The Substance Abuse and Mental Health Administration (SAMHSA) recognized housing first as a best evidence-based practice, and funds for training and replicating the model across the United States were made available (2010). The housing-first model has also been replicated in others countries, where modifications, such as peer-driven communal housing, have also been successful.

An autonomous, peer-run, or consumer-choice model for homelessness disrupts the new social control surveillance, and recognition for the model's success was hard won. The same resistance to innovative suggestions, restrictions to access, and creeping social control of the homeless that I encountered in my study were also encountered by Tsemberis and his colleagues when they started implementing the model twenty years ago. Moreover, while this highly acclaimed, evidence-based model is available in the northern United States, as well as in Canada, Japan, France, and other countries, it was not yet replicated in the state where the women in my study lived. Many of the women had dual diagnoses of mental health problems and drug addiction, but they rarely received even temporary housing, and the idea of being autonomous while receiving help was only a dream. For the homeless women who were affected daily by the lack of services available in their area, the reality was a tragic nightmare.

Restorative and Transformative Justice

Restorative justice is a movement challenging the criminal justice system to focus on the needs of all concerned in wrongdoing: the victims, the communities, and the offenders (Zehr 2002). Social justice advocate Howard Zehr writes, "If we expect them [offenders] to assume their responsibilities, to change their behavior, to become contributing members of our communities, their needs, says restorative justice, must be addressed as well" (ibid., 16). While restorative justice has empirical support of success, it typically is not practiced in the criminal justice system. Moreover, when applied, restorative justice programs typically address the needs of the victim only, and few, if any, are concerned about the needs of the offender.

A similar concept, known as transformative justice, describes a transformation process that takes restoration a step further (Morris 2000). A transformative interaction between the victim, the offender, and law enforcement facilitates the expression of feelings and their transformation into a shared quest for the "common good." Using a systems approach, a transformative process actively includes actors from the larger community in pursuit of identifying the root of the offense rather than the offense or offender alone.

Women who use methamphetamine essentially become perpetual offenders when they are incarcerated and then stigmatized as ex-felons and blocked from social reintegration. Their felony record precludes them from finding employment and benefiting from government programs (food stamps, housing vouchers, Medicaid) designed for the most marginalized; they cannot obtain financial aid for education, and they cannot pass a background check that will allow them a stable place to live. Left with no mainstream resources, they are isolated within their own communities; yet if the activities prevalent in the communities involve alcohol and drug use, they feel isolated *from* their community as well. Invariably, the women engage in self-defeating crime to survive. A restorative process aims to restore the offenders/victims to their place in the community.

While the socially conscious might agree that policy makers need to address the human suffering depicted in these pages, the fiscal realities of contemporary postmodern society demand better solutions for drug users than continued incarceration and the revolving door of treatment and drug use. Rather than banishment of the unwanted, "more meaningful alternatives to arrest and incarceration would include greater provision of low-income housing, universal health care coverage, and more effective social service and harm-reduction programs. Such strategies represent the hope for a better future for those in need, as well as a more inclusive and humane polity" (Beckett and Herbert 2008, 30). To achieve such a polity, transformative justice outlines a process that includes the participation and collaboration of all stakeholders, and dialogue and respect for all community members. Restorative justice adds to this process the insights of the most marginalized and vulnerable—in this case, the drug-using women.

Female-Initiated Programs

The more the women talked about their methamphetamine use within the context of their lives, the more "the inner conversations that make up thinking" in their minds emerged to reveal "their inner lives as well as their external lives" (Collins 2004, 99). Nowhere was this more evident than when they discussed their experiences of child molestation, rape, and domestic violence. Based on the revelations of their inner lives, it was clear that the community around them did not adequately acknowledge these issues where and when they occurred.

Rape occurred when they were young, before they used drugs, while they used drugs, after they used drugs, and when they were old. It was never their fault, but they were told otherwise. Although rape is always violent because it is forced (even if the woman is unconscious), law enforcement and most social service staff have internalized the idea that there are two kinds of rape and one is worse than the other: "simple rape," which does not officially involve physical violence, and "aggravated rape," which involves physical violence (Goode 2011). Allowing rape to officially be divided into a softer and harder defined rape essentially neutralizes the essence of rape and its effect on the minds of the public. The rapist who commits simple rape is typically never charged or if charged, rarely convicted.

It is this kind of social response to rape that makes the women's stories even more tragic, because the women internalized the idea that "simple rape" is not so bad. Few of these rapes were reported to the police. If a woman was brave enough to report it, she was not taken seriously. Some of women tended to trivialize the rape, as if it were normal—just one of those things that happens. Others spoke very little about it. Some cried years after the experience, still feeling the shame and pain.

Rape crisis centers distribute literature stating that regardless of the circumstance—whether you are drinking or using drugs, what you are wearing, or where you go at night—rape is not your fault. But this is not the reality women find in courts, among law enforcement, among medical staff, and among the politicians who promise to uphold the law. For example, one ER doctor told a young woman who was raped at a party that it was better if she did not get a blood test to see if she had been given a date-rape drug, because if any other drugs were found, it could be used against her. Remarkably, one of the cruelest and most insensitive remarks came from a female representative in the state senate, a lawyer, who said to a twenty-year-old female rape victim, "There are worse rape cases for the state to prosecute than yours." Yet because she ran on a women's rights platform, the local rape crisis center supported her and did nothing to address the inconsistency between what she said and what she did for women in real situations. The demeaning attitudes of people who have power and are responsible for defending women who were raped uphold the status quo. There is a reason the women I had interviewed remained silent about their own rape—they were not heard when they tried to speak.

Peer-run initiatives for rape, domestic violence, and child abuse organizations should be the goal. Rape centers and domestic violence homes need to be staffed by the women whose knowledge of rape and domestic violence is experiential, and who would never tell a rape victim that her rape was not as bad as another woman's rape. Listening to these women allows more appropriate and effective solutions to be proposed. According to SAMHSA (2010), "peer advocates offer deep understanding and empathy to the people they serve. They each know the system and have been there themselves. They know how to link people to Medicaid services, work with doctors, and find safe and affordable housing."

The women I interviewed often knew what was needed to address their problems effectively, and I heard a number of female-initiated solutions. For example, many women with children desired to be better educated so they could find employment that provided a living wage and heath insurance. One solution proposed was a computer center—perhaps located in local library—where online degree programs offered by colleges and universities could be accessed, and laptop computers could be borrowed to study and complete homework. Many traditional state universities and colleges now have fully online programs that women can take advantage of at home or at a local center. We know that the best predictor of children's educational attainment is that of their mothers, so funding college courses for mothers helps ensure a better life for the future generation as well. However, women with felony drug convictions are barred from government financial aid for higher education. For them to have access to most educational programs, the restrictions on Pell Grant funding regarding drug charges should be lifted. In order to implement this suggestion and many of the previous solutions proposed here, and to begin to address the problems associated with drug use, we need to end the war on drugs.

END THE WAR ON DRUGS

As I was writing this final chapter, the latest Global Commission on Drugs policy report (2011) was released. The commissioners who wrote the report included former heads of state such as the former presidents of Brazil,

Colombia, and Mexico, a former United States secretary of state, a former secretary of the German Ministry of Health, a former secretary general of the United Nations, a former chairman of the U.S. Federal Reserve, and many other esteemed experts in the field of drug policy, economic strategy, and global health. The policy recommendations in the report were congruent with the policy implications I presented in this chapter. The authors recommended policies based on public health and social justice, which complement my proposal for harm-reduction strategies and transformative-justice processes; their recommendations for the decriminalization of drugs and more, new, and better models for drug treatment corresponded to my call for social recovery, treatment on demand, peer-run homes, and female-initiated programs. Showing how a forty-year war on drugs has failed even to curtail drug supply and consumption and has instead led to the incarceration, destruction, and untimely deaths of countless of millions of people globally, the commission concluded with a mandate to "replace drug policies and strategies driven by ideology and political convenience with fiscally responsible policies and strategies grounded in science, health, security and human rights" (Global Commission on Drugs 2011, 3).

When I started this study I did not know that a global recession would occur within year. I suspected that I would find some impoverished women in the suburbs who used methamphetamine, but I was shocked by the extent of their poverty, the widespread effects of incarceration, and the lack of social and health care services for suburban poor families. With a newly elected president and a newly appointed "drug czar," I thought we would replace the criminalization of drug use with evidence-based programs for treatment, prevention, and harm reduction. Instead, by the end of the study, the already destitute conditions of drug-using networks had worsened, and the need for treatment and preventative care had increased. Meanwhile, drug laws and policies had not changed, despite all evidence showing that our current policy was misguided and had failed.

I end this book with hope for the future, praise for the innovative programs that already exist, and practical suggestions for how to extend the best evidence-based initiatives. The bright side is that innovative programs based on harm reduction, social justice, and respect for all humanity have been evolving despite the deep financial tear in the fabric of the economy and our politicians' steadfast refusal to support drug policy reform. Although not the only change needed, a change in drug policy that ends the war on drugs would facilitate the expansion of effective initiatives and programs, such as those presented in this chapter.

The women I interviewed began using methamphetamine for functional or recreational reasons, yet the criminalization of their use resulted in social isolation, and they eventually used to heal or forget. When I asked an older female ex-felon how women with felony convictions support themselves, her response depicted the depths of her despair: "By selling your soul to the devil." Many women in this study referred to methamphetamine as the devil: "That's the devil in methamphetamine, it's because it makes you happy, and you don't know why, and you don't really care." Another warned me: "This is the devil's dandruff. You're fighting something beyond." She was very close to the truth; however, it was not the metaphorical destroyer of life but the symbolic violence, structural inequalities, and segregating social stigmatization resulting from a criminal record that pushed these women into the abyss. The Global Commission on Drugs policy report ended with a warning and plea that I humbly but emphatically reiterate in closing: "Act urgently: the war on drugs has failed, and policies need to change now" (2011, 17).

Appendix A

Methodological Process

Data for this book were drawn from two sequential studies on methamphetamine use in the suburbs funded by the National Institute on Drug Abuse (NIDA), at the National Institutes of Health (NIH). The first study used a cross-sectional design; the second study was a longitudinal design that included the baseline component of the first study with the addition of follow-up interviews and focus groups.

The goal of the first study was to gain a better understanding of emerging trends among methamphetamine users in the suburbs, focusing on how users initiate, maintain, moderate, remit or resume use of methamphetamine over the life course. When preliminary analysis of the data revealed that the suburban setting increased risk factors for female drug users, I designed a second study to collect additional data to gain a more in-depth understanding of methamphetamine use by suburban women. The specific aims in this study were (1) to expand our exploration of the turning points in drug use trajectories among suburban women; (2) to provide a more comprehensive understanding of the risks and protective factors that impact the transmission of HIV, HCV, and other infectious diseases that may be specific to female methamphetamine users living in the suburbs; and (3) to assess HIV risk awareness, risk behaviors, health care utilization and accessibility over time for women in our sample.

I was the principal investigator (PI) on both studies; the second study included a coinvestigator, a nursing professor. A number of research assistants, drawn primarily from undergraduate programs in my university, were trained to help with data collection and analysis. My university's Institutional Review Board (IRB) approved the study methods, and NIDA provided a *certificate of confidentiality*, which protected study data and researchers from court subpoena.

A mixed-methods design was used to collect the data, with a focus on the qualitative component. Mixed-methods designs are relatively new, and norms for data collection and analysis are still in development (Ragin 2008). I employed what is called a concurrent mixed methods design (Teddlie and Yu 2007). Combining both qualitative and quantitative data collection and analysis offers several advantages to conducting research on hidden populations, including greater flexibility, creativity, validity, and reliability (Shaw 2005).

RECRUITMENT

Active and former (inactive) methamphetamine users were drawn from the suburban counties surrounding a large metropolitan area in southeastern United States through intensive ethnographic fieldwork. Beyond establishing a presence in the community, we used a combination of targeted, snowball, and theoretical sampling methods to find study participants (Glaser and Strauss 1967; Strauss and Corbin 1998; Watters and Biernacki 1989). The first study, conducted from 2007 to 2009, enrolled 50 active and 50 inactive users of methamphetamine. Of these 35 were female. The second study, conducted from 2009 to 2011, used the same recruitment methods and added 30 females to the sample of suburban methamphetamine users.

Active users were defined as having used methamphetamine at least one time in the past month. Inactive users were defined as having used methamphetamine for at least six consecutive months in the past but not using in the last month. To be eligible, participants had to be residing in the suburbs of the city at the time of use and be eighteen or older at the time of the interview.

To ensure a diverse sample, we employed various methods and targeted different social settings during our fieldwork. About one-third of the study participants were recruited through face-to-face contact while we were in the field, and about one-third saw our fliers or were given our research cards and called the study number. The others were recruited through snowball sampling, a method used to reach overlapping networks.

Fieldwork

Ethnographic research requires the researcher to spend hours in the field to become familiar with the settings and people (Bourgois 2003; Sterk-Elifson 1993). Since our study included a large area of twenty-eight counties, we often employed community consultants, also called outreach workers or key informants, who were people we met while in the field who lived in the community and could provide access to drug-using networks (Lambert, Ashery, and Needle 1995; Shaw 2005). Community consultants helped us by establishing trust through an introduction, or by referring a participant to the study. For example, a community consultant could bring us to insider user settings, where no one would have talked to us had we not been with the consultant (Becker 1953). They were paid a small fee for spending a few hours with us in the field or when they referred someone who qualified for participation in the study.

Fliers

We posted fliers in strategic public sites and distributed cards with the study information and contact phone number while we were engaged in community outreach. Flier designs varied but generally included the following information:

Female Methamphetamine Users Needed for a University Research Study

A sociology professor is seeking female participants for a health study to learn how methamphetamine affects the lives of people living in the suburbs.

PAID INTERVIEWS $30 Cash

ANONYMOUS

100% CONFIDENTIAL

NO NAMES ARE COLLECTED

For More Information Please Call Miriam [Study Phone #]

Fliers were typically small, about five inches by seven inches, and left in stacks in stores, gas stations, and other commercial areas, with permission. We also hung larger fliers around college campuses, on coffeehouse bulletin boards, and at public places.

Snowball Sampling

Snowball sampling, also called chain referral, involved asking participants and interested inquirers to refer another potential participant to the study. If the people they referred qualified and participated in the study, the person who referred them received a small cash referral compensation of ten dollars. We limited referrals to three or four per person and carefully screened those who were referred.

Screening

A screening process was used to ensure that participants pass the eligibility criteria to enroll in the study. Screening consisted of asking questions about age, drug use in the past thirty days, use of methamphetamine in the past six months, and the county where the potential participant resided. To establish validity regarding use of methamphetamine, more focused questions were asked, such as those relating to price, appearance, and effects of the drug. Legitimate questions regarding eligibility were interspersed with questions that would not disqualify a respondent, (number of children, number of years living in the area) so that those who referred people to the study could not guess the eligibility requirements and prep their referrals. No identifying materials, such as name and address, were collected at any time.

When we met potential participants for the study in the field or they contacted us through the study phone number, we discussed the study goals and time commitment, how the interview would be conducted, anonymity and confidentiality issues, and the monetary reimbursement for their participation. A consent form was read and agreed to before collecting any data. For the first study the consenting process was oral; for the second study, which included follow-up interviews, we collected a signed consent that was not linked to the study data. Data material was identified with a study number.

While the study design seems straightforward, the reality of conducting research on illegal and stigmatized behaviors, especially in the suburbs, has aspects that can only be learned by doing. Our fieldwork typically involved going out all day to find field sites, distribute fliers, and talk to people who might know anything about methamphetamine use in the area. In the evening and night we frequented bars, clubs, and twenty-four-hour diners. Unlike clinical research described in textbooks or portrayed on television, where participants show up at an office or are interrogated in an institutional setting, our ethnographic interviews started and often remained in the field. We might arrange to meet participants at a specified location (a library, fast food restaurant, bar, or park) and sometimes waited for hours; sometimes they would never arrive. The lives of drug users can be chaotic, and participants may change their minds about coming to the interview, not have transportation, or otherwise be detained. We usually met in public places first, until we became better acquainted, and then we might be invited to the participant's home. Other times we were invited to parties, typically in motel rooms, where we would meet more people who wanted to participate in the study.

We quickly developed trust with the participants we initially met face-to-face, but this was a little more difficult to do with those who called on the phone. Once we met, we usually convinced them we had no connection with the criminal justice system. Being funded by the NIH greatly helped, since the focus of the study was on health and not legal issues. Many participants had health problems or needed treatment and were glad to contribute to this research. In the second study, one of the aims was to help find resources for the women, which was a motivator to participate. However, many participants said they mainly wanted to participate to help others. For example, one woman made sure we wrote down the names of good lawyers she knew to give to other methamphetamine users we interviewed. Another women wanted me to write the name of the doctor who had helped her so "the world would know."

Data Collection

Beyond the extensive ethnographic field notes that provided the foundational data, three types of research instruments were used in the cross-sectional design: (1) a life history matrix; (2) a drug history matrix; and (3) an audio recorded open-ended in-depth interview.

Life History Matrix

I conducted the interviews in the first study with a research assistant in training, who later conducted some interviews on his own. We collected an overview of the participant's life history data using a life history matrix (see figure A.1), a research tool designed to focus the participant on retrospective life events. This process also helped to develop rapport with the participant and established an additional validating strategy (Bruckner and Mayer 1998). The life history matrix was completed with pencil by the interviewer asking questions while allowing the participant to visually follow along and offer suggestions. This part of the interview lasted about twenty to thirty minutes.

Drug History Matrix

The interviewer collected a complete drug history using pencil and paper on a matrix, which included information on first use of each drug, past six-months use, past thirty-day use, and routes of administration (see figure A.2). The drug history took about twenty to thirty minutes to complete. Information collected on the matrix informed the rest of the data collection and served as an additional validating tool.

In-Depth Interviews

In-depth interviewers were recorded using a small digital recording device. I informed the participant when I started the recording. Although we had prepared a semistructured in-depth interview guide, I typically employed these questions only when there was a lull in the interview. By the time I had collected the data on the matrices, most participants were very eager to share their stories.

The major themes in the interview included the context of drug use, time of use, interaction with others, social roles, and health issues. Transitions and turning points identified by the drug history and life history were examined, with reasons for initiating, continuing use, cessation, and relapse more fully explored. As is often the case in qualitative interviews, the interviews developed a path of their own directed by the unique experiences of each participant. The recorded interviews lasted about two hours and participants were reimbursed for their time at the end of the interview (twenty-five dollars for the first study; thirty and forty dollars for the second study). A larger incentive was provided in the second study since it was a longitudinal design; the amount was increased for the second and third interviews to further ensure their participation in follow-up interviews, since participant retention is a known difficulty in longitudinal research. The choice of cash or gift certificate was offered, but most chose the cash. Reimbursement for participants

Age													
DATE													
Work history (licit and illicit)													
Medical history													
Family													
Partners													
Social Life													
Residence													
Education													
Religion/ spirituality													
Treatment history													
Law Involvement													
Substance use													

A.1. Life History Matrix # _____ Age: _____ Race: _____ Sex: _____ . Source: Miriam Boeri.

Drug	If ever used; age of first use/regular use	If no longer use; age stopped use	Past 6 months use in approximate number of days used	Past 30 days use in number of days used	Past 7 days use in number of days used	Route of administration S = smoke N = nasal O = oral I = injection A = anal Circle most used	
						Ever	Past 6 months
Tobacco							
Alcohol							
Marijuana							
LSD/mushrooms							
Ecstasy							
Other club drugs							
Pills (uppers)							
Pills (narcotics)							
Pills (other)							
Cocaine							
Crack							
Heroin							
Methamphetamine							
Crank							
Crystal							
Ice							
Price							
Other drugs*							

*Specify any "other":
NOTES:
A.2. Drug History Matrix #_____ Age:_____ Race:_____ Sex:___. Source: Miriam Boeri.

has been shown to be ethical and useful when collecting research on hidden and stigmatized behaviors (Wiebel 1990).

I either brought food for the respondent or offered to buy a snack after the interview, which often involved walking to or driving the participant to a nearby coffeehouse or diner. During this time, additional rapport was built and more details were revealed. I wrote notes on my reflections of the interviews within forty-eight hours.

PRELIMINARY ANALYSIS

Data analysis began with the first few interviews using the constant-comparison method commonly employed in grounded theory (Charmaz 2005; Strauss and Corbin 1998). The in-depth interviews were transcribed word for word. The computer program QSR NVivo was used for storing, managing, and coding the qualitative data. The quantitative data from the drug histories were entered into a statistical software program for social sciences (SPSS).

The field notes, life histories and drug histories, interviewer notes, and in-depth interviews were used to triangulate the data through an iterative model of analysis (Boeri 2007; Nichter et al. 2004). As the data were collected and after they were entered into computer programs, we compared the responses on the various forms of data to gain a clearer understanding of the phenomenon and to inform the continuing data collection and analysis.

LONGITUDINAL DATA COLLECTION

In the second study I increased the number of women by adding 30 new female cases. Data were collected at three points in time from the same female participants: (1) a first interview; (2) a follow-up interview; and (3) a focus group interview. Not all women participated in the focus group since they could choose to be part of a focus group or take a another follow-up interview alone.

First (Baseline) Interview

The first (baseline) interview used the same data collection instruments as the first study: a life history matrix; a drug history matrix; and a semistructured, audio-recorded, in-depth interview. A short risk-behavior inventory was included in this study. All participants were asked questions during the first in-depth interview regarding their knowledge of and access to local health provider services, including drug treatment and awareness of HIV-risks and other drug-related risks. A resource list of social service, health care, shelters, and other services was downloaded from a Web site and made available to participants at the end of the interview. The first resource list we used was one developed by a local nonprofit consortium as a referral list of nonprofit organizations and public social service agencies in the area. We quickly learned we had to personalize this resource list for each participant and added information targeted for specific needs. For example, the SAMHSA treatment locator Web site was often accessed to find treatment facilities in the area that matched the eligibility and financial constraints of each participant. I collected all first interview data. Participants were given thirty dollars cash or equivalent gift certificate for their time.

Follow-up Interviews

During the follow-up interviews, I updated the drug use matrix and risk-behavior inventory and conducted a follow-up qualitative interview, specifically to see how they used the resource list we provided. The transcribed in-depth interviews from the baseline interview generated follow-up questions.

The follow-up interviews were typically conducted between one month and six months after the first interview. My original plan was to conduct follow-up interviews between three months and six months, but I quickly learned that many of our female interviewees were in such a precarious situation (being homeless, on probation or parole) that we might lose them in a few weeks. Therefore, when I identified women with whom I thought we might lose contact, I conducted their follow-up interviews at the next available date. For a few women it was within a month and for others it was as long as eight months.

The individual follow-up interview included an update of the drug use and risk-behavior matrices and a short, recorded interview on what had occurred in the participant's life since the previous interview. An updated health care, social services, and drug treatment resource list developed by the research assistants was given to each participant. Follow-up interviews typically took only about one-half hour. Two female research assistants conducted a few of the follow-up interviews, and some were done by phone.

Focus Group Interviews

Focus groups were conducted at our university research room on a weekend day when few people were around. The coinvestigator facilitated the focus groups with the help of two female research assistants while I watched and took notes. I also typically picked up the participants in my car or met them to guide them to the room.

The focus group started with an opening brief introduction by the facilitator using the participants' study number; if they desired they could use a pseudonym instead. The research assistants led an initial ice-breaker game aimed to explore access to risk awareness and utilization of social services and health care providers. During this game, participants were shown large placards with the names of various service resources. They were handed a stack of multicolor cards with the following responses printed on them:

PINK—used service last year and was pleased.

BLUE—wanted to use it, but was prevented.

YELLOW—referred for an appointment but did not go.

BLACK—used service, but needs not meet or displeased.

WHITE—did not know service existed, but could have used it.

The women were asked to match their response cards to the resource cards. Immediately after the game we discussed why certain response cards were matched with each resource.

We found the card game to be very effective, providing more than merely an ice-breaker. In fact, the women became so engrossed in identifying the right card that much discussion occurred during the game itself. After the first focus group we included a new preprinted response card that read *I would like to talk more about this service* to ensure that women who were shy or reticent would have a change to talk about a particular problem accessing a resource.

After the discussion of the ice-breaker results, the facilitator led the focus group using an interview guide that served as a framework on which to maximize group discussion and interaction. Questions prompted discussion on recent health, HIV-related awareness, prevention experiences, needs assessment, use of the resource list, and experiences in gaining access to health care and treatment. Resources and approaches that were found to be ineffective were discussed, and suggestions for better strategies were explored.

Refreshments were available when a break was needed. The entire interview was recorded and the discussions were transcribed. Participants were given forty dollars in cash or a gift certificate for their time. All researchers present at the focus group wrote reaction notes within forty-eight hours.

Although we anticipated focus groups consisting of four to six members, in reality we found it difficult to arrange a day and time for our participants to meet. The first focus group consisted of four women in the same network. In order to ensure they all arrived on time, I picked them up and drove them to the meeting and back. The remaining focus groups were more difficult to organize, mainly because not all lived nearby and transportation was often an issue. The smallest focus group involved two participants; however, we discovered that even two people provided very insightful information. They often encouraged each other to be more open and thoughtful, and challenged responses tactfully.

We conducted seven focus groups. The reasons why some women did not participate in a focus group included moving too far away from the research study area, losing contact, or difficulty finding a two-hour slot of free time. We knew of three women who were incarcerated for probation violation and could not complete all the interviews. One woman returned to participate in a focus group after she was released from jail.

VALIDITY AND RELIABILITY

The multimethod design and targeted sampling used in this study added to the validity of the data (Lambert, Ashery, and Needle 1995; Pach and Gorman 2002; Rhodes and Moore 2001). We compared information collected from various sources and cross-checked suspicious responses with colleagues and experts, without revealing any identity. The inclusion of follow-up interviews and focus group interviews also added to the overall validity of the data collected in the second study (Deren et al. 2003). Any inconsistencies found were further explored through an iterative process in follow-up interviews and field observations.

Previous research shows that drug users tend to report valid information in qualitative interviews (Rosenbaum 1981; Weatherby et al. 1994). However, if any cases exhibited extensive inconsistencies between data sources, they were not included in the analysis and were removed from the data files. In this study, only two cases were eliminated.

Throughout the fieldwork, recruitment, and data collection, I strove to establish good rapport with the women and empathize with them as much as possible. When I could not understand their experience because it was so foreign to my own, I let them know that it was I who lacked knowledge and I needed their help to understand. I often was immersed in the field for weeks and became involved quite a few times with the personal sufferings of those I studied. Although my empathy and respect were genuine and not displayed merely to obtain data, showing compassion and understanding is also known to increase the validity of the study findings (Shaw 2005).

DATA ANALYSIS

I conducted analysis of the data for this book according to the modified or constructivist approach, called a "reconstructed" version of grounded theory (Charmaz 2005). This started by acknowledging that researchers do not live in a vacuum but instead have preconceived ideas, theories, and biographies that inform their analysis. During analysis, I tried to gain a better

understanding of how the women defined situations and solutions to problems. My analysis followed the guidelines set out by Charmaz for conducting
research that advances social justice goals (2005, 507–535). First I read and
reread the data looking for what was going on in the women's lives. I coded
the data using a free coding frame and then organized this into patterns.
Throughout the analysis I looked for linking processes and situated the
processes and action in social and historical context.

While the women's voices were the heart of the findings, they were supported by memos containing reflections from my field notes, theoretical perspectives, political and economic exigencies, and own life experiences.
Theoretical explanations for the complex interplay between structure and
agency, and the social processes that influenced behavior, were illustrated by
a representative case or specific vignettes from the women's lives.

Coding

I trained two research assistants who helped develop the coding outline
(called a "tree" in NVivo) used to code the data collected in the first study,
which included the first 35 women. We used "free coding" first to gain a
better understanding of the drug career or trajectory (Boeri, Harbry, and
Gibson 2009). We met numerous times to discuss and compare our coding
categories until an outline was developed that incorporated all of our codes
and interpretations. After 21 transcripts were coded, we had a basic tree of 10
codes (called "nodes" in NVivo) and 18 free codes. I used these codes to
analyze the data from the second study, adding an eleventh main code called
"access to services" and numerous free codes based on the rich material from
the focus groups. The transcripts for the first, second, and third interviews
were combined and coded as one case. Each main code provided over
a hundred of pages of direct quotes that were subsequently organized by
themes.

Theoretical coding was an important part of the coding process and
resulted in additional codes used for the book beyond the original tree. The
drug career typology discussed in appendix B was employed as a coding tool.
Each transcript (that is, each woman's life story) was coded by what phase she
was in at the time of the interview as well as past phases indicated in her life
history. Each case was also coded by the conceptual sets: suburban youth class
(SYC); suburban working middle-class (SWMC); and suburban poor (SP).
The aggregated sample demographics and theoretical coding for the female
participants are shown in table A.1.

TABLE A.1

Sample Demographics and Drug Career Status

Demographic	N	%*
N = 65		
Race/Ethnicity		
African American	2	0.03
Latina	4	0.06
American Indian	1	0.02
White	58	0.89
Conceptual Set		
Suburban Youth Culture	20	0.31
Suburban Working Middle Class	19	0.29
Suburban Poor	26	0.4
Career Phase Status (last 3 months)		
Controlled Occasional User	8	0.12
Weekend Warrior	0	0.0
Habitué	3	0.5
Marginal User	3	0.5
Problem Addict	4	0.6
Using Dealer Runner	0	0.0
Using Hustler Sex Worker	1	0.2
Junkie	1	0.2
Relapsing Addict Junkie	18	0.28
Former User	27	0.42
Age	18–51 *(range)*	33.5 *(mean)*

* Rounded up.

SOURCE: Miriam Boeri

Appendix B

The Drug Career Typology

The career model has been used by to explain deviant careers as well as main-stream careers (Becker 1953 and 1963; Biernacki 1986; Faupel 1991; Laub and Sampson 2003; Rosenbaum 1981; Waldorf 1973). Building on the tradition of drug use as a career, I used the concepts of social roles, social control, and self-control to develop a typology of career phases. The nine phases of the typology help identify and explain transitions and turning points in a drug-user career (Boeri 2004). Before presenting the typology here, I provide a brief overview of social role, social control, and self-control theories.

Social Role Theory

Social roles are the behaviors, responsibilities, activities, and privileges belonging to a particular social status. Roles are used to organize personal activities, provide guidelines for behavior, and act as a point of reference. The self has been conceptualized as multiple role identities, and identity as internalized role designation (Stryker and Serpe 1994). Therefore, it can be assumed that role loss and role transition provide new guidelines for behaviors and help form a new identity. A successful acquisition of a new role results in a new role identity through a mutual transformation of both self and role.

In chapter 3 I discussed the importance of identifying turning points and transitions in the drug trajectory (Boeri et al. 2011). The concepts of role acquisition and role loss provide an additional tool for understanding turning points in drug use. We know that problematic use of drugs is associated with a loss of social roles (Agar 1973; Faupel 1991; Stephens 1991). As adults lose mainstream roles (for example, work and parenting roles), they acquire new ones or return to previously held roles. This process is known as role transition. Roles can be both conventional and unconventional. Drug users who lose their mainstream conventional roles have less motivation to abstain from activities that place them at risk. The drug user who is alienated from mainstream society can regain social role stability by becoming involved in an unconventional drug-using role, which may also motivates the user to maintain more control over his or her drug use. For example, by becoming dealers some women regained control over economic difficulties, and this increased their motivation to use drugs in a more controllable manner.

The control mechanism of drug-using roles is rarely discussed in the literature on drug treatment, with a few exceptions. For example, Edward Preble and John Casey (1969) argue that, contrary to the widely held belief that heroin is used as an escape, heroin provides individuals with a purpose in life and a pattern of consistent behavior. Such activity can be rewarding and meaningful, especially for those to whom legitimate role opportunities are not available.

Social roles should be understood as constructed within a historical and structural context that constrains the behavior of individuals (Mills 1959). Social structure can be viewed as the sum total of recurrent patterns of interaction that are eventually reified, a process called the "social construction of reality" (Berger and Luckmann 1966). In terms of interaction ritual (IR) chains theory, these roles are ritualized and provide emotional energy (EE) that work as a reinforcement agent (Collins 2004). It is important to understand these processes occur with both conventional and unconventional roles.

SOCIAL CONTROL THEORY

Social control theory, as originally developed by Travis Hirschi (1969), was extended and modified into a variety of theories whose foundational concepts include social bonding, social learning, and attachment to social roles (Akers 1998 and 2000). More recent developments include a life-course perspective (Laub and Sampson 2003).

Classic social control theory focused on the mechanisms that explain why people do *not* engage in illegal or deviant behaviors rather than why they do. Social bonding involves attachment, commitment, involvement, and belief in conventional social relationships and activities (Hirschi 1969). Ronald Akers (1999) argued that these bonding concepts are conceptually contained under two components of social learning theory: differential association and differential reinforcement. Edwin Sutherland (1939) proposed differential association to show how deviance—or anomie as conceptualized by Robert Merton (1938 and 1968)—and its opposite, conformity, is learned through association with others who are more or less deviant or conforming.

What is important about the early theories of deviance is that in both the theory of anomie and the theory of differential association, the focus shifted between the individual and society. Interestingly, classic social control theory as first proposed by Hirschi (1969) gave analytical preeminence to social aspects of delinquency for the first time. Instead of developing this interplay between what can be conceptualized as aspects of agency (self-control) and structure (social control), Hirschi relegated social control (structural and relational influences) to a minor role in his revised theory of self-control, developed with Michael Gottfredson. Future modifications of social control, therefore, spent valuable time focused not on understanding the interplay between agency and structure but instead in reaction to self-control theory, which became the dominant theory used in criminological studies for many years.

Robert Sampson and John Laub (1993 and 2003) turned the social control gaze directly back on the complex and shifting processes that occur between agency and structure in their conceptualization of an age-graded theory of informal social control. They proposed a life-course version of social control that includes "personal agency and situated choice, routine activities, aging, macro-level events, and local culture and community context" (2003, 293). In so doing, the authors allow for self-control (agency or individual choice) to be analyzed along with structure or environmental influences.

SELF-CONTROL THEORY

During the last half century, drug abuse was understood and framed primarily in the context of a "loss of control" (Cloward and Ohlin 1960). According to Gottfredson and Hirschi (1990), self-control was hypothesized to develop in childhood and to remain relatively stable throughout the life course. In other words, once low self-control is established, the individual will lack self-control throughout life. Self-control theory became one of the dominant theories used by criminologists for many years, linking low self-control with engaging in illegal behaviors such as using and dealing drugs.

In contrast, ethnographic and life-course studies show that drug users who have lost control can learn to regain controlled drug use behavior (Biernacki 1986; Laub and Sampson 2003; Zinberg 1984). Self-control theory fails to consider a continuum of self-control and ignores within-individual changes in self-control over time; it also does not distinguish among salient domains. For example, a person may have low self-control in some areas of life but not in others. Control within the drug-using role is also an option. A drug user may control his or her drug use by using less or not using during workdays. Users also gain control by changing the route of administration, such as from injecting to snorting, and by substituting a problematic drug with another drug. Older heroin users who have learned how to control their use often pass these "habit management behaviors" on to newer users (Acker 2002).

A TYPOLOGY OF DRUG CAREER PHASES

This typology is based on the dimensions of social roles and self-control, indicating levels of either maintaining or not maintaining desired social roles and control over drug use. Social control theory informs the relationship between these two dimensions, conceptualized as phases of a drug user's trajectory

(Boeri 2004). Since the typology applies only to drug users, and not to former drug users, control over drug use does not mean the individual ceased all
drug use. Instead control indicates the user was able to maintain her desired
social roles without much interference from drug use. For example, if a
mother wanted to use methamphetamine in a controlled manner, she might
wait until the children spend the weekend with the grandparents to use
methamphetamine on Friday night and have the drug out of her system by
the time the children come home on Sunday night. The relationship between
control of drug use and maintaining social roles applies to both conventional
and unconventional roles. As explained earlier, a dealer could not remain a
dealer for long if she used all of her dope. Self-control, therefore, is possible
even while engaged in drug-using roles. The typology illustrated in table B.1
represents the following conceptualization of the relationship between social
roles and self-control.

Social roles most salient to the user are identified as either mainstream conventional social roles (family role, partner role, work role) or unconventional
roles associated with the drug-using career (drug user, sex worker, dealer, hustler). Three possible dimensions of social roles are identified: (1) maintains

TABLE B.1

Drug Career Typology

Career Category	Roles	Control
Controlled Occasional User	+	+
Weekend Warrior	+	+/−
Habitué	+/−	+
Marginal User	+	−
Problem Addict	+/−	−
Using Dealer/Runner	−	+
Using Hustler/Sex Worker	−	+/−
Junkie	−	−
Relapsing Addict/Junkie	+/−	+/−
Former User	*NA*	*NA*

+ Maintaining conventional social roles other than drug-using role; maintaining
control of drug use—lost salient conventional social roles; loss of control of drug use.

+/− Indicates sporadic salience of conventional and unconventional social roles;
intermittent control and loss of control of drug use.

SOURCE: Miriam Boeri

salient conventional roles; (2) does not maintain salient conventional roles; or (3) combines a salient drug-user role and other salient conventional roles.

The property of control signifies the control the drug user maintains over drug-use behavior. The dimensions of self-control are defined as being able to maintain enough control so as not to lose all salient conventional roles, or once those are lost, not to lose salient drug roles. The three dimensions of control are: (1) maintains control; (2) does not maintain control; or (3) has irregular periods of control and out-of-control.

The coding scheme based on roles and control, shown in table B.1, is represented by plus (+) and minus (−) combinations. A plus (+), minus (−), or plus/minus (+/−) symbol is used to indicate the users' placement along the dimensions of roles and control. Each woman's chart representing her drug career was marked with a symbol (+, −, or +/−) according to her reported social roles and sense of control for the last ninety days (three months). When the user indicated a role or roles that were more salient than the drug-using or drug-related role, I marked the interview transcript with a plus (+) for the role category. When the unconventional drug roles or drug-related roles, such as drug dealing, running, or hustling for drugs, were most salient in the respondent's current life, the interview transcript was marked with a minus (−) in the social role category. If the user indicated a recent pattern of sporadic salience of a drug role and another social role, I marked a plus/minus (+/−). Likewise, for the user's reported control of drug use, I marked a plus (+) when all indicators in the data signified controlled use of drugs, a minus (−) when a loss of control was indicated, and a plus/minus (+/−) when the user reported a pattern of sporadic control and loss of control in the preceding three months.

Once all conventional roles were lost and no longer salient in the woman's life, a shift in the relationship between roles and control occurred. Instead of control signifying that the user had enough restraint to maintain conventional roles, it now indicates that the user must keep enough control over drug use in order to maintain a salient unconventional role that supplies drugs or money for drugs. Thus, the plus (+) indicated the woman could control her drug use enough that her salient unconventional role was not lost. If all roles were lost, the woman entered a phase with no roles and no control. Current phases were identified for the last thirty to ninety days, but phases throughout the life history might last for years.

Nine distinct phases include every possible combination of social roles and self-control. Each phase was identified with a label that illustrated what was going on in that particular phase. As much as possible, I used terms that were employed by the users themselves. The typology includes the following nine phases and descriptions based on maintaining social roles and control over drug use.

Controlled Occasional User [+ , +]

In this phase, the user maintains social roles and maintains control of drug use. A sense of control is defined by users as the ability to use drugs occasionally while continuing to function uninterrupted in salient conventional roles. In other words, drug use does not interfere with other mainstream social role responsibilities. This phase is often referred to as "functional use."

Weekend Warrior [+ , + / −]

The user maintains salient conventional roles in this phase but experiences intermittent control and loss of control of drug use. In this phase drugs are used on weekends or only at parties, typically during nonwork days. The work role or other conventional role is salient. However, during the short periods of use, behavior may be out of control, such as using more than planned or engaging in risky behaviors while using drugs.

Habitué [+ / − , +]

In this phase, the user maintains salient conventional roles and unconventional drug roles but also maintains control of drug use. The user in this phase has a self-acknowledged habit and is able to maintain it along with salient social roles in conventional life. Moreover, the drug user role is not as salient or important in their lives. Their use is controlled.

Marginal User [+ , −]

Users in this phase maintain salient conventional roles but experience a loss of control of drug use. However, they did not include any unconventional role as a salient role, which distinguishes this phase from that of the habitué. A loss of control is seen as a precursor to being unable to fulfill other social roles due to drug use. In this phase the users acknowledge that their uncontrolled drug use might soon interfere with their conventional roles.

Problem Addict [+ / − , −]

In this phase, users maintain conventional roles and salient unconventional roles, but they have lost control of drug use. The term "addict" is commonly used to describe anyone from an occasional user to a hard-core user. However, as used here, the term refers to a phase in which users not only described themselves as having lost control but also indicated a problem keeping salient conventional roles in their lives. At this point, they recognized their drug use as an addiction that required daily attention and interfered with maintaining functional social roles in mainstream society. "Addict" is a derogatory term, and I want to note that I did not choose this term to use; the people I interviewed used the term to describe someone who had a problem with drug use.

Using Dealer/Runner [−,+]

Users in this phase have lost salient conventional roles, but they maintain control of drug use. Users discover that no other roles are as salient as the drug-related unconventional role, usually a dealer or runner, but they control drug use so that it does not interfere with their dealer or runner role. A runner is the person who runs drugs between the dealer and the user; the term is often employed figuratively to indicate a small-supply dealer. It is in this phase that a shift in the relationship between roles and control occurs: once all conventional roles are lost, the meaning of control over drug use changes. Instead of control signifying that the user has enough restraint to maintain conventional roles, it now indicates that the user must keep enough control over drug use to maintain a salient unconventional role.

Using Hustler/Sex Worker [−,+/−]

In this phase, users have no other salient conventional role and have intermittent control and loss of control of drug use. A hustle is usually an illegal activity. A hustler who uses drugs often is hustling to obtain money for more drugs. Users in this phase had less control of drug use than the using dealers and runners; nevertheless, they had to maintain some control of use in order to complete the hustle. The pattern of control in this category was one of periodic control and loss of control. In some cases, the hustler or sex worker previously engaged in dealing or running. In other cases, they were still running drugs as one of their many hustles, but they could not keep regular clients who trusted them.

Junkie [−,−]

Users in this phase have no other salient role but being a drug user and have lost all control of their drug use. The term "junkie" was employed by participants in the study and appears frequently in scholarly work, mainly when referring to heroin users. It implies an addict at the lowest level in the drug-user hierarchy, and this is how the women I interviewed used this term. In this phase, every area of life revolves mainly around drug use. These are the users who have exhausted all resources and sources of help except for public shelter and treatment facilities. Lack of any social routines or activities other than drug using and drug seeking is the most evident characteristic of the junkie. Most often, the term evokes a homeless individual living on streets begging, panhandling, and using charity and soup kitchens. Periodic sex work and drug running during this phase may provide short-lived, precarious roles. Because of the environmental and symbolic violence that often accompanies this role, most women do not stay in this phase very long.

Relapsing Addict/Junkie [+ / −, + / −]

In this phase, the user maintains salient conventional and salient drug roles intermittently and experiences intermittent control and loss of control of drug use. Users often spend years in a revolving door of treatment, clean time, regaining control of their drug use, then losing control again. The recurring pattern shows that during treatment they learn how to maintain control over their use and lose it soon after leaving treatment. The user in a relapsing addict/junkie phase has recently maintained other salient roles and recently also lost them. For some addict/junkies, complete abstinence is too difficult to maintain.

SUMMARY

The drug career typology was used to identify phases of the drug trajectory. The phases described above are not developmental in the sense that one does not start as a controlled occasional user and go through all the stages to the end. Instead, the user can start at any phase, although a controlled phase is more typical as a starting point. The user may skip phases or stay in one phase the entire career. Unfortunately, users who are in the beginning phases of this typology are typically not studied, do not end up on our indicators of drug use, such as treatment facilities and jails, and do not participate in many drug studies. They make up a more hidden population of users, especially those who start and remain in a controlled phase. While few women in the studies were in the controlled phases at the time of the interviews, their life histories indicated that they had been in the past, some for long periods of time.

The typology proved useful for describing different kinds of drugs users based on the phases of drug use illustrated in their lives in the last three months. Distinguishing categories of users in this way allows intervention and treatment for problematic drug use to be focused on areas most in need and on those who need it. It also provides a measure of assessment to know when intervention might be most helpful.

References

Abadinsky, Howard. 1997. *Drug Abuse: An Introduction*. Chicago: Nelson Hall.

Acker, Jean Caroline. 2002. *Creating the American Junkie: Addiction Research in the Classic Era of Narcotic Control*. Baltimore: Johns Hopkins University Press.

Adler, Freda. 1975. *Sisters in Crime: The Rise of the New Female Criminal*. New York: McGraw-Hill.

Adler, Patricia A. 1993. *Wheeling and Dealing: An Ethnography of an Upper Level Drug Dealing and Smuggling Community*. New York: Columbia University Press.

Agar, Michael. 1973. *Ripping and Running: A Formal Ethnography of Urban Heroin Addicts*. New York: Seminar Press.

———. 2003. "The Story of Crack: Towards a Theory of Illicit Drug Trends." *Addiction Research & Theory* 11 (1): 3–29. doi:10.1080/1606635021000059042.

Akers, Ronald L. 1991. "Addiction: The Troublesome Concept." *Journal of Drug Issues* 21 (4): 777–793.

———. 1998. *Social Learning and Social Structure: A General Theory of Crime and Deviance*. Boston: Northeastern University Press.

———. 1999. *Criminological Theories: Introduction, Evaluation*. Los Angeles, CA: Roxbury.

Allard, Scott W. and Benjamin Roth. 2010. "Strained Suburbs: The Social Service Challenges of Rising Suburban Poverty." Metropolitan Policy Program. Washington, DC: Brookings Institution.

Anderson, Elijah. 1999. *Code of the Street: Decency, Violence, and the Moral Life of the Inner City*. New York: W. W. Norton.

———. 2004. "The Cosmopolitan Canopy." *Annals of the American Academy of Political and Social Science* 595:14–31.

Anderson, Tammy L. 2005. "Dimensions of Women's Power in the Illicit Drug Economy." *Theoretical Criminology* 9 (4): 371–400.

Anderson, Tammy L., and Judith Levy. 2003. "Marginality among Older Injectors in Today's Illicit Drug Culture: Assessing the Impact of Ageing." *Addiction* 98 (6): 761–770.

Anglin, M. Douglas, Cynthia Burke, Brian Perrochet, Ewa Stamper, and Samia Dawud-Noursi. 2000. "History of the Methamphetamine Problem." *Journal of Psychoactive Drugs* 32 (2): 137–141.

Bailey, Lucy. 2005. "Control and Desire: The Issue of Identity in Popular Discourses of Addiction." *Addiction Research & Theory* 13 (6): 535–543. doi:10.1080/16066350500338195.

Barr, Alasdair M., William J. Panenka, G. William MacEwan, Allen E. Thornton, Donna J. Lang, William G. Honer, and Tania Lecomte. 2006. "The Need for Speed:

An Update on Methamphetamine Addiction." *Journal of Psychiatry Neuroscience* 31 (5): 301–313.

Barrick, Christopher, and Gerard J. Connors. 2002. "Relapse Prevention and Maintaining Abstinence in Older Adults with Alcohol-Use Disorders." *Drugs & Aging* 19 (8):583–594.

Becker, Howard S. 1953. "Becoming a Marihuana User." *American Journal of Sociology* 59 (3): 235–242.

————. 1963. *Outsiders: Studies in the Sociology of Deviance*. New York: The Free Press.

Beckett, Katherine, and Steve Herbert. 2008. "Dealing With Disorder: Social Control in the Post-industrial City." *Theoretical Criminology* 12 (1): 5–30. doi:10.1177/1362480607085792.

Berger, Peter, and Thomas Luckmann. 1966. *The Social Construction of Reality: A Treatise in the Sociology of Knowledge*. New York: Doubleday.

Biernacki, Patrick. 1986. *Pathways from Heroin Addiction: Recovery without Treatment*. Philadelphia: Temple University Press.

Blankenship, Kim M., and Stephen Koester. 2002. "Criminal Law, Policing Policy, and HIV Risk in Female Street Sex Workers and Injection Drug Users." *Journal of Law, Medicine and Ethics* 30 (4): 548–559. doi:10.1111/j.1748-720x.2002.tb00425.x.

Boeri, Miriam W. 2004. "'Hell I'm an Addict, but I Ain't No Junkie': An Ethnographic Analysis of Aging Heroin Users." *Human Organization* 63 (2): 236–245.

————. 2007. "A Third Model of Triangulation: Continuing the Dialogue with Rhineberger, Hartmann and Van Valey." *Journal of Applied Social Science* 1 (1): 42–48.

Boeri, Miriam W., David Gibson, and Liam Harbry. 2009. "Cold Cook Methods: An Ethnographic Exploration on the Myths of Methamphetamine Production and Policy Implications." *International Journal of Drug Policy* 20 (5): 438–443. PMCID:19195870. doi:10.1016/j.drugpo.2008.12.007.

Boeri, Miriam, Liam Harbry, and David Gibson. 2009. "A Qualitative Exploration of Trajectories among Suburban Users of Methamphetamine." *Journal of Ethnographic & Qualitative Research* 3 (3): 139–151. PMCID:PMC3088870.

Boeri, Miriam, Aukje Lamonica, and Liam Harbry. 2011. "Social Recovery, Social Capital, and Drug Courts." *Practicing Anthropology* 33 (1): 8–13.

Boeri, Miriam W., Claire E. Sterk, and Kirk W. Elifson. 2008. "Reconceptualizing Early- and Late-Onset: A Life Course Analysis of Older Heroin Users." *Gerontologist* 48 (5): 637–645. doi:10.1093/geront/48.5.637.

Boeri, Miriam W., and Benjamin D. Tyndall. 2012. "A Contextual Comparison of Risk Behaviors among Older Adult Drug Users and Harm Reduction in Suburban versus Inner-City Social Environments." *Journal of Applied Social Science* 6 (1): 72–91. doi:10.1177/1936724411431035.

Boeri, Miriam, Benjamin Tyndall, and Denise Woodall. 2011. "Suburban Poverty: Barriers to Services and Injury Prevention among Marginalized Women Who Use Methamphetamine." *Western Journal of Emergency Medicine* 12 (3): 284–292. PMCID:PMC3117602.

Boeri, Miriam, Thor Whalen, Benjamin Tyndall, and Ellen Ballard. 2011. "Drug Trajectory Patterns among Older Drug Users." *Substance Abuse and Rehabilitation* 2:89–102. doi:10.2147/SAR.S14871.

Boshears, Paul, Miriam Boeri and Liam Harbry. 2011. "Addiction and Sociality: Perspective from Methamphetamine Users in Suburban USA." *Addiction Research & Theory* 19 (4): 289–301. doi:10.3109/160663359.2011.566654.

Bourdieu, Pierre. 1984. *Distinction: A Social Critique of the Judgement of Taste*. Cambridge: Harvard University Press.

———. 1986. "The Forms of Capital." In *Handbook of Theory and Research for the Sociology of Education*, ed. John G. Richardson, 241–258. New York: Greenwood Press.

———. 2001. *Masculine Domination*. Stanford, CA: Stanford University Press.

———. 2004. *Science of Science and Reflexivity*. Chicago: University of Chicago Press.

Bourgois, Philippe. 1999. "Theory, Method, and Power in Drug and HIV-Prevention Research: A Participant Observer's Critique." *Substance Use & Misuse* 34 (14): 2155–2172.

———. 2002. "Ethnography's Troubles and the Reproduction of Academic Habitus." *Qualitative Studies in Education* 15 (4): 417–420. doi:10.1080/09518390210145471.

———. 2003 [1996]. *In Search of Respect: Selling Crack in El Barrio*. New York: Cambridge University Press.

Bourgois, Philippe, Bridget Prince, and Andrew Moss. 2004. "The Everyday Violence of Hepatitis C among Young Women Who Inject Drugs in San Francisco." *Human Organization* 63 (3): 253–264.

Boyd, Susan C. 1999. *Mothers and Illicit Drugs: Transcending the Myths*. Toronto: University of Toronto Press.

Brecht, Mary-Lynn, Lisa Greenwell, and M. Douglas Anglin. 2005. "Methamphetamine Treatment: Trends and Predictors of Retention and Completion in a Large State Treatment System (1992–2002)." *Journal of Substance Abuse Treatment* 29 (4): 295–306. doi:10.1016/j.jsat.2005.08.012.

Bren, L. 2006. "Some Cold Medicines Move behind the Counter." *FDA Consumer Magazine* 40 (4): 18–19.

Bruckner, Erika, and Karl Ulrich Mayer. 1998. "Collecting Life History Data: Experiences from the German Life History Study." In *Methods of Life Course Research: Qualitative and Quantitative Approaches*, ed. Janet Z. Giele and Glen H. Elder Jr., 152–181. Thousand Oaks, CA: Sage Publications.

Campbell, Nancy D. 2000. *Using Women: Gender, Drug Policy and Social Justice*. New York: Routledge.

Centers for Disease Control and Prevention (CDC). 2006. "Recommended HIV/AIDS, Sexually Transmitted Disease (STD), and Viral Hepatitis Prevention Services, by Risk Population." *Morbidity and Mortality Weekly Report* (MMRW) 55 (RR-16).

———. 2008. "Cases of HIV Infection and AIDS in Urban and Rural Areas of the United States, 2006." *HIV/AIDS Surveillance Supplemental Report* 13 (2). http://www.cdc.gov/hiv/topics/surveillance/resources/reports/2008supp_vol13no2/.

———. 2010. "HIV-Associated Behaviors among Injecting-drug users—23 cities, United States, May 2005–February 2006." *Morbidity and Mortality Weekly* 58 (13): 329–333.

Charmaz, Kathy. 2005. "Grounded Theory in the 21st Century." In *The SAGE Handbook of Qualitative Research*, ed. Norman K. Denzin and Yvonna S. Lincoln, 507–535. Thousand Oaks, CA: Sage Publications.

Chesney-Lind, Meda, and Randall Sheldon. 1992. *Girls, Delinquency and Juvenile Justice*. Pacific Grove, CA: Brooks/Cole Publishing.

Cloud, William, and Richard Granfield. 2001. *Recovery from Addiction: A Practical Guide to Treatment, Self-help and Quitting on Your Own*. New York: New York University Press.

Cloward, Richard, and Lloyd Ohlin. 1960. *Delinquency and Opportunity: A Theory of Delinquent Gangs*. New York: The Free Press.

Cohen, Stanley. 1985. *Visions of Social Control*. Cambridge, UK: Polity Press.

Coleman, James S. 1990. *Foundations of Social Theory*. Cambridge: Harvard University Press.

Collins, Randall. 2004. *Interaction Ritual Chains*. Princeton, NJ: Princeton University Press.

Compton, Wilson M., Yonette F. Thomas, Kevin P. Conway, and James D. Colliver. 2005. "Developments in the Epidemiology of Drug Use and Drug Use Disorders." *American Journal of Psychiatry* 162 (8): 1494–1502. doi:10.1176/appi.ajp.162.8.1494.

Connell-Carrick, Kelli. 2007. "Methamphetamine and the Changing Face of Child Welfare: Practice Principles for Child Welfare Workers." *Child Welfare* 86 (3): 125–143.

Denzin, Norman, and Yvonne Lincoln. 1994. *The SAGE Handbook of Qualitative Research*. Thousand Oaks, CA: Sage Publications.

Deren, Sherry, Denise Oliver-Velez, Ann Finlison, Rafaela Robles, Jonny Andia, Hector M. Colon, Sung Yeon Kang, and Michele Shedlin. 2003. "Integrating Qualitative and Quantitative Methods: Comparing HIV-Related Risk Behaviors among Puerto Rican Drug Users in Puerto Rico and New York." *Substance Use & Misuse* 38 (1): 1–24.

Deschenes, Elizabeth, Connie Ireland, and Christine Kleinpeter. 2009. "Enhancing Drug Court Success." *Journal of Offender Rehabilitation* 48 (1): 19–36. doi:10.1080/10509670802577473.

Dluzen, Dean E., and Bin Liu. 2008. "Gender Differences in Methamphetamine Use and Responses: A Review." *Gender Medicine* 5 (1): 24–35. doi:10.1016/S1550-8579(08)80005-8.

Dole, Vincent P. 1980. "Addictive Behavior." *Scientific American* 243:138–154.

Donaldson, Mark, and Jason H. Goodchild. 2006. "Oral Health and the Methamphetamine Abuser." *American Journal of Health-System Pharmacists* 63:2078–2082. doi:10.2146/ajhp060198.

Edlin, Brian R., and Michael R. Carden. 2006. "Injection Drug Users: The Overlooked Core of the Hepatitis C Epidemic." *Clinical Infectious Diseases* 42 (5): 673–676. doi:10.1086/49960.

Edlin, B. R., K. H. Seal, J. Lorvick, A. H. Kral, D. H. Ciccarone, L. D. Moore, and B. Lo. 2001. "Is It Justifiable to Withhold Treatment for Hepatitis C from Illicit-Drug Users?" *New England Journal of Medicine* 345:211–215.

Elder, Glen H., Jr. 1985. *Life Course Dynamics: Trajectories and Transitions, 1968–1980*. Ithaca, NY: Cornell University Press.

Eliason, Michele J. 2006. "Are Therapeutic Communities Therapeutic for Women?" *Substance Abuse Treatment, Prevention, and Policy* 1 (3). doi:10.1186/1747-597X-1-3.

Ettore, Elizabeth. 1992. *Women and Substance Use*. New Brunswick, NJ: Rutgers University Press.

Faupel, Charles E. 1991. *Shooting Dope: Career Patterns of Hard-Core Heroin Users*. Gainesville: University of Florida Press.

Felland, Laurie. E., Johanna R. Laeur, and Peter J. Cunningham. 2009. "Suburban Poverty and the Healthcare Safety Net." *Research Brief* 13. Washington, DC: Center for Studying Health System Change.

Geertz, Clifford. 1973. *The Interpretation of Cultures*. New York: Basic Book.

Gibson, Barry, Sam Acquah, and Peter G. Robinson. 2004. "Entangled Identities and Psychotropic Substance Use." *Sociology of Health & Illness* 26 (5): 597–616. doi:10.1111/j.0141-9889.2004.00407.x.

Glaser, Barney G., and Anselm Strauss. 1967. The *Discovery of Grounded Theory: Strategies for Qualitative Research*. New York: Aldine.

Global Commission on Drugs. 2011. *War on Drugs: The Report of the Global Commission on Drug Policy.* Accessed June 2011 at www.globalcommissionondrugs.org/.

Goetz, Andrew C. 2007. "One Stop, No Stop, Two Stop, Terry Stop: Reasonable Suspicion and Pseudoephedrine Purchases by Suspected Methamphetamine Manufacturers." *Michigan Law Review* 105:1573–1596.

Golub, Andrew, Bruce D. Johnson, Eloise Dunlap, and Stephen Sifaneck. 2004. "Projecting and Monitoring the Life Course of the Marijuana/Blunts Generation." *Journal of Drug Issues* 34 (2): 361–388.

Goode, Erich. 2011. *Deviant Behavior.* Upper Saddle River, NJ: Prentice Hall.

Gottfredson, Michael R., and Travis Hirschi. 1990. *A General Theory of Crime.* Stanford, CA: Stanford University Press.

Granfield, Robert. 2004. "Addiction and Modernity: A Comment on a Global Theory of Addiction." *Nordic Studies on Alcohol and Drugs* 44:27–32.

Granfield, Robert, and William Cloud. 2001. "Social Context and 'Natural Recovery:' The Role Of Social Capital in the Resolution of Drug-associated Problems." *Substance Use & Misuse* 36 (11): 1543–1570.

Grusky, David B., Bruce Western, and Christopher Wimer, eds. 2011. *The Great Recession.* New York: Russell Sage.

Habermas, Jurgen. 1985. *The Theory of Communicative Action: Reason and the Rationalization of Society.* Boston: Beacon Press.

Haight, Wendy, Teresa Jacobsen, James Black, Linda Kingery, Kathryn Sheridan, and Cray Mulder. 2005. "'In these Bleak Days:' Parent Methamphetamine Abuse and Child Welfare in the Rural Midwest." *Children and Youth Services Review* 27 (8): 949–971.

Hammersley, Richard, and Marie Reid. 2002. "Why the Pervasive Addiction Myth is Still Believed." *Addiction Research & Theory* 10 (1): 7–30. doi:10.1080/1606635 0290001687.

Hannan, Dan. 2005. "Meth Labs: Understanding Exposure Hazards and Associated Problems." *Professional Safety* 50 (6): 24–31.

Hirschi, Travis. 1969. *Causes of Delinquency.* Berkeley: University of California Press.

Hoffmann, Heath. 2003. "Recovery Careers of People in Alcoholics Anonymous: Moral Careers Revisited." *Contemporary Drug Problems* 30:647–683.

Hora, Peggy, William Schma, and John Rosenthal. 1999. "Therapeutic Jurisprudence and the Drug Court Movement: Revolutionizing the Criminal Justice System's Response to Drug Abuse and Crime in America." *Notre Dame Law Review* 74 (2): 439–537.

Hser Yih-Ing, Elizabeth Evans, and Yu Chuang Huang. 2005. "Treatment Outcomes among Women and Men Methamphetamine Abusers in California." *Journal of Substance Abuse Treatment* 28 (1): 77–85. doi:10.1016/j.jsat.2004.10.009.

Hughes, Kahryn. 2007. "Migrating Identities: The Relational Constitution of Drug Use and Addiction." *Sociology of Health & Illness* 29 (5): 673–691. doi:10.1111/ j.1467-9566.2007.01018.x.

Inciardi, James A. 1995. "Crack, Crack House Sex, and HIV Risk," *Archives of Sexual Behavior* 24 (3): 249–269. doi:10.1007/BF01541599.

Inciardi, James A., and Anne E. Pottieger. 1998. "Drug Use and Street Crime in Miami: An (almost) Twenty-year Retrospective." *Substance Use & Misuse* 33 (9): 1839–1870.

Inciardi, James, A. Dorothy Lockwood, and Anne. E. Pottieger. 1993. *Women and Crack Cocaine.* New York: Macmillan.

Justice Policy Institute. 2009. "Pruning Prisons: How Cutting Corrections Can Save Money and Protect Public Safety." May. Washington, DC: U.S. Department of Justice.

Katz, Michael B. 1989. *The Undeserving Poor: From the War on Poverty to the War on Welfare.* New York: Pantheon Books.

King, Ryan S., and Jill Pasquarella. 2009. "Drug Courts: A Review of the Evidence." *The Sentencing Project, Research and Advocacy for Reform.* Washington, DC.

Klitzman, Robert L., Harrison G. Pope Jr., and James I. Hudson. 2000. "MDMA (Ecstasy) Abuse and High-risk Sexual Behaviors among 169 Gay and Bisexual Men." *American Journal of Psychiatry* 157 (7): 1162–1164. doi:10.1176/appi.ajp.157.7.1162.

Kwiatkowski, Carol F., and Robert E. Booth. 2003. "HIV Risk Behaviors among Older American Drug Users." *Journal of Acquired Immune Deficiency Syndromes* 33:S131–S137.

Lambert, Elizabeth Y., Rebecca S. Ashery, and Richard H. Needle. eds. 1995. *Qualitative Methods in Drug Abuse and HIV Research.* NIDA Research Monograph, 157 NIH Publication No. 95-4025. Washington, DC: U.S. Government Printing Office.

Laub, John H., and Robert J. Sampson. 1993. "Turning Points in the Life Course: Why Change Matters in the Study of Crime." *Criminology* 31 (3): 301–325. doi:10.1111/j.1745-9125.1993.tb01132.x.

———. 2003. *Shared Beginnings, Divergent Lives: Delinquent Boys to Age 71.* Cambridge: Harvard University Press.

Laudet, Alexandre B. 2008. "The Road to Recovery: Where are We Going and How Do We Get There? Empirically-Driven Conclusions and Future Directions for Service Development and Research." *Substance Use & Misuse* 43 (12–13): 2001–2020. doi:10.1080/10826080802293459.

Lende, Daniel H., Terri Leonard, Claire E. Sterk, and Kirk Elifson. 2007. "Functional Methamphetamine Use: The Insider's Perspective." *Addiction Research & Theory* 15 (5): 465–477. doi:10.1080/16066350701284552.

Leshner, Alan. 1997. "Addiction is a Brain Disease, and It Matters." *Science* 278 (5335): 45–47. doi:10.1126/science.278.533545.

Leshner, Alan, and George F. Koob. 1999. "Drugs of Abuse and the Brain." *Proceedings of the Association of American Physicians,* 111 (2): 99–108. doi:10.1046/j.1525-1381.1999.09218.x.

Lindesmith, Alfred R. 1938. "A Sociological Theory of Drug Addiction" *American Journal of Sociology* 43 (4): 593–613.

Lineberry, Timothy W., and J. Michael Bostwick. 2006. "Methamphetamine Abuse: A Perfect Storm of Complications." *Mayo Clinical Proceedings* 81 (1): 77–84. doi:10.4065/81.1.77.

Lockhart, William H. 2005. "Building Bridges and Bonds: Generating Social Capital in Secular and Faith Based Poverty-to-Work Programs." *Sociology of Religion* 66 (1): 45–60. doi:10.2307/4153115.

Lofland, John, David Snow, Leon Anderson, and Lyn Lofland. 2006. *Analyzing Social Settings: A Guide to Qualitative Observation and Analysis.* Belmont, CA: Thomson/Wadsworth.

Lorvick, Jennifer, Alexis Martinez, Lauren Gee, and Alex H. Kral. 2006. "Sexual and Injection Risk among Women Who Inject Methamphetamine in San Francisco." *Journal of Urban Health* 83 (3): 497–505. doi:10.1007/s11524-006-9039-4.

MacLeod, Jay. 1995. *Ain't No Makin' It: Aspirations and Attainments in a Low-Income Neighborhood.* Boulder, CO: Westview Press.

Maher, Lisa. 1997. *Sexed Work: Gender, Race, and Resistance in a Brooklyn Drug Market.* Oxford: Clarendon Press.

May, Candace. 2008. "Drug Courts: A Social Capital Perspective." *Sociological Inquiry* 78 (4): 513–535. doi:10.1111/j.1475-682X.2008.00261x.

Mbopi-Kéou, François-Xavier, Pierre Ongolo-Zogo, Fru Angwafo III, Peter M. Ndumbe, and Laurent Belec. 2007. "High Impact of Mobile Units for Mass HIV Testing in Africa." *AIDS* 21 (14): 1994–1996.

McElrath, Karen, Dale D. Chitwood, and Mary Comerford. 1997. "Crime Victimization among Injection Drug Users." *Journal of Drug Issues* 27 (4): 771–783.

McGovern, George. 1997. *Terry: My Daughter's Life and Death Struggle with Alcoholism.* New York: Penguin Books.

Morgan, Patricia and Karen Ann Joe. 1996. "Citizens and Outlaws: The Private Lives and Public Lifestyles of Women in the Illicit Drug Economy." *Journal of Drug Issues* 26 (1): 125–142.

Morris, Ruth Rittenhouse. 2000. *Stories of Transformative Justice.* Toronto: Canadian Scholars' Press.

National Institutes of Health (NIH). 2005. *Community Epidemiology Work Group: Epidemiological Trends in Drug Abuse,* vol. 1, June 2004. Rockville, MD: National Institute of Drug Abuse (NIDA), U.S. Department of Health and Human Services. NIH Publication No. 05-5364A.

Neaigus, Alan, Samuel R. Friedman, Richard Curtis, Don C. Des Jarlais, R. Terry Furst, Benny Jose, Patricia Mota, Bruce Stepherson, Meryl Sufian, Thomas Ward, and Jerome W. Wright. 1994. "The Relevance of Drug Injectors' Social and Risk Networks for Understanding and Preventing HIV Infection." *Social Science and Medicine* 38 (1): 67–78. doi:10.1016/0277-9536(94)9030-8.

Nichter, Mark, Gilbert Quintero, Mimi Nichter, Jeremiah Mock, and Sohaila Shakib. 2004. "Qualitative Research: Contributions to the Study of Drug Use, Drug Abuse and Drug Use(r)–Related Interventions." *Substance Use & Misuse* 39 (10–12): 1907–1969.

O'Brien, Charles P. 2003. "Research Advances in the Understanding and Treatment of Addiction." *American Journal on Addictions* 12 (S2): S36–S47. doi:10.1111/j.1521-0391.2003.tb00555.x.

O'Connor, Catherine A., Carol Patsdaughter, Cecelia G. Grindel, Paulo F. Taveira, and Judith L. Steinberg. 1998. "A Mobile HIV Education Program: Bringing Services to Hard-to-Reach Populations." *AIDS Patient Care STDs* 12 (12): 931–937. doi:10.1089/apc. 1998. 12.931.

Office of National Drug Control Policy. 2012. "In-Custody Treatment and Offender Reentry." Accessed May 2012 at www.whitehouse.gov/ondcp/in-custody-treatment-and-reentry

Ostrow, David. 2000. "The Role of Drugs in the Sexual Lives of Men Who Have Sex with Men: Continuing Barriers to Researching the Question." *AIDS and Behavior* 4 (2): 205–219. doi:10.1023/A:1009520809581.

Pach A., III, and E. Michael Gorman. 2002. "An Ethno-epidemiological Approach for the Multi-site Study of Emerging Drug Abuse Trends: The Spread of Methamphetamine in the United States of America." *Bulletin on Narcotics* 54 (1 and 2): 87–102.

Page, J. Bryan. 1990. "Shooting Scenarios and Risk of HIV-1 Infection." *American Behavioral Scientist* 33 (4): 478–490. doi:10.1177/0002764290033004008.

Page, J. Bryan, and Merrill Singer. 2010. *Comprehending Drug Use: Ethnographic Research at the Social Margins.* New Brunswick, NJ: Rutgers University Press.

Peele, Stanton, Charles Bufe, and Archie Brodsky. 2000. *Resisting 12-Step Coercion: How to Fight Forced Participation in AA, NA or 12-Step Treatment.* Tucson, AZ: Sharpe Press.

Portes, Alexander. 1998. "Social Capital: Its Origin and Application in a Modern Sociology." *Annual Review of Sociology* 22:1–24.

Potera, Carol. 2005. "Meth's Pollution Epidemic." *Environmental Health Perspectives* 113 (9): A589. PMCID:PMC1280434.

Potvin, Louise, Sylvie Gendron, Angele Billodeau, and Patrick Chabot. 2005. "Integrating Social Theory into Public Health Practice." *American Journal of Public Health* 95 (4): 591–595. doi:10.2105/AJPH.2004.048017.

Poundstone, K. E., Steffanie A. Strathdee, and David D. Celentano. 2004. "The Social Epidemiology of Human Immunodeficiency Virus/Acquired Immunodeficiency Syndrome." *Epidemiological Reviews* 26 (1): 22–35. doi:10.1093/epirev/mxh005.

Preble, Edward, and John J. Casey. 1969. "Taking Care of Business—The Heroin Addict's Life on the Street." *International Journal of Addictions* 4 (1): 1–24.

Putnam, Robert D. 2000. *Bowling Alone: The Collapse and Revival of American Community*. New York: Simon and Schuster.

Ragin, Charles C. 2008. *Redesigning Social Inquiry: Fuzzy Sets and Beyond*. Chicago: University of Chicago Press.

Rawson, Richard A., Rachel Gonzales, Jeanne L. Obert, Michael J. McCann, and Paul Brethen. 2005. "Methamphetamine Use among Treatment-seeking Adolescents in Southern California: Participant Characteristics and Treatment Response." *Journal of Substance Abuse Treatment* 29 (2): 67–74.

Reding, Nick. 2009. *Methland: The Death and Life of an American Small Town*. New York: Bloomsbury.

Reinarman, Craig. 2001. "The Achievement of Addiction: Discursive Construction of Phenomenological Reality." Paper presented at the annual meeting of the Society for the Study of Social Problems, August. Anaheim, CA.

———. 2005. "Addiction as Accomplishment: The Discursive Construction of Disease." *Addiction Research & Theory* 13 (4): 307–320. doi:10.1080/16066350500077728.

Reinarman, Craig, and Harry G. Levine, eds. 1997. *Crack in America: Demon Drugs and Social Justice*. Berkeley: University of California Press.

Rhodes, Tim, and David Moore. 2001. "On the Qualitative in Drug Research: Part One." *Addiction Research & Theory* 9 (4): 279–297.

Romero-Daza, Nancy, Margaret Weeks, and Merrill Singer. 2003. "'Nobody Gives a Damn if I Live or Die': Violence, Drugs, and Street-Level Prostitution in Inner-City Hartford, Connecticut." *Medical Anthropology* 22 (3): 233–259. doi:10.1080/01459740306770.

Rosenbaum, Marsha. 1981. *Women on Heroin*. New Brunswick, NJ: Rutgers University Press.

Sampson, Robert J., and John H. Laub. 1993. *Crime in the Making: Pathways and Turning Points through Life*. Cambridge: Harvard University Press.

Schensul, Stephen, Jean J. Schensul, and Margaret LeCompte. 1999. *Essential Ethnographic Methods: Observations, Interviews and Questionnaires*. Walnut Creek, CA: AltaMira Press.

Schensul, Jean J., Kim Radda, Margaret Weeks, and Scott Clair. 2002. "Ethnicity, Social Networks and HIV Risks in Older Drug Users." *Advances in Medical Sociology* 8:167–197. doi:10.1016/S1057-6290(02)80026-2.

Schuller, Tom. 2007 "Reflections on the Use of Social Capital." *Review of Social Economy* 65 (1): 11–28. doi:10.1080/00346760601132162.

Semple, Shirley, Jim Zians, Igor Grant, and Thomas L. Patterson. 2005. "Impulsivity and Methamphetamine Use." *Journal of Substance Abuse Treatment* 29 (2): 85–93. doi:10.1016/j.jsat.2005.05.001.

Sexton, Rocky L., Robert G. Carlson, Carl G. Leukefeld, and Brenda Booth. 2006. "Patterns of Illicit Methamphetamine Production ('Cooking') and Associated Risks in the Rural South: An Ethnographic Exploration." *Journal of Drug Issues* 36 (4): 853–876.

————. 2008. "Trajectories of Methamphetamine Use in the Rural South: A Longitudinal Qualitative Study." *Human Organization* 67 (2): 181–193.

Shaner, J. W., N. Kimmes, T. Saini, and P. Edwards. 2006. "'Meth Mouth': Rampant Caries in Methamphetamine Abusers." *AIDS Patient Care and STDs* 20 (3): 146–150. doi:10.1089/apc.2006.20.146.

Shaw, Victor N. 2005. "Research with Participants in Problem Experience: Challenges and Strategies." *Qualitative Health Research* 15 (6): 841–854. doi:10.1177/1049732305275639.

Sheridan, Janie, Sara Bennett, Carolyn Coggan, Amanda Wheeler, and Karen McMillan. 2006. "Injury Associated with Methamphetamine Use: A Review of the Literature." *Harm Reduction Journal* 3 (14): 1–8.

Singer, Merrill. 1994. "AIDS and the Health Crisis of the U.S. Urban Poor: The Perspective of Critical Medical Anthropology." *Social Science and Medicine* 39 (7): 931–948. doi:10.1016/0277-9536(94)90205-4.

————. 2006. *Something Dangerous: Emergent and Changing Illicit Drug Use and Community Health.* Long Grove, IL: Waveland Press.

Sloboda, Zili, Eric Rosenquist, and Jan Howard. 1997. "Introduction: Drug and Alcohol Abuse in Rural America." In *Rural Substance Abuse: State of Knowledge and Issues,* ed. Elizabeth B. Robertson, Zili Sloboda, Gayle M. Boyd, Lula Beatty, and Nicholas Kozel, 1–5. NIDA Research Monograph No. 168, NIH Publication No. 97-4177. Washington, DC: U.S. Government Printing Office.

Sobell, Linda. 2007. "The Phenomenon of Self-Change: Overview and Key Issues." In *Promoting Self-Change from Addictive Behaviors: Practical Implications for Policy, Prevention, and Treatment,* ed. Harald Klingemann, and Linda Carter Sobell, 1–30. New York: Springer. doi:10.1007/978-0-387-71287-1_1.

Stefancic, Ana, and Sam Tsemberis. 2007. "Housing First for Long-Term Shelter Dwellers with Psychiatric Disabilities in a Suburban County: A Four-Year Study of Housing Access and Retention." *Journal of Primary Prevention* 28 (3–4): 265–279. doi:10.1007/s10935-007-0093-9.

Stephens, Richard C. 1991. *The Street Addict Role: A Theory of Heroin Addiction.* Albany: SUNY Press.

Sterk, Claire E. 1999. *Fast Lives: Women Who Use Crack Cocaine.* Philadelphia: Temple University Press.

————. 2000. *Tripping and Tricking: Prostitution in the Era of AIDS.* New York: Social Change Press.

Sterk-Elifson, Claire. 1993. "Outreach among Drug Users: Combining the Role of Ethnographic Field Assistant and Health Educator." *Human Organization* 52 (2): 162–168.

Stewart, Eric, Kirk Elifson, and Claire E. Sterk. 2004. "Integrating the General Theory of Crime into an Explanation of Violent Victimization among Female Offenders." *Justice Quarterly* 21 (1): 159–181. doi:10.1080/07418820400095771.

Strauss, Anselm, and Juliet Corbin. 1998. *Basics of Qualitative Research: Techniques and Procedures for Developing Grounded Theory.* Thousand Oaks, CA: Sage Publications.

Stryker, Sheldon, and Richard Serpe. 1994. "Identity, Salience, and Psychological Centrality: Equivalent, Overlapping, or Complementary Concepts?" *Social Psychology Quarterly* 57 (1): 16–35.

Substance Abuse and Mental Health Services Administration (SAMHSA). 1999. *Brief Interventions and Brief Therapies for Substance Abuse.* Treatment Improvement Protocol (TIP) Series, no. 34, Center for Substance Abuse Treatment. Rockville, MD: U.S. Substance Abuse and Mental Health Services Administration.

————. 2007. *Results from the 2006 National Survey on Drug Use and Health: National Findings*. NSDUH Series H-32, DHHS Publication No. SMA07-4293. Rockville, MD: Office of Applied Studies.

————. 2009. *Substance Abuse Treatment: Addressing the Specific Needs of Women*. Treatment Improvement Protocol (TIP) Series 51. HHS Publication No. SMA09-4426. Rockville, MD: Substance Abuse and Mental Health Services Administration, U.S. Department of Health and Human Services.

————. 2010. *Permanent Supportive Housing: The Evidence*. HHS Publication No. SMA10-4509. Rockville, MD: Center for Mental Health Services, Substance Abuse and Mental Health Services Administration, U.S. Department of Health and Human Services.

Surratt, H. L., and James L. Inciardi. 2004. "HIV Risk, Seropositivity and Predictors of Infection among Homeless and Non-homeless Sex Workers in Miami, Florida, USA." *AIDS Care* 16 (5): 594–604. doi:10.1080/095401204100017163967.

Sutherland, Edwin H. 1939. *Principles of Criminology*. Philadelphia: Lippincott.

Sylvestre, Diana. 2005. "Approaching Treatment for Hepatitis C Infection in Substance Users." *Clinical Infectious Diseases* 41 (S1): S79–82. doi:10.1086/429501.

Sylvestre, Diana, and Joan Zweben. 2007. "Integrating HCV Services for Drug Users: A Model to Improve Engagement and Outcomes." *International Journal of Drug Policy* 18 (5): 406–410. doi:10.1016/j.drugpo.2007.01.010.

Taylor, Avril. 1993. *Women Drug Users: An Ethnography of a Female Injecting Community*. Oxford: Clarendon Press.

Teddlie, Charles, and Fen Yu. 2007. "Mixed Methods Sampling: A Typology with Examples." *Journal of Mixed Methods Research* 1:77–100.

Teruya, Cheryl, and Yih-Ing Hser. 2010. "Turning Points in the Life Course: Current Findings and Future Directions in Drug Use Research." *Current Drug Abuse Reviews* 3 (3): 189–195. doi:10.2174/1874473711003030189.

Thomas, William I. 1966. [1918]. *W. I. Thomas on Social Organization and Social Personality: Selected Papers*, ed. Morris Janowitz. Chicago: University of Chicago Press.

Tirrell, Meg. 2011. "Hepatitis C: 'Silent Epidemic' in U.S. Needs More Funding." Bloomberg News, May 25. Accessed August 9, 2011, from http://www.bloomberg.com/news/2011-05-25/hepatitis-c-silent-epidemic-in-u-s-needs-more-funding-researcher-says.html.

Tsemberis, Sam. 1999. "From Streets to Homes: An Innovative Approach to Supported Housing for Homeless Adults with Psychiatric Disabilities." *Journal of Community Psychiatry* 27 (2): 225–241. doi:10.1002/(SICI)1520-6629(19903)27:2<225::AID-JCOP9>3.0CO;2-Y.

United Nations Office on Drugs and Crime (UNODC). 2005. *World Drug Report: Analysis*, vol. 1. New York: United Nations Publication.

————. 2007. *World Drug Report*. New York: United Nations Publication.

Urbina, Antonio, and Kristina Jones. 2004. "Crystal Methamphetamine, Its Analogues, and HIV Infection: Medical and Psychiatric Aspects of a New Epidemic." *Clinical Infectious Diseases* 38 (6): 890–894. doi:10.1086/381975.

Wacquant, Loïc. 1998. "Negative Social Capital: State Breakdown and Social Destitution in America's Urban Core." *Journal of Housing and the Built Environment* 13 (1): 25–40. doi:10.1007/BF02496932.

————. 2008. *Urban Outcasts: A Comparative Sociology of Advanced Marginality*. Malden, MA: Polity Press.

————. 2009. "The Body, the Ghetto, and the Penal State." *Qualitative Sociology* 32 (1): 101–129. doi:10.1007/s11133-008-9112-2.

Waldorf, Dan. 1973. *Careers in Dope.* Englewood Cliffs, NJ: Prentice Hall.

Ward, Stephanie Francis, Molly McDonough, Steven Keeva, Margaret Teebo, Jason Krause, and Steve Seidenberg. 2006. "Flying Under the Radar." *ABA Journal* 92 (1): 34–36. http://www.abajournal.com/magazine/article/flying_under_the_radar1/.

Watters, John and Patrick Biernacki. 1989. "Targeted Sampling: Options for the Study of Hidden Populations." *Social Problems* 36 (4): 416–430.

Weatherby, Norman, Richard H. Needle, Helen Cesari, Robert Booth, Clyde McCoy, John Watters, Mark Williams, and Dale Chitwood. 1994. "Validity of Self-reported Drug Use among Injection Drug Users and Crack Cocaine Users Recruited through Street Outreach." *Evaluation and Program Planning* 17 (4): 347–355.

Weinberg, Darin. 2000. "Out There: The Ecology of Addiction in Drug Abuse Treatment Discourse." *Social Problems* 47 (4): 606–621.

Weisheit, Ralph, and William White. 2009. *Methamphetamine: Its History, Pharmacology, and Treatment.* Center City, MN: Hazelden Publishing.

West, Heather C., William J. Sabol, and Sarah J. Greenman. 2010. "Prisoners in 2009." *Bureau of Justice Statistics Bulletin*, December. NCJ 231675. Washington, DC: U.S. Department of Justice.

Westermeyer, Joseph, and Amy E. Boedicker. 2000. "Course, Severity, and Treatment of Substance Abuse among Women versus Men." *American Journal of Drug and Alcohol Abuse* 26 (4): 523–535. doi:10.1081/ADA-100101893.

Wiebel, W. Wayne. 1990. "Identifying and Gaining Access to Hidden Populations." In *The Collection and Interpretation of Data from Hidden Populations*, ed. Elizabeth Lambert, 4–11. National Institute on Drug Abuse Research Monograph 98. DHHS Publication No. (ADM) 90-1678. Washington, DC: U.S. Government Printing Office.

Williams, Clint, and Jill Young Miller. 2006. "Officials to Study Toll of Meth." *Atlanta Journal Constitution*, March 20.

Wilson, William Julius. 1987. *The Truly Disadvantaged: The Inner City, the Underclass, and Public Policy.* Chicago: University of Chicago Press.

Winick, Charles. 1962. "Maturing Out of Narcotic Addiction." *Bulletin on Narcotics* 14:1–7.

Zehr, Howard 2002. *The Little Book of Restorative Justice.* Intercourse, PA: Good Books.

Zerai, Assata, and Rae Banks. 2002. *Dehumanizing Discourse, Anti-Drug Law and Policy in America: A "Crack Mother's" Nightmare.* Burlington, VT: Ashgate.

Zinberg, Norman E. 1984. *Drug, Set, and Setting: The Basis for Controlled Intoxicant Use.* New Haven, CT: Yale University Press.

INDEX

About the Author

Miriam Boeri holds a Ph.D. in sociology from Georgia State University. A paper from her dissertation, "Hell I'm and Addict, but I Ain't No Junkie," won the Peter K. New Award from the Society for Applied Anthropology in 2002. She has worked as a researcher on various drug studies at Emory University. Her research studies on older drug users and suburban methamphetamine use were supported by funding from the National Institute on Drug Abuse, an institute with the National Institutes of Health. She specializes in ethnographic research among hidden and marginalized populations, with the goal of reducing the adverse health effects associated with drug use, such as the transmission of HIV/AIDS, hepatitis C, and sexually transmitted diseases, and the harmful social effects of drug use, such as incarceration, social isolation, unemployment, and violence. Her papers have been published in leading academic journals and she has contributed book chapters in the field of drug research.

CPSIA information can be obtained at www.ICGtesting.com
Printed in the USA
LVOW12s2159141013

356935LV00005B/203/P